IMAGES
of America

HURRICANE AGNES IN THE WYOMING VALLEY

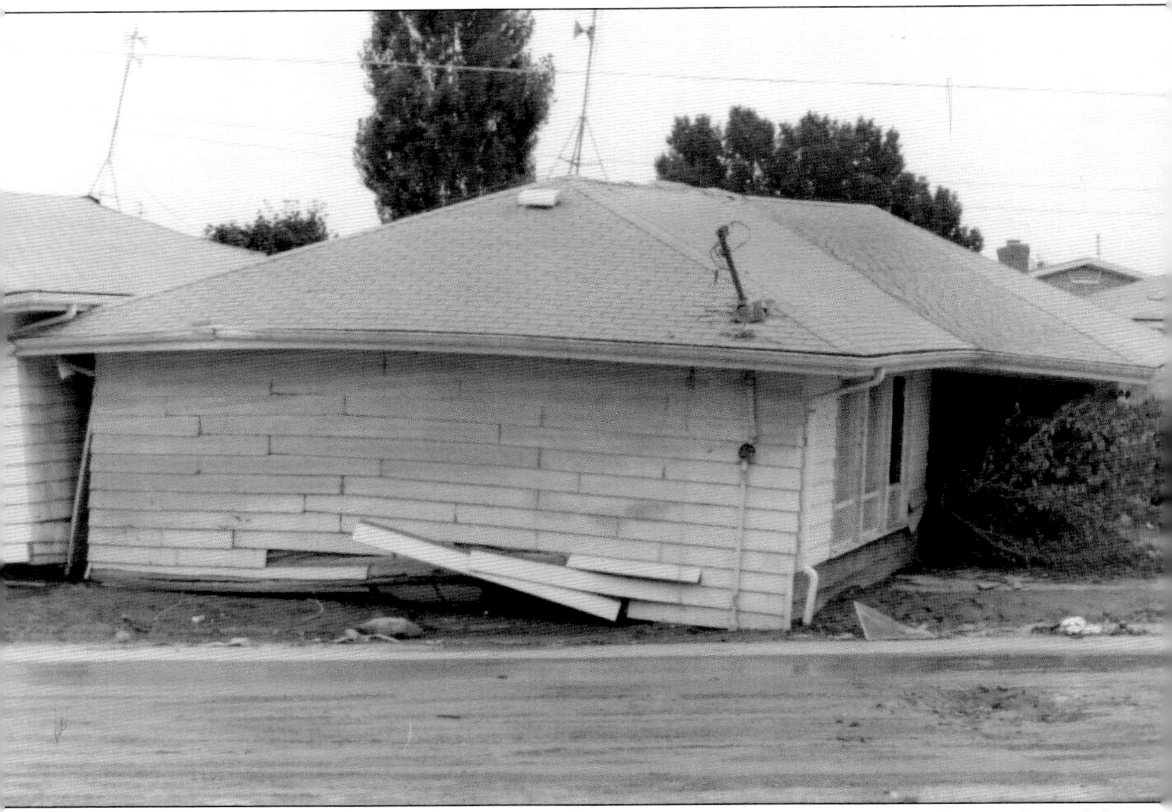

For most residents of northeastern Pennsylvania, the Susquehanna River is a place to boat, fish, or enjoy the scenery. Though a long river, most stretches are relatively shallow. This changed on June 23, 1972. As this image clearly demonstrates, the immense power of a raging river, over 40 feet deep, and its current are capable of jarring homes from their foundations, if not destroying them entirely. This structure is one of thousands that did not escape the wrath of Hurricane Agnes. (Courtesy of Sheldon Glahn.)

On the Cover: As residents stand on the dike in the background, a home sits in the foreground, a victim of Hurricane Agnes and the subsequent flooding of the Susquehanna River, which began June 23, 1972. As this picture shows, many homes simply could not be saved. Homeowners often described the area as a war zone. One noted how strange it was to leave the damage and head into the Back Mountain, where residents out of the flood zone were cutting their grass, relaxing on their porches, and doing other day-to-day activities citizens in the lower areas would have to wait some time to engage in again. (Courtesy of Sheldon Glahn.)

IMAGES
of America

HURRICANE AGNES IN THE WYOMING VALLEY

Bryan Glahn

ARCADIA
PUBLISHING

ISBN 978-1-4671-2605-2

Published by Arcadia Publishing
Charleston, South Carolina

Printed in the United States of America

Library of Congress Control Number: 2016959052

For all general information, please contact Arcadia Publishing:
Telephone 843-853-2070
Fax 843-853-0044
E-mail sales@arcadiapublishing.com
For customer service and orders:
Toll-Free 1-888-313-2665

Visit us on the Internet at www.arcadiapublishing.com

To my parents: your images and your stories make this book yours; I was just the secretary.

CONTENTS

Acknowledgments

The main credit for this book goes to Sheldon and Bonita Glahn, my parents. Were it not for your images and, most importantly, your stories, this book could not have been written. I realized, at the completion of this work, that much of this is our family's story, told through the eyes of your camera and with your words. I will always cherish the nights we spent reliving an event that, though the calendar says took place six years before my birth, feels like yesterday to you. To my grandmother, Ruth Glahn, thank you for the pictures and your tales of the flood. Although it saddens me Grampa is not here to see this book, he helped write it. To Molly and Chuck Malpass, you have one of the greatest stories in the history of Wyoming Valley. Thank you for your photographs and snacks, and I apologize again for taking out part of your driveway while backing out. Special thanks to Mary Lou Stancavage, for helping me (again) and driving two hours out of your way to introduce me to George and Sherene Barilla, the latter of whom I thank for your humor, graciousness, and chili. Nancy Lychos and Matthew Schooley, of the Forty Fort Cemetery Association, were a tremendous help with images. Joseph Hizny was a great help with his tales of the cleanup. Maureen Cech, archivist from Misericordia University, thank you and your staff for all your work in providing me with pictures and sources. Thank you to Stephen Kondrad, Georgetta Potoski, and Albert Dragon from the Plymouth Historical Society for the great pictures and conversation. And finally, to my wife, Jennifer, thank you for taking on extra babysitting duties so I could research and write.

INTRODUCTION

No one knows how many times the Susquehanna River has flooded in the millions of years it has coursed through the Wyoming Valley of northeastern Pennsylvania. As the industrialization of the United States was in full swing in the 1800s, many small communities began to solidify along the banks of the normally serene river. As the way of life switched from agrarian to anthracite, the population grew. The one constant, however, was the Susquehanna, provider of food, water, and transportation for as long as humans have lived on her shores. But the very river that made life possible in the area can also be responsible for inflicting tremendous damage on those who choose to live there. The first accurate data reveals that in March 1784, the water reached 30 feet in Wilkes-Barre, Pennsylvania, which was eight feet above flood stage. Although the river leaves her banks often, some floods over the years were particularly devastating: 31 feet in 1902 and again in 1904, 33 feet in 1936, and 32 feet in 1946. Recognizing the need for protection, man has attempted to keep the river in her banks, constructing a levy system on either side to hold back the water from the thousands of homes and businesses in the flood zone. As of 1968, over $15 million had been spent on the dikes in Kingston, Forty Fort, Plymouth, Wilkes-Barre, and Hanover to protect people and property. In June 1972, the residents of the cities, boroughs, and municipalities along the Susquehanna River would learn that their engineering efforts were not enough. Hurricane Agnes, now classified as a 175- to 200-year storm, was about to ravage the Wyoming Valley.

Although the Susquehanna River stood at roughly 4.5 feet on June 21, 1972, which was higher than normal, she would soon rise to 40 feet. Despite the impending arrival of Hurricane Agnes, many if not most residents were not immediately concerned. Having been told if they did not get water in the flood of 1936 they would not now, many felt no need to plan for evacuation nor securement of their homes. This delay would prove disastrous. Though officials initially thought the river would crest at 37 feet, predictions by some of 40 feet soon became a reality. At 5:00 on the morning of Friday, June 23, the sirens began to blow, as radio and television joined in to beg residents to get out . . . now.

Yet even as water swirled in the Forty Fort Cemetery and graves washed many miles away, residents still stood and watched, rather than plan their escape. Curious onlookers were taking pictures of caskets floating away, in some cases hitting trees and popping open to reveal corpses. As the Forty Fort Cemetery was continually gutted, many residents began to fear for the worst. Only a few hours before the full wrath of Agnes was to unfold on the Wyoming Valley, Forty Fort resident Sheldon E. Glahn recalled the words of his late father, A. Sheldon Glahn, a Red Cross volunteer and active community member, who, upon returning to his home on Bidlack Street to find his family nonchalantly preparing dinner, exclaimed, "If we don't get out now, we're getting out in a boat."

Although most residents evacuated by automobile, Glahn's prediction proved prophetic. For many citizens of the valley, their return trip to their property was made by water. As floodwater still inundated the area, a variety of vessels were utilized to view the destruction. Whether it was rescuing citizens who did not or could not evacuate, surveying damage, or reentering their homes, the roadways of the Wyoming Valley looked more like the streets of Venice, Italy.

As water receded and streets became passable, a new threat emerged—mud. "My God the mud," Bonnie Stinson exclaimed. "It seemed like the more we sprayed, the more mud there was." Aided by the National Guard, citizens began the agonizing process of trying to put their lives and homes back together. Perhaps most difficult was knowing that irreplaceable photographs and mementos were gone forever, washed away by waters that few thought could get so high.

Meanwhile, in the Back Mountain area, two different stories emerged. In the midst of such drama, a young couple, Charles Malpass and Molly Hourigan, had their wedding day interrupted by Hurricane Agnes. With some deliberation, it was decided late at night that the wedding must go on. Phone calls were made, a church procured, and on June 24, 1972, a ceremony was thrown together, with a reception to follow. On the grounds of College Misericordia in Dallas, displaced flood victims were getting a reception of their own, treated to enormous generosity and hospitality thanks to the campus staff. The Nesbitt Hospital in Kingston relocated to the campus, where a makeshift medical center was created. While temporarily homeless residents dined, attended worship, or watched their children play, they worried about their homes and how they were going to afford to rebuild their shattered lives.

The federal government provided an answer to the second part of that question. Though laws have since been changed, in the aftermath of the flood of 1972, federal loans with one-percent interest rates were available, with the first $5,000 free. Many residents were able to use these funds to make their homes even better than before the flood. The greatest economic benefit came at the local level. Cities were able to rebuild outdated sewer systems in Swoyersville and revitalize downtown Wilkes-Barre while other areas benefited from new curbs, roads, and recreational areas. Although citizens such as Eugene Foriano of Forty Fort lamented "we gained nothing" from loans that, were it not for the flood, they would never have had to take on, overall, the area was better after the disaster than before. With current interest rates and legal loopholes now closed, another Agnes would likely have a more negative effect on the region. Many residents now have flood insurance, though they hope to never need it. In 2001, another storm, this time named Lee, caused locals to panic. Evacuations were ordered, volunteers sandbagged, and the Susquehanna rose to over 40 feet while residents held their collective breath to see if the levy would hold. It did, and for the most part the area was spared. But for anyone alive during Hurricane Agnes, it brought back vivid memories. "It felt like 1972 all over again," Bonnie Glahn described. "Had it happened again, I don't think I could come back." For many, though, Agnes was a test that, though difficult, they passed. Neighbors, government officials, and complete strangers worked side by side, building a bond that did not exist before June 1972. Although many questioned how they could ever recover, they did, rebuilding their homes and coming back stronger than before. Ingrained in their psyche, however, are the sounds of sirens, the smell of mud, and the visions of dead bodies floating down the streets. For many citizens in the small cities along the Susquehanna River, their lives will always be defined in two parts: before "the flood," and after.

One

Agnes is Born

From Tropical Storm to Hurricane

Although the date of June 23, 1972, is etched into the mind of every resident of the Wyoming Valley, the instrument of destruction that would forever alter the lives and economy of northeastern Pennsylvania began on June 11, as convection was first recorded over the Caribbean Sea. As a polar front dropped in from the northwest, a depression was forming over the Yucatan Peninsula. By June 15, a tropical storm had developed. Three days later, a hurricane named Agnes made landfall in Florida. With an initial downgrade to a tropical storm, Agnes affected parts of Florida, Georgia, and South Carolina. Mother Nature was not finished, however. Despite this slight weakening, Agnes regained her strength as she tracked over North Carolina. The storm system continued to intensify on June 22 in the northwest Atlantic. For residents of northeastern Pennsylvania, their lives were about to be forever changed.

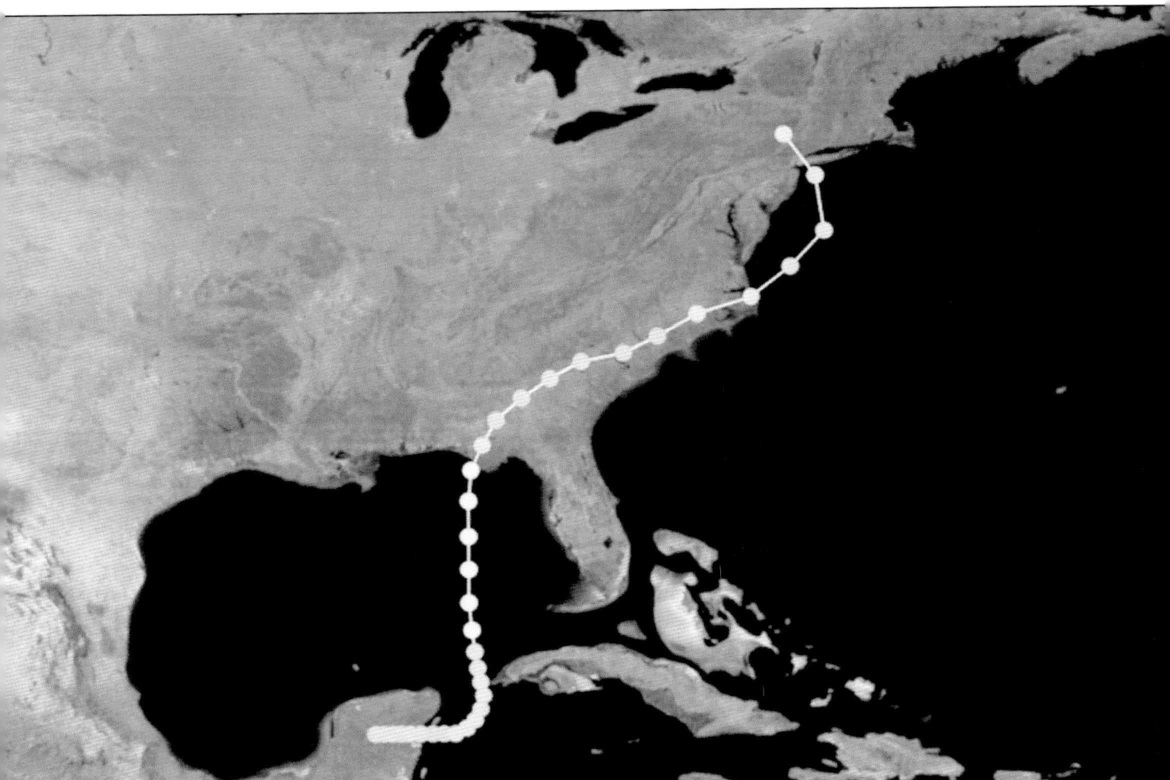

Satellite imagery from the National Hurricane Center shows the track of Hurricane Agnes in 1972. Contrary to perception, Agnes was not technically a hurricane when she hit land. Aircraft recorded her winds at 86 miles per hour, which, though high, made her barely a Category 1 storm. However, the National Hurricane Center still referred to Agnes as a hurricane so people would not get complacent. Alone, Hurricane Agnes would have been a minor event, but she had help in the form of two storms that dumped over a dozen inches of rain on some parts of the area, causing rivers and streams to swell. In the Atlantic Ocean, a high-pressure system kept Agnes from going out to sea while two storms over land drew Agnes to northeastern Pennsylvania, where she overstayed her welcome. Ultimately, 48 square miles in the Wyoming Valley would soon be under water. (Courtesy of NASA and the National Hurricane Center.)

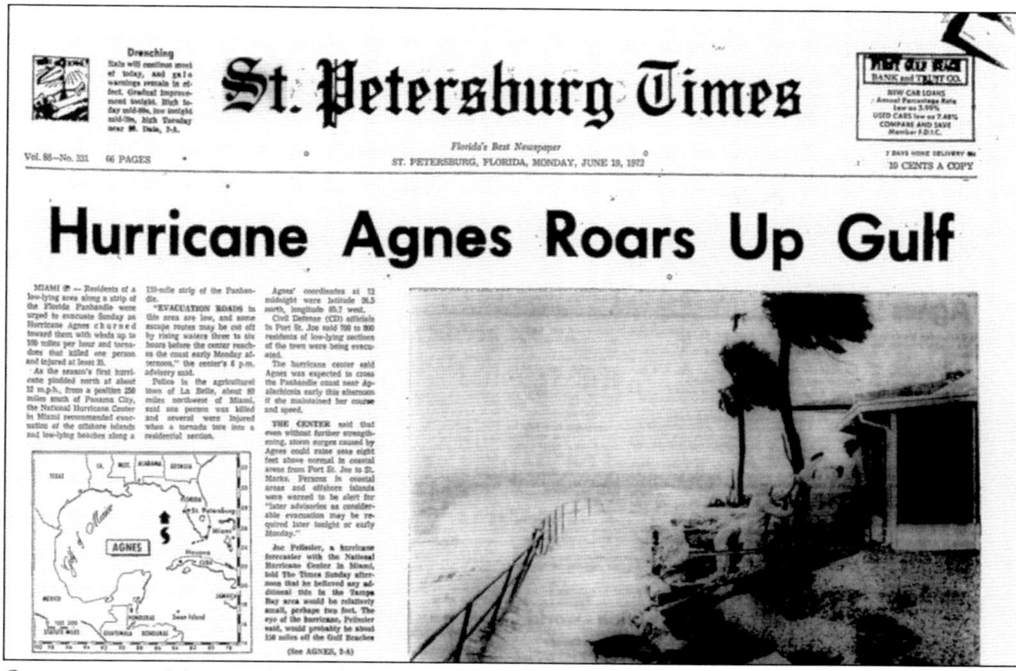

Drenching
Rain will continue most of today, and gale warnings remain in effect. Gradual improvement tonight. High today mid-80s, low tonight mid-70s, high Tuesday near 80. Data, 2-A.

St. Petersburg Times

Florida's Best Newspaper

Vol. 88—No. 331 66 PAGES ST. PETERSBURG, FLORIDA, MONDAY, JUNE 19, 1972 10 CENTS A COPY

Hurricane Agnes Roars Up Gulf

MIAMI (AP) — Residents of a low-lying area along a strip of the Florida Panhandle were urged to evacuate Sunday as Hurricane Agnes churned toward them with winds up to 100 miles per hour and tornadoes that killed one person and injured at least 35.

As the season's first hurricane plodded north at about 12 m.p.h., from a position 250 miles south of Panama City, the National Hurricane Center in Miami recommended evacuation of the offshore islands and low-lying beaches along a 110-mile strip of the Panhandle.

"EVACUATION ROADS in this area are low, and some escape routes may be cut off by rising waters three to six hours before the center reaches the coast early Monday afternoon," the center's 6 p.m. advisory said.

Police in the agricultural town of La Belle, about 80 miles northwest of Miami, said one person was killed and several were injured when a tornado tore into a residential section.

Agnes' coordinates at 12 midnight were latitude 26.3 north, longitude 85.7 west.

Civil Defense (CD) officials in Port St. Joe said 700 to 800 residents of low-lying sections of the town were being evacuated.

The hurricane center said Agnes was expected to cross the Panhandle coast near Apalachicola early this afternoon if she maintained her course and speed.

THE CENTER said that even without further strengthening, storm surges caused by Agnes could raise seas eight feet above normal in coastal areas from Port St. Joe to St. Marks. Persons in coastal areas and offshore islands were warned to be alert for "later advisories as considerable evacuation may be required later tonight or early Monday."

Joe Pelissier, a hurricane forecaster with the National Hurricane Center in Miami, told The Times Sunday afternoon that he believed any additional tide in the Tampa Bay area would be relatively small, perhaps two feet. The eye of the hurricane, Pelissier said, would probably be about 150 miles off the Gulf Beaches

(See AGNES, 2-A)

Originating in Mexico, Agnes first made landfall in the United States on Sunday, June 18, 1972, when the Florida panhandle was struck by the storm. The headline above from the *St. Petersburg Times* reflects the event. Though not technically a hurricane when she arrived in Florida, Agnes was still a powerful storm. At right, the front page of *The Scranton Times* warns residents of northeastern Pennsylvania to brace for the worst. Although Agnes herself was not a deadly threat, several storms converged, which would ultimately keep Agnes in place to unleash well over a foot of rain on the Wyoming Valley. Many citizens made the same comment, verbatim, in regard to the arrival of the storms: "It just rained and rained and rained." (Both, courtesy of the Osterhout Free Library.)

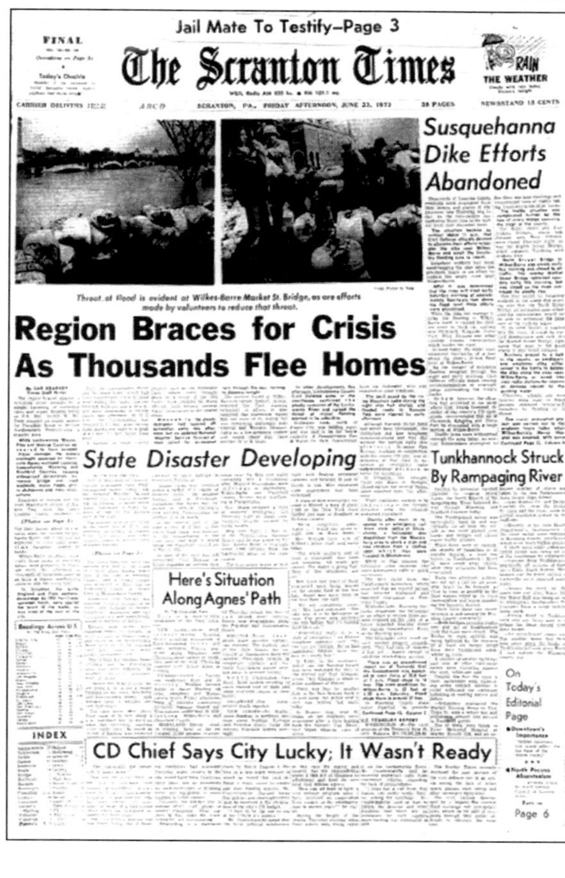

Jail Mate To Testify—Page 3

FINAL

The Scranton Times

RAIN
THE WEATHER

SCRANTON, PA., FRIDAY AFTERNOON, JUNE 23, 1972

Susquehanna Dike Efforts Abandoned

Threat of flood is evident at Wilkes-Barre Market St. Bridge, as are efforts made by volunteers to reduce that threat.

Region Braces for Crisis As Thousands Flee Homes

State Disaster Developing

Tunkhannock Struck By Rampaging River

Here's Situation Along Agnes' Path

On Today's Editorial Page

INDEX

CD Chief Says City Lucky; It Wasn't Ready

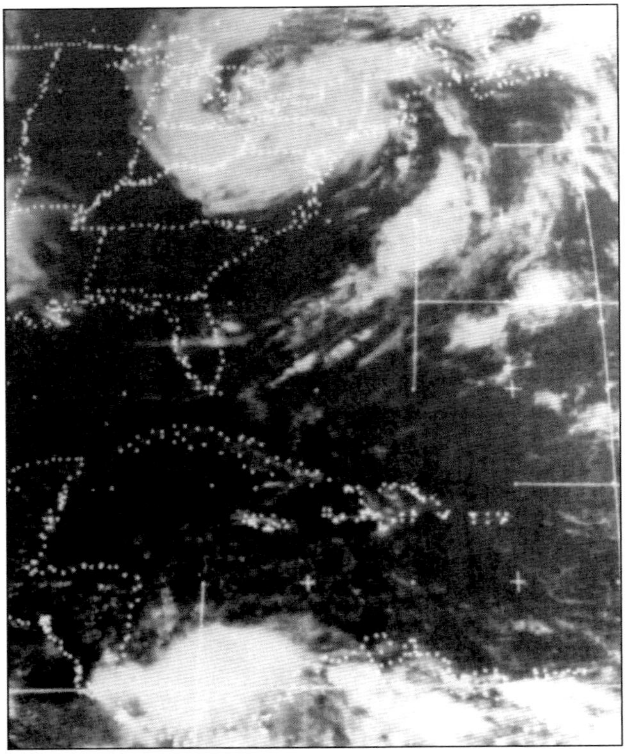

Satellite imagery shows Hurricane Agnes inflicting her rage on the East Coast of the United States. Initially striking Florida on June 18, 1972, Hurricane Agnes would be pushed inland and soon unleash unprecedented damage on the East Coast, especially Pennsylvania. At the time, Hurricane Agnes was the most expensive storm to ever hit the United States. As she tracked up the eastern seaboard, Agnes set her sights on northeastern Pennsylvania. Though at first many residents were not concerned, on Thursday, June 22, officials called for residents in low-lying areas to evacuate. Initial river crest predictions were low, but Agnes would soon create the worst flood in the recorded history of the Wyoming Valley. (Both, courtesy of National Oceanic and Atmospheric Administration.)

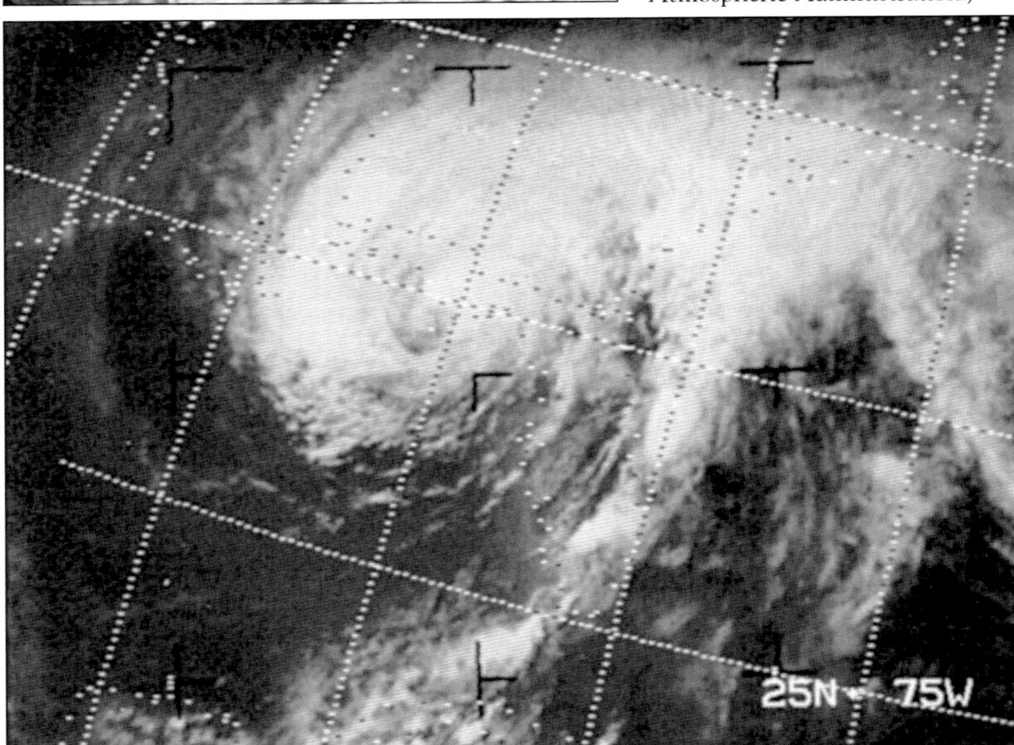

TABLE 3

COSTS OF LOCAL FLOOD PROTECTION PROJECTS

PROJECT	FEDERAL COST	ESTIMATED LOCAL COST	TOTAL COST*	YEAR COMPLETED
Kingston-Edwardsville	$ 5,072,900	$ 379,000	$ 5,451,900	1943
Plymouth	1,911,700	117,000	2,028,700	1948
Swoyersville-Forty Fort	2,718,700	283,000	3,001,700	1957
Wilkes-Barre & Hanover Township	4,486,500	216,000	4,702,500	1952
TOTAL	$14,189,800	$ 995,000	$15,184,800	

* Costs to June 1968

Source: Susquehanna River Basin Study; June 1970.

-8-

Data from June 1968 shows that over $15 million had been spent to protect northeastern Pennsylvania from flooding. Previously, the 1936 flood had been classified as a 100-year storm. However, in light of Agnes and new research, the flood of 1936 is now considered a 33-year storm. Never in recorded history had anyone seen a flood like 1972. (Courtesy of Plymouth Historical Society.)

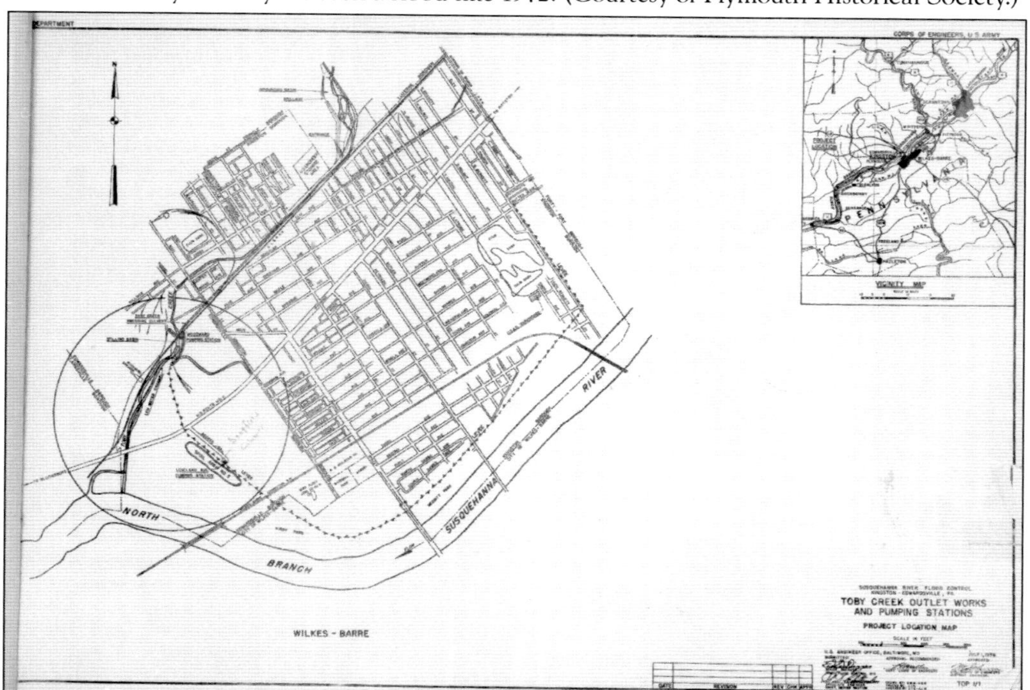

This is a blueprint for flood control in Edwardsville. Despite a history of flooding, local towns can never really tame the river. Despite being 36 feet high, the levy system could not hold back the floodwaters of Agnes. Even now, officials are constantly tweaking plans and making sure the dike system works properly, for it is not a matter of if, but when, the Susquehanna River will flood again. (Courtesy of Library of Congress.)

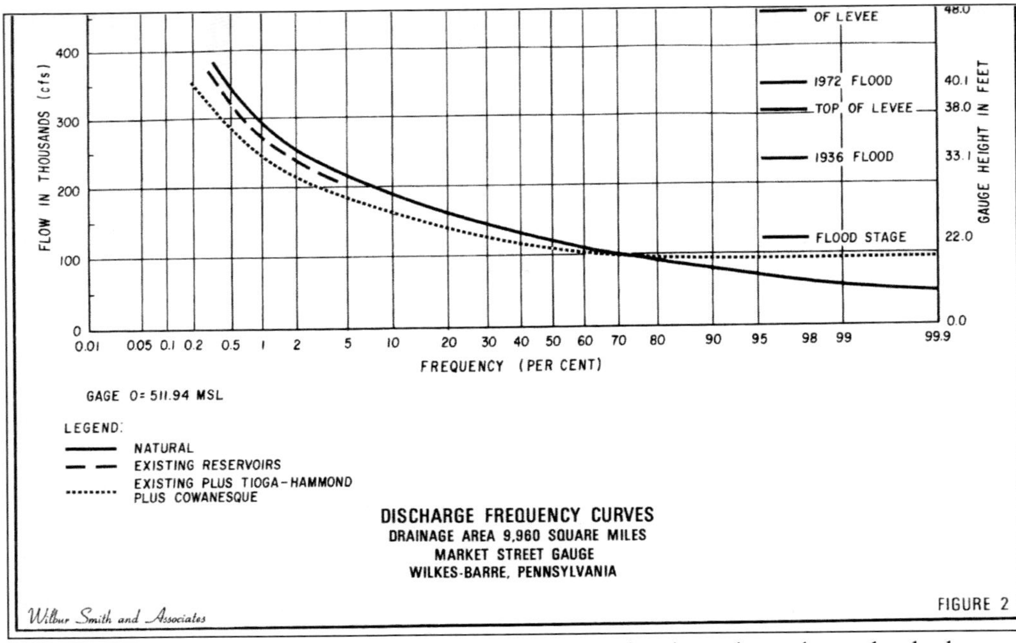

DISCHARGE FREQUENCY CURVES
DRAINAGE AREA 9,960 SQUARE MILES
MARKET STREET GAUGE
WILKES-BARRE, PENNSYLVANIA

FIGURE 2

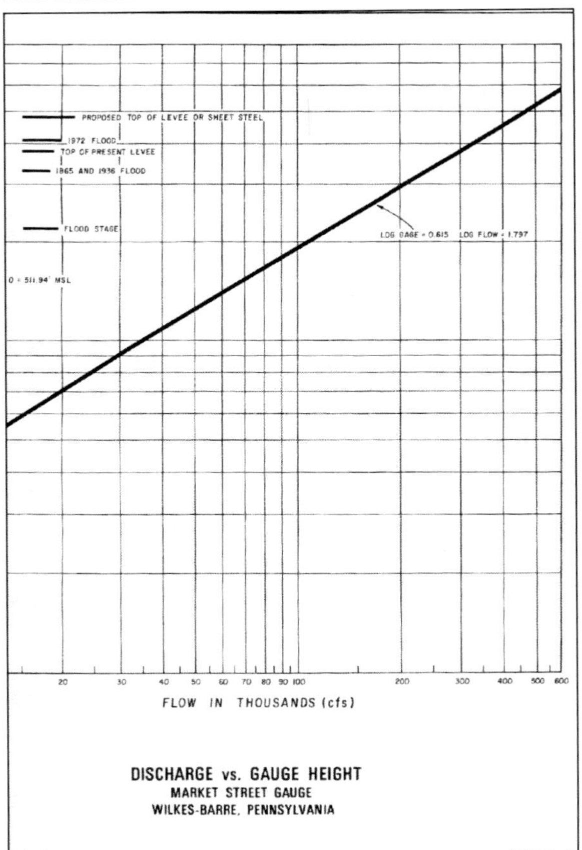

DISCHARGE vs. GAUGE HEIGHT
MARKET STREET GAUGE
WILKES-BARRE, PENNSYLVANIA

FIGURE 3

The chart above shows the discharge frequency of Hurricane Agnes as measured at the Market Street Bridge gauge. Scientists classify a flow rate of 290,000 cubic feet per second to be a 100-year storm. At 345,000 cubic feet per second, Agnes was determined to be a 175- to 200-year storm. Accurate flood records for the Susquehanna River are only available from the mid-1800s on. At left, the discharge versus gauge height is shown, also at Market Street. As of June 1968, over $15 million had been spent on flood control. Despite these efforts, Agnes caused local officials to examine and adapt their approach to flood control. (Both, courtesy of Plymouth Historical Society.)

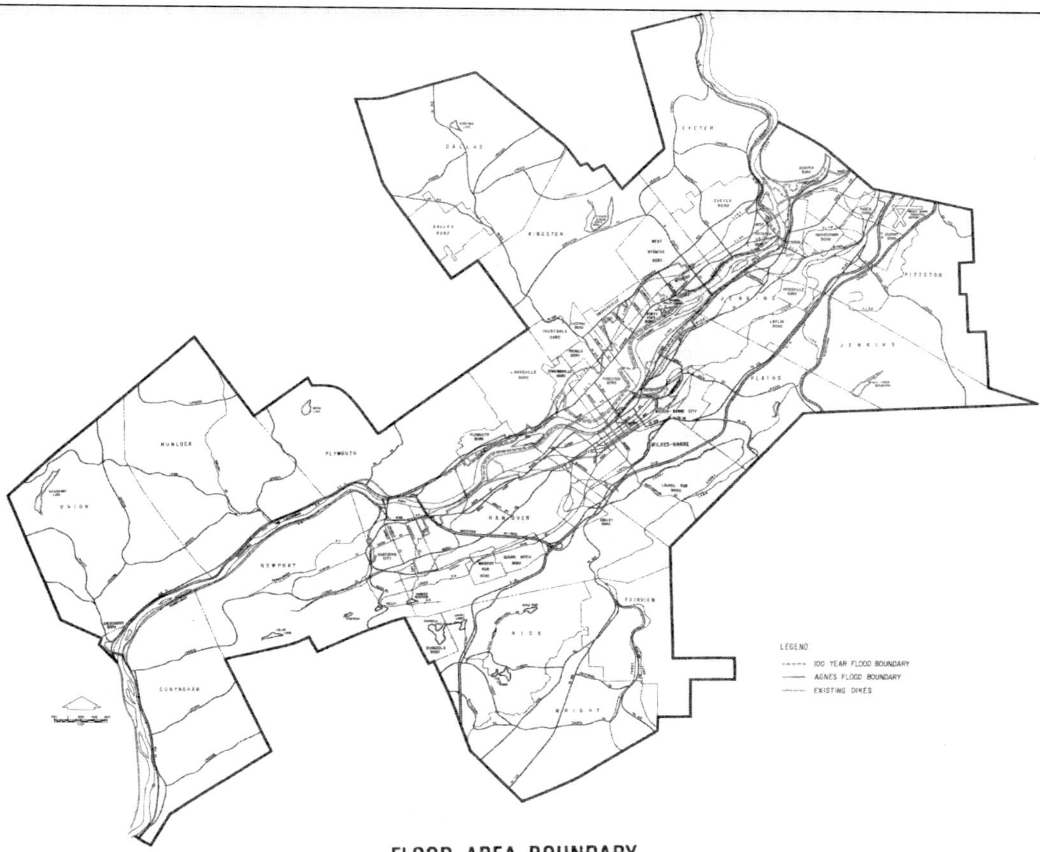

Smith and Associates **FLOOD AREA BOUNDARY** FIGURE 1

This map shows the boundary of the effects of Hurricane Agnes. Due to the "linear city" that stretches from Carbondale to Nanticoke, the impact of Agnes was far reaching. Areas in the flood zone were simply devastated. Even areas not affected by water were impacted economically, as the entire region attempted to put their lives back together. Despite the significant damage, the federal government paid much of the bill. This would be unheard of today. Unlike in the 1970s, today, local agencies would be required to pick up at least 25 percent of the tab. Legal loopholes had to be closed after Agnes, which means a storm of such magnitude would cost far more today than in 1972. (Courtesy of Plymouth Historical Society.)

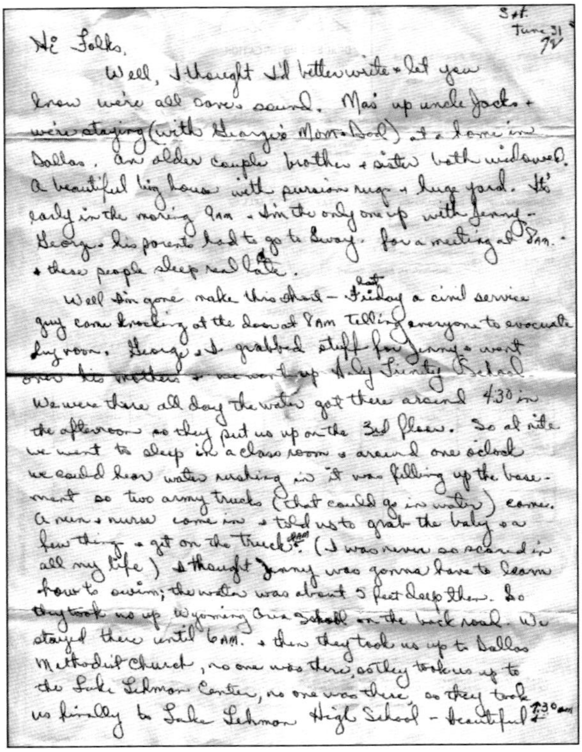

Sat.
June 31
72

Hi Folks,

Well, I thought I'd better write & let you know we're all save & sound. Ma's up uncle Jack's & we're staying (with George's Mom & Dad) at a home in Dallas. An older couple brother & sister both widowed. A beautiful big house with persian rugs & huge yard. It's early in the moring 9AM & I'm the only one up with Jenny – George & his parents had to go to Sway. for a meeting at 8AM. & these people sleep real late.

Well I'm gonna make this short – Friday last a civil service guy came knocking at the door at 8AM telling everyone to evacuate by noon. George & I grabbed stuff for Jenny & went over his mother's & we went up Holy Trinity School. We were there all day the water got there around 4:30 in the afternoon so they put us up on the 3rd floor. So at nite we went to sleep in a class room & around one o'clock we could hear water rushing in it was filling up the basement so two army trucks (that could go in water) came. A man & nurse came in & told us to grab the baby & a few things & get on the truck 2AM. (I was never so scared in all my life) I thought Jenny was gonna have to learn how to swim; the water was about 5 feet deep then. So they took us up Wyoming Area School on the back road. We stayed there until 6AM. & then they took us up to Dallas Methodist Church, no one was there, so they took us up to the Lake Lehman Center, no one was there, so they took us finally to Lake Lehman High School – beautiful 7:30am

Scribbled on the back of Department of Transportation forms, this letter, dated Saturday, June 31, 1972, was penned by Sherene Barilla of Swoyersville, describing the effect Agnes had on her family. While her husband, George, helped with sandbagging efforts, the Barilla family waited, until they were told to evacuate Friday morning. Though at first they did not anticipate leaving, they soon found themselves grabbing the baby, so to speak, and a few personal items as they hastily left their home. "I was never more scared in my life," Barilla wrote, as she was helped into an Army truck with water already covering its enormous tires. Sherene, George, and the rest of her family were evacuated to the Lake-Lehman High School in the Back Mountain. Although treated well at the shelter, the Barillas would nervously wait to return to their home and see what damage had been done. (Both, courtesy of Sherene and George Barilla.)

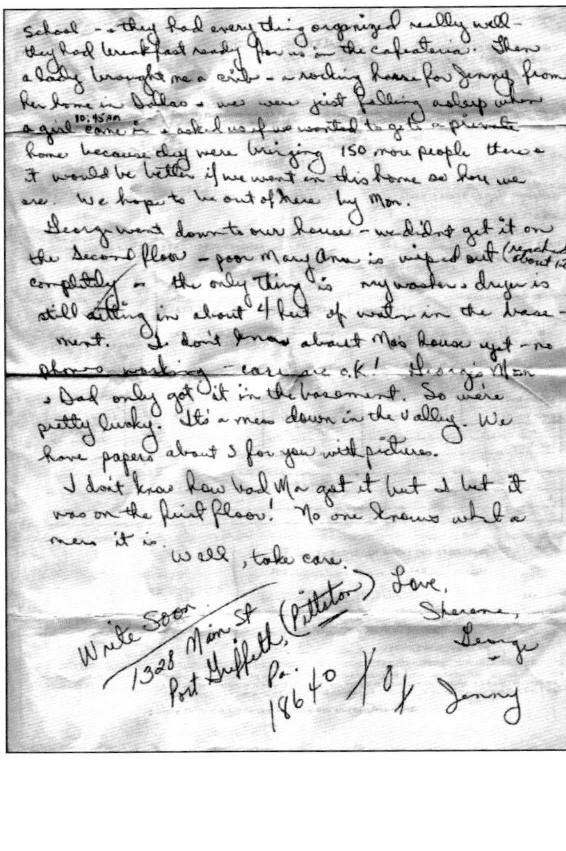

School – & they had every thing orgnized really well – they had breakfast ready for us in the cafeteria. Then a lady brought me a crib – a rocking horse for Jenny from her home in Dallas & we were just falling asleep when a girl came in 10:45AM & asked us if we wanted to go to a private home because they were bringing 150 more people there & it would be better if we went in this home so here we are. We hope to be out of here by Mon.

George went down to our house – we didn't get it on the second floor – poor Mary Ann is wiped out completly (reached about 12') – the only thing is my washer & dryer is still sitting in about 4 feet of water in the basement. I don't know about Ma's house yet – no phones working – cars are o.k! George's Mom & Dad only got it in the basement. So we're pretty lucky. It's a mess down in the valley. We have papers about 3 for you with pictures.

I don't know how bad Ma got it but I bet it was on the first floor! No one knows what a mess it is.

Well, take care.

Love,
Sherene,
George
+
Jenny

Write Soon
1328 Main St
Port Griffith, (Pittston)
Pa.
18640

Two

The Forty Fort Cemetery

A River Wakes the Dead

Located between River Street and Wyoming Avenue, the Forty Fort Meeting House has been standing since approximately 1806, with the first church service dating to 1807. While the structure was used for church services and various social gatherings for the living, the cemetery around it served as a final resting place for prominent and ordinary citizens alike, as well as, legend has it, Native Americans. This rest would be disturbed on June 23, 1972, however, as Hurricane Agnes delivered the first and most infamous blow to the Wyoming Valley. As residents watched with curiosity that soon turned to horror, the Susquehanna River tore through the dike and flood wall in the rear of the cemetery. As the water continued to surge and spin, tombstones were tossed around like feathers, large mausoleums were knocked off their foundations, and bodies were strewn for miles, most never to be recovered. The damage at the Forty Fort Cemetery was the first visual for many residents of the Wyoming Valley, as several storm systems parked themselves over northeastern Pennsylvania. It would also be the last image to leave the minds of many.

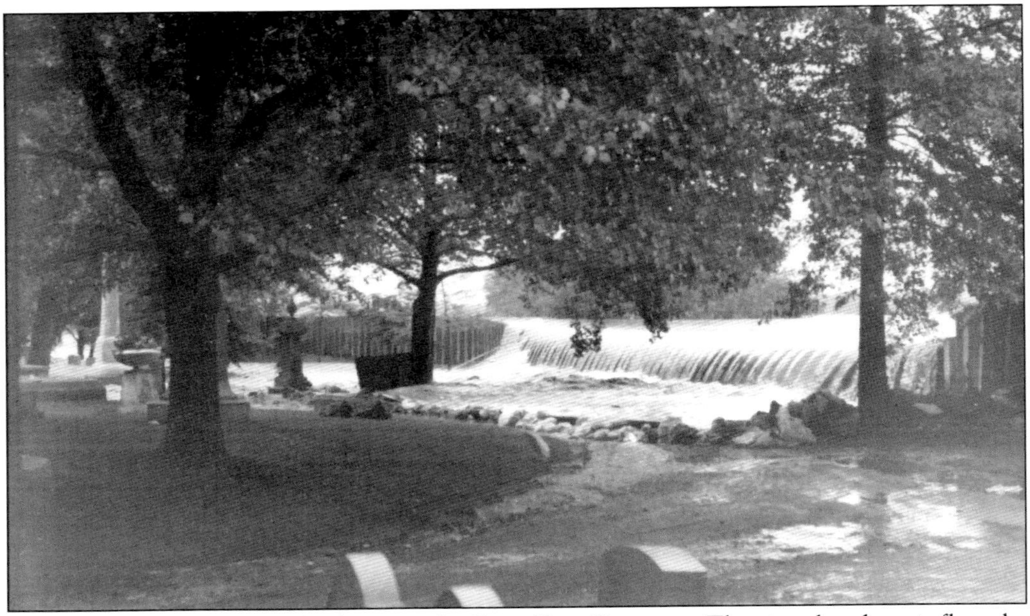

Floodwaters rage through the fence at the Forty Fort Cemetery. The river bends as it flows by Forty Fort, which created a whirlpool that disinterred thousands of graves. It is perhaps the most graphic reminder of the flood for the residents who had bodies deposited in their yards. One common theme was that the flood did not discriminate between the living and the dead or the rich and the poor. (Courtesy of Forty Fort Cemetery Association.)

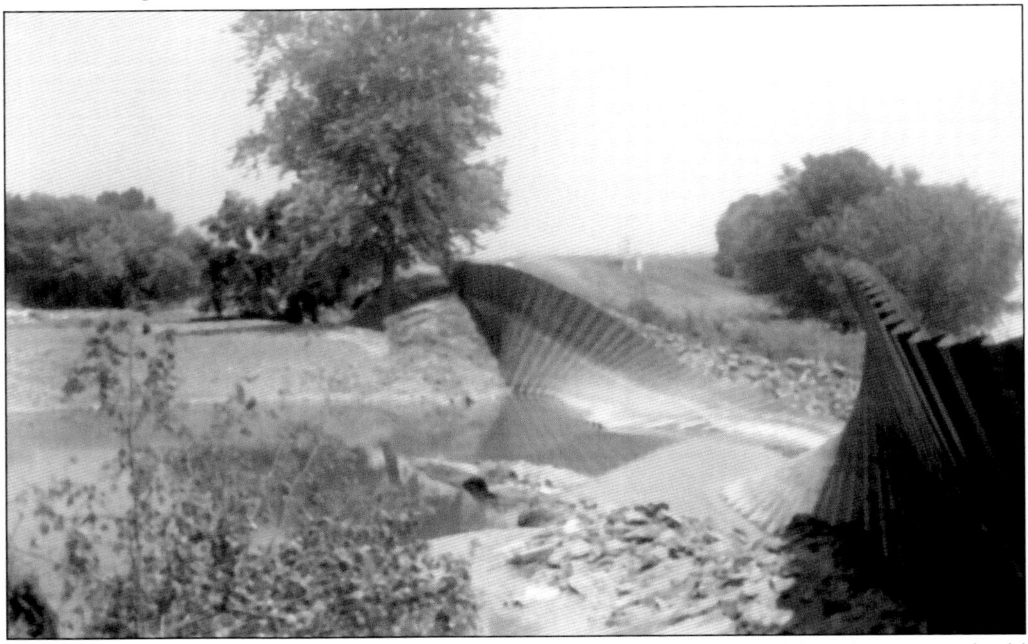

A twisted flood wall sits on River Street in Forty Fort, a reminder that although man can build a levy system, Mother Nature's force can destroy it. The waters of the Susquehanna River were flowing so quickly that at one point, the Coast Guard was unable to get a 19-foot boat across the current. (Courtesy of Forty Fort Cemetery Association.)

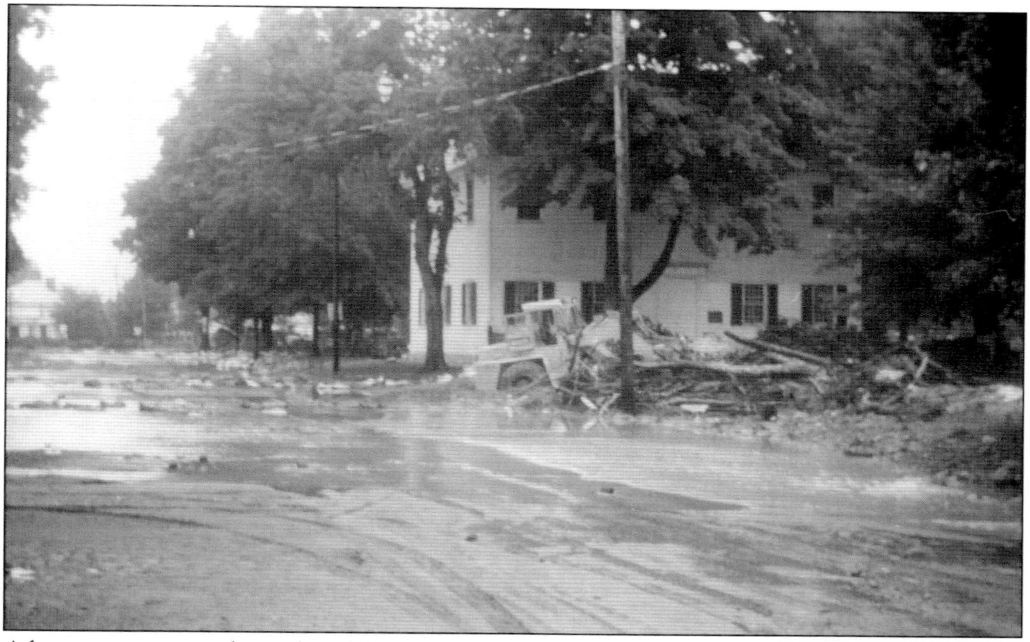

A large excavator works to clear debris in front of the Forty Fort Meeting House, which is adjacent to the cemetery. Miraculously, the meetinghouse was spared from severe damage. The cemetery itself fared far worse, as the floodwaters ravaged the area, causing incredible destruction to the graves there. (Courtesy of Forty Fort Cemetery Association.)

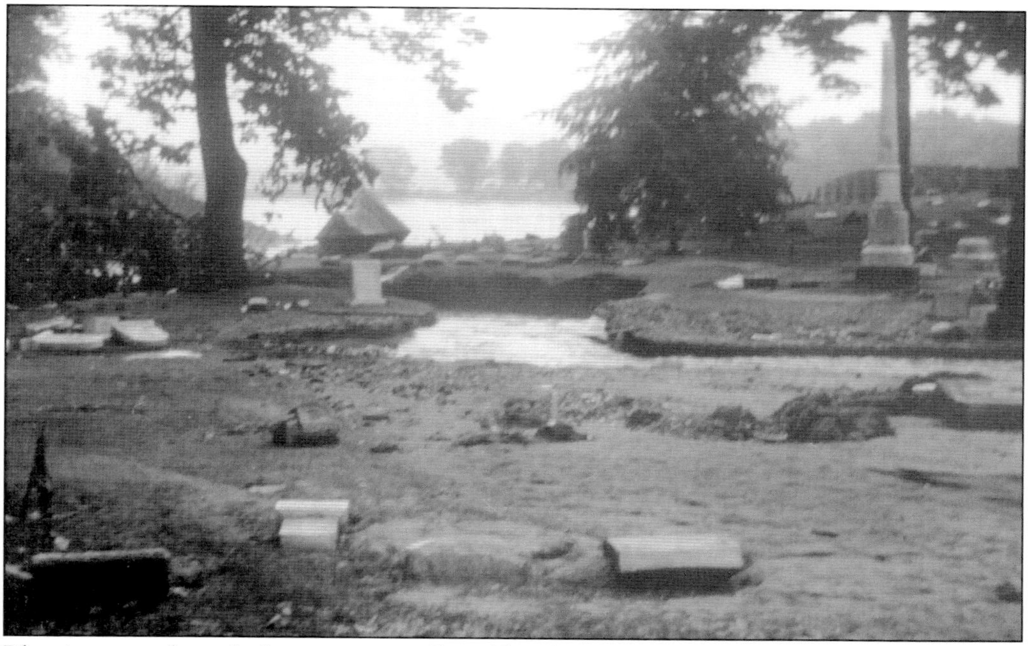

The river cuts through the cemetery in Forty Fort, leaving toppled headstones in its wake. The manner in which Hurricane Agnes caused the normally placid Susquehanna River to slice through the levy system at the Forty Fort Cemetery and redistribute corpses throughout the area is one of the most chilling memories for citizens. (Courtesy of Forty Fort Cemetery Association.)

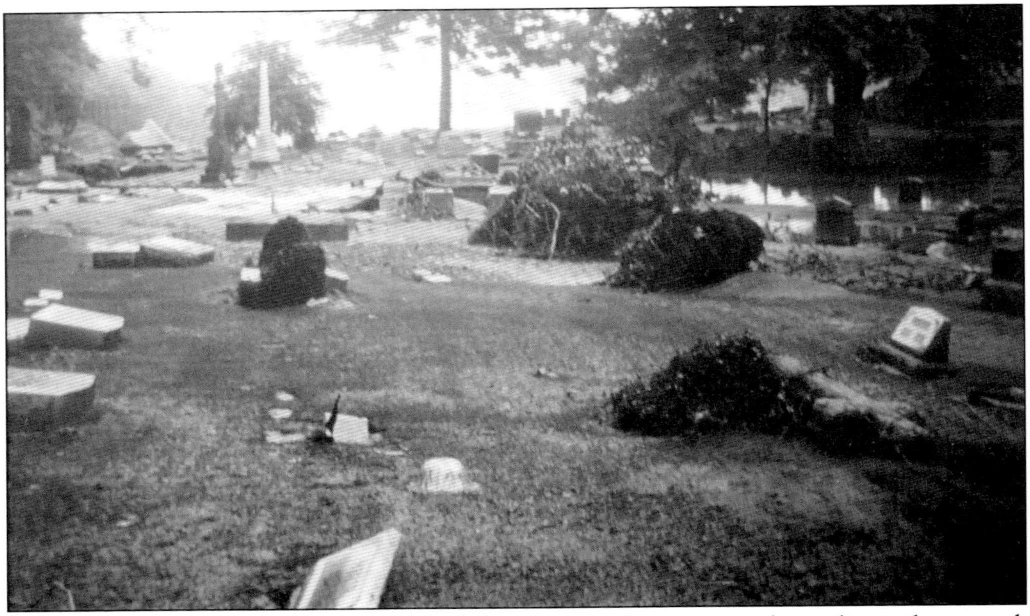

The twisted fence is seen in the back left of this photograph, as uprooted trees lie on the ground. Despite being made of iron and buried in several feet of cement, the structure was no match for the waters of Agnes. The soft ground, saturated from days of rain, allowed the Susquehanna River to effortlessly cut underneath the dike, though eventually the top level was washed away as well. (Courtesy of Forty Fort Cemetery Association.)

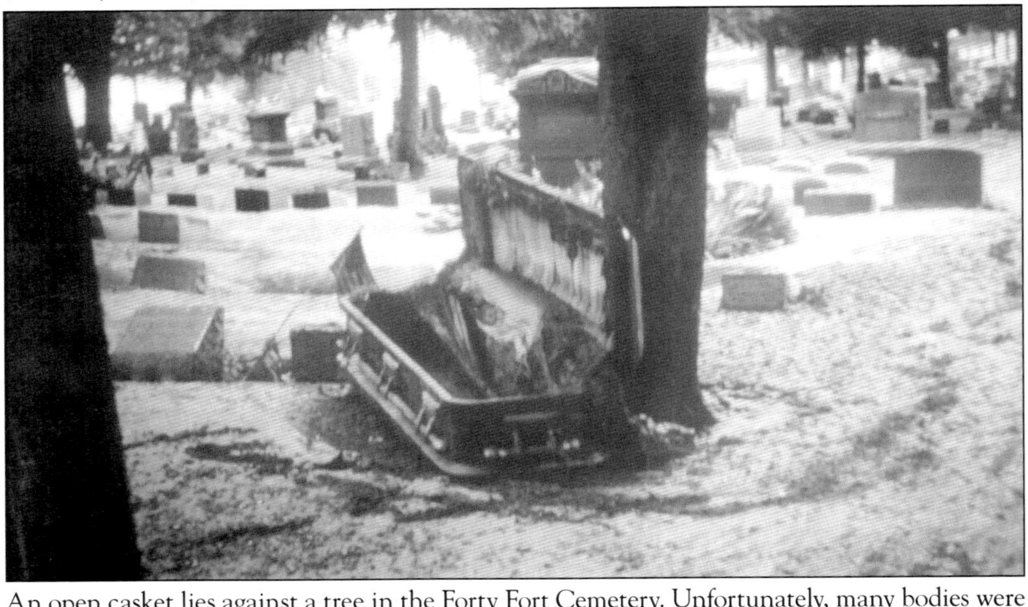

An open casket lies against a tree in the Forty Fort Cemetery. Unfortunately, many bodies were unable to be properly identified, so remains were reburied in a common grave. Many burial records were lost in the flood. Trespassers were warned to stay out of the area; however, curiosity got the better of some locals who ventured into the cemetery anyway. Upon seeing the corpses littered throughout the grounds, many would later regret their visit. (Courtesy of the Forty Fort Cemetery Association.)

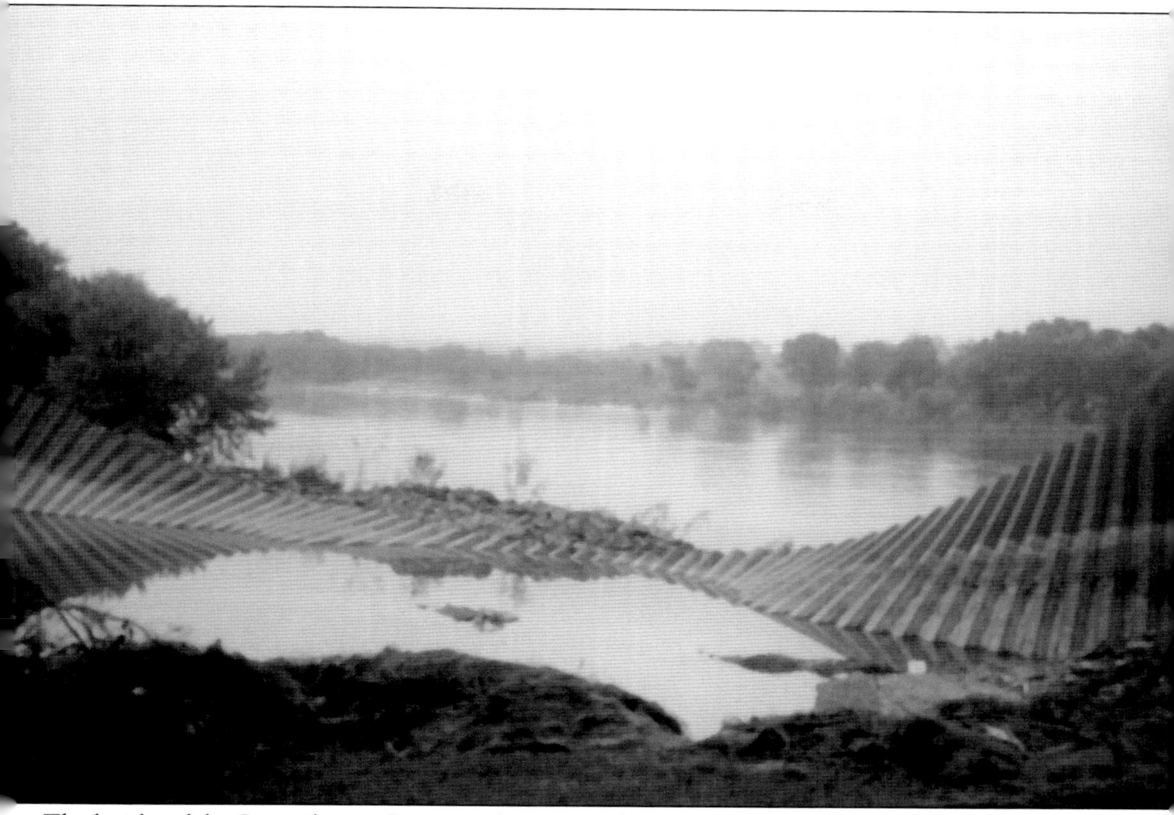

The height of the Susquehanna River can be seen in this picture. Although the levy system was nearly 40 feet high, the water touched the top. The mangled remains of this fence were no match for the power of the flood. Few residents imagined rain and a tropical storm could turn their towns into such chaos. (Courtesy of the Forty Fort Cemetery Association.)

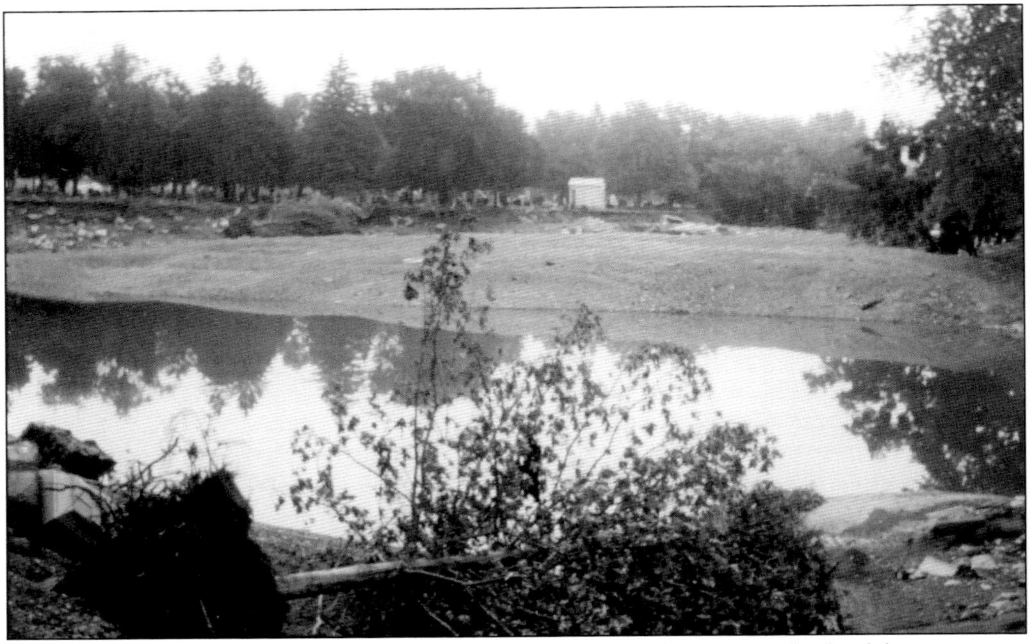

Receding waters begin to reveal what is left of the Forty Fort Cemetery in both of these pictures. Deputy coroner Joseph Shaver was instrumental in helping identify the remains as best he could. Several years later, a state in the Midwest reached out to him to see if he could be of assistance in again identifying remains after a flood. Although he offered his expertise, he would not personally visit the site. "Once was enough," he stated. One can only imagine what he must have seen trying to identify and collect the hundreds if not thousands of human remains unearthed during the flood of 1972. (Both, courtesy of Forty Fort Cemetery Association.)

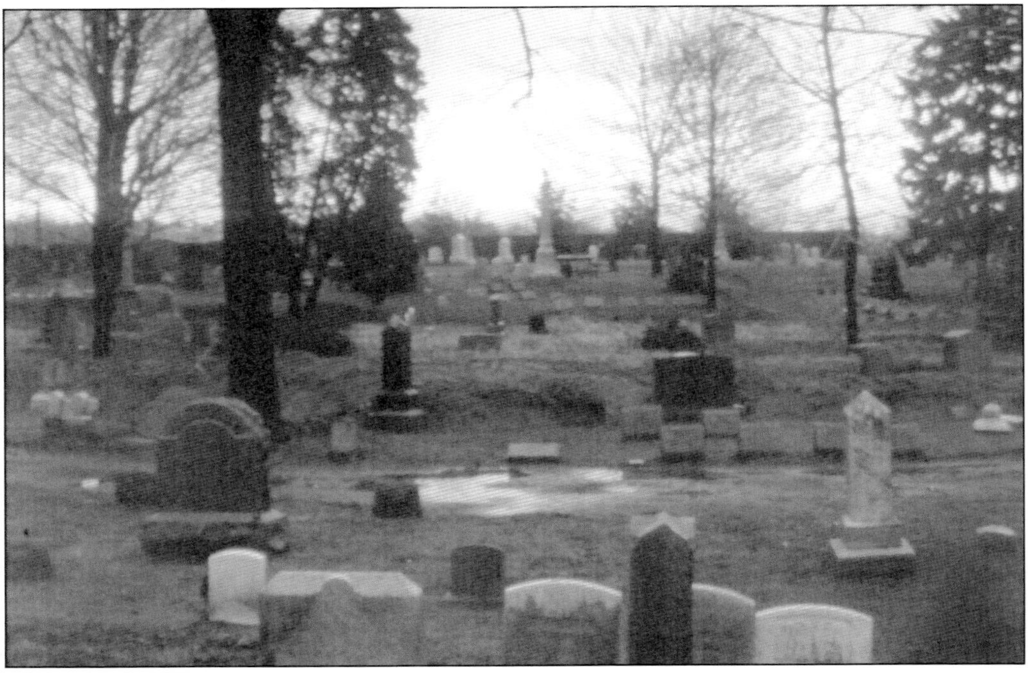

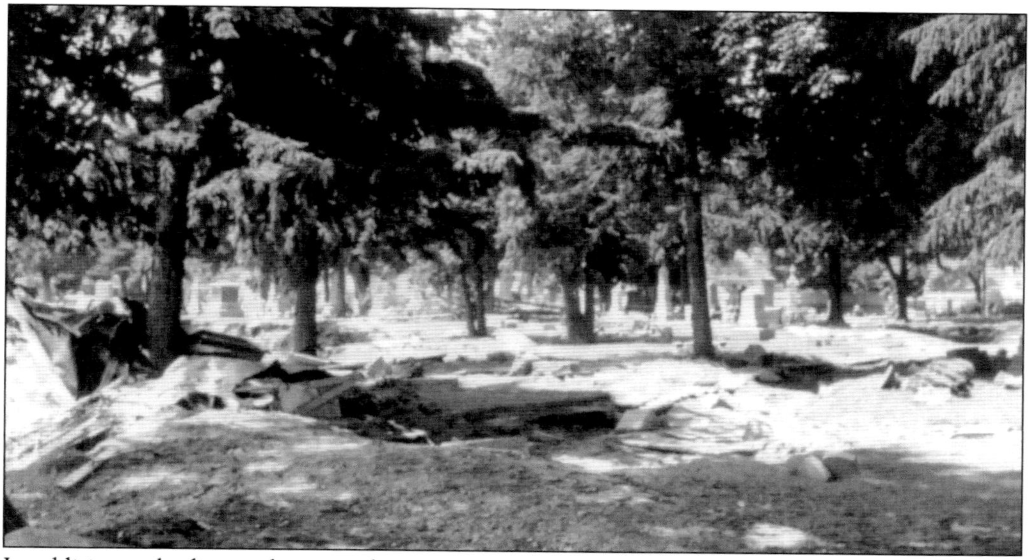

In addition to bodies in the immediate vicinity of the cemetery, the current distributed remains for some distance in the surrounding cities. Residents described with both amusement and horror how neighborhood dogs would sometimes return home with bones, their origins not always clear. One homeowner even found a human femur while rebuilding their residence some years after. Some residents recalled seeing the bodies floating at night, dreading daylight when the scene was more visible. A morgue was set up at the Swetland Homestead in Wyoming, an area untouched by water. There the task of identification began. (Courtesy of Forty Fort Cemetery Association.)

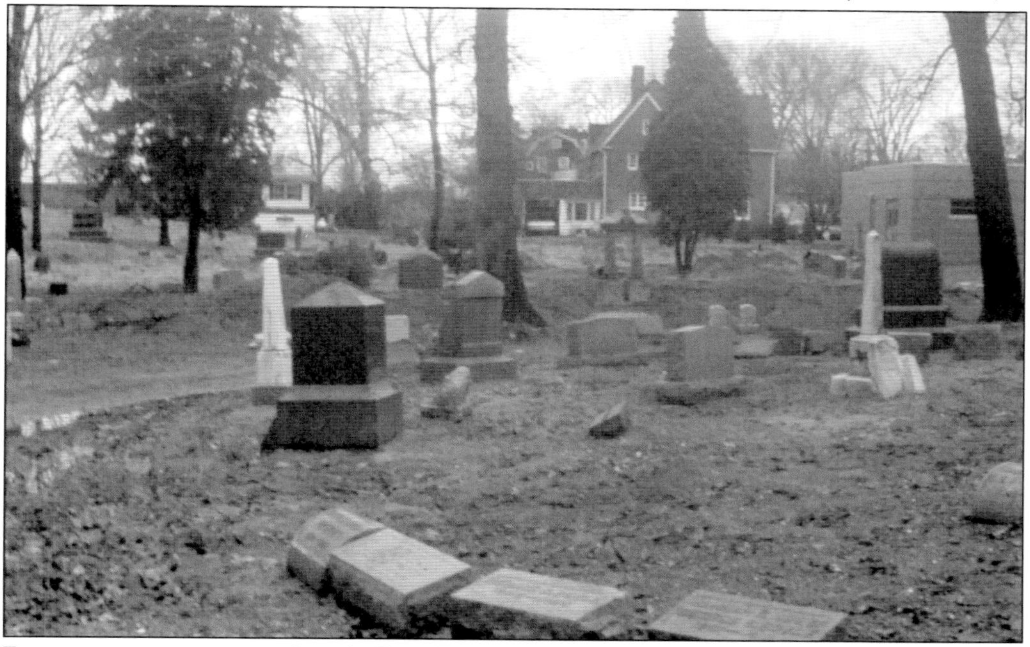

For many, seeing an icon such as the Forty Fort Cemetery in such disarray was almost as upsetting as the damage to their homes. This area of the cemetery did not have as much damage to tombstones, though it would take some time to replant grass and restore it to its original condition. (Courtesy of Forty Fort Cemetery Association.)

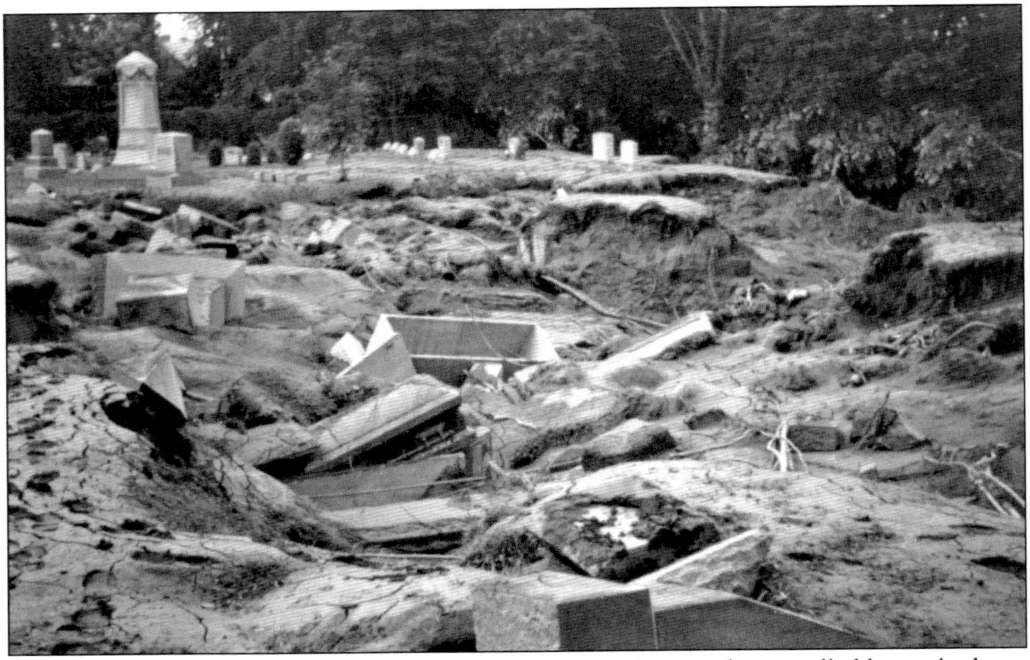

Caskets and tombs were scattered throughout Forty Fort. One resident recalled how a body sat covered by a blanket for some time near the fence. Passersby were both shocked and curious about such things, with one resident even lifting the blanket to show their child the corpse. The child's tears led onlookers to question the judgement of the mother. It was one thing to come back to the area and witness firsthand the property damage inflicted by Agnes. But to see dead bodies floating; to find corpses in garages, homes, and lawns; or to find human bones on their property was too much for many. (Both, courtesy of Forty Fort Cemetery Association.)

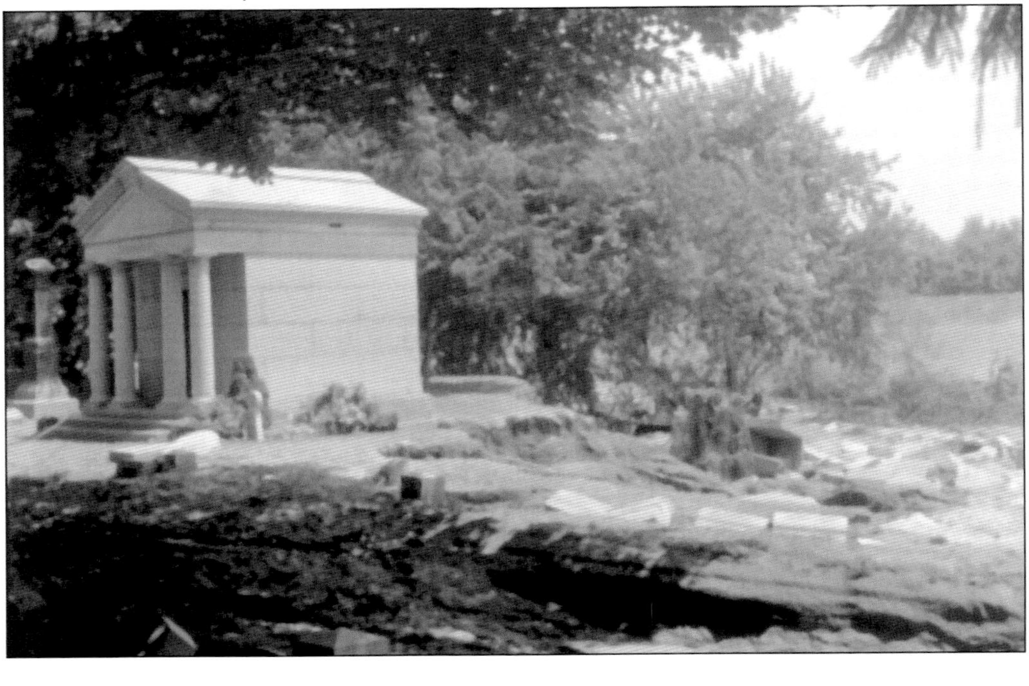

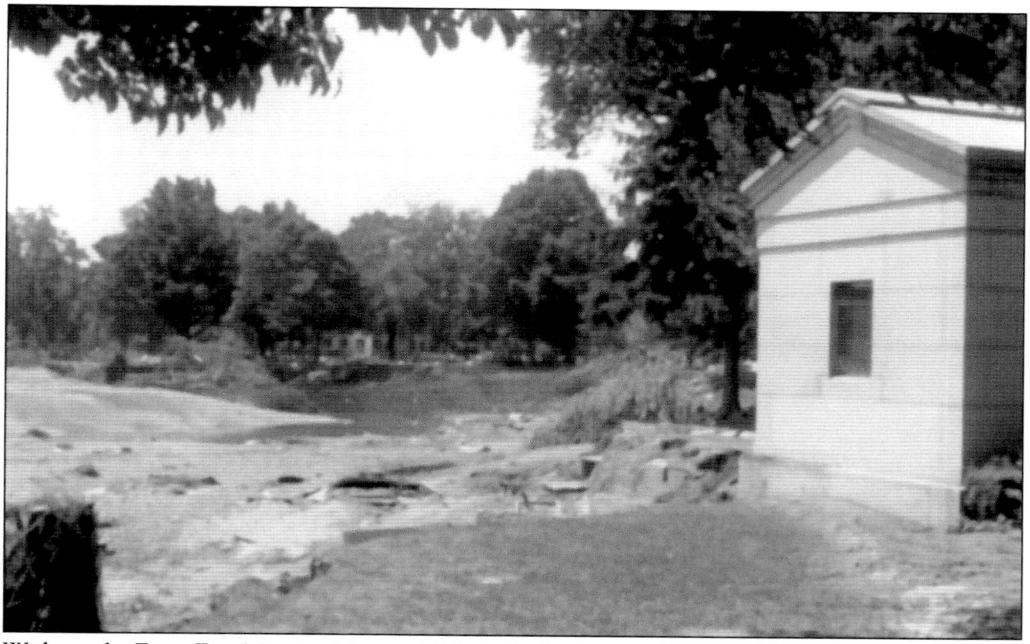

Without the Forty Fort Meeting House visible in the background, one could not identify this picture as one of the historic Forty Fort Cemetery. Stones weighing hundreds if not thousands of pounds were uprooted and thrown around the vicinity, a reminder of the immense power of the flood of 1972. Many graves were from the 1800s. (Courtesy of the Forty Fort Cemetery Association.)

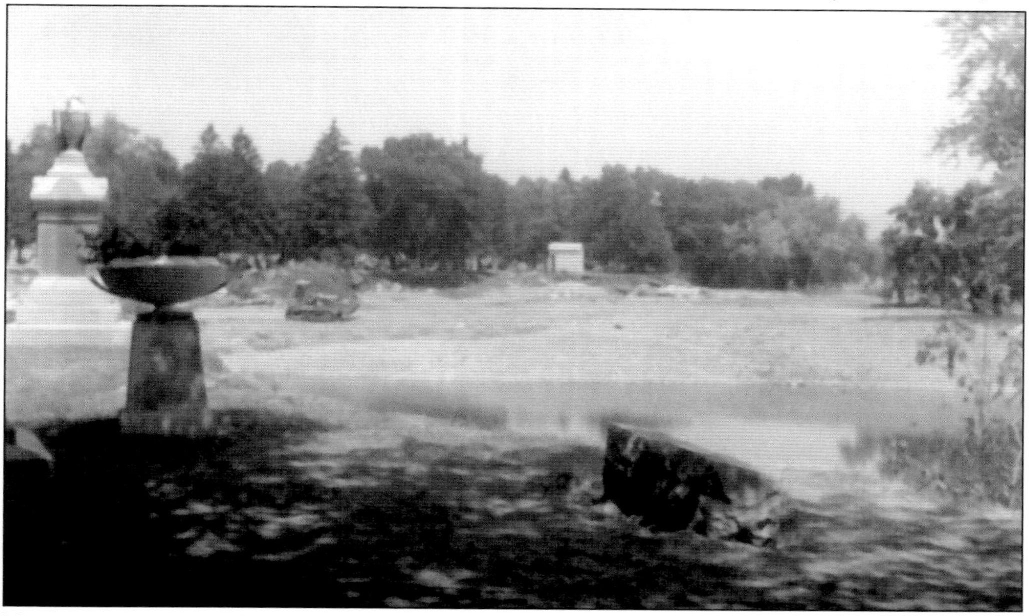

Heavy equipment, such as this bulldozer, worked after Agnes to rebuild the cemetery. The first order of business was to fill in the "moon crater," as one citizen described the giant hole left by Agnes. Large trucks dumped load after load of dirt to help the cemetery rebuild. From there, the ground was leveled and grass was planted; today, the site bears no evidence of the carnage that existed in 1972. (Courtesy of Forty Fort Cemetery Association.)

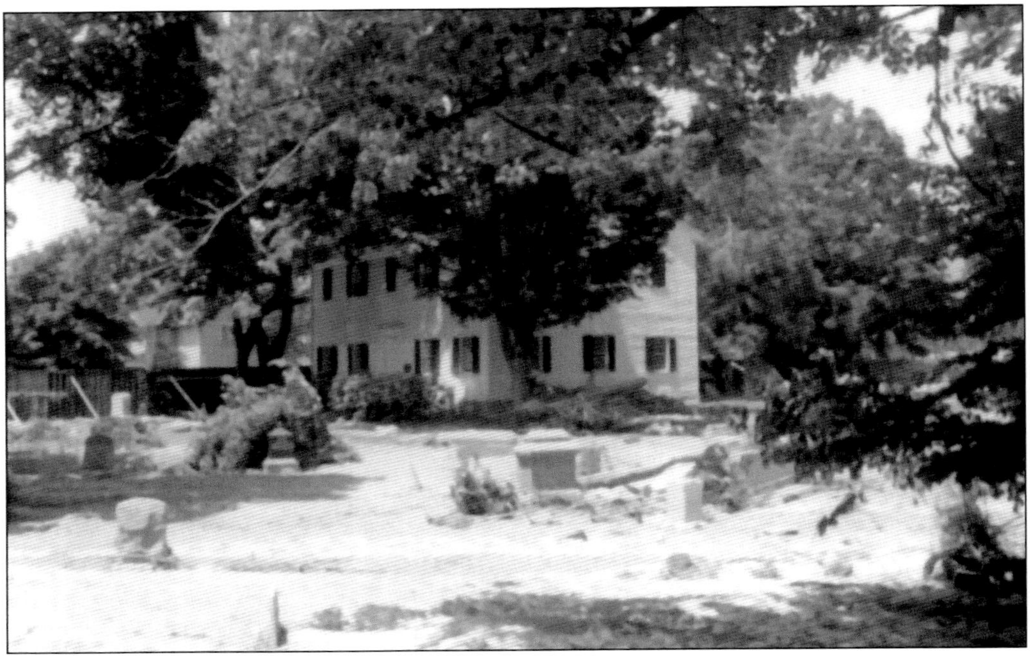

In both images, the Forty Fort Meeting House is seen with debris around it with the structure itself surviving Hurricane Agnes relatively unscathed. Built in approximately 1806, the building likely survived many floods. However, never before had she seen one such as Agnes. Amazingly, the meetinghouse was spared all but minimal damage. The rest of the cemetery, however, was a war zone. Coroner Dr. George E. Hudock Jr. oversaw the grim task of trying to identify remains. (Both, courtesy of Forty Fort Cemetery Association.)

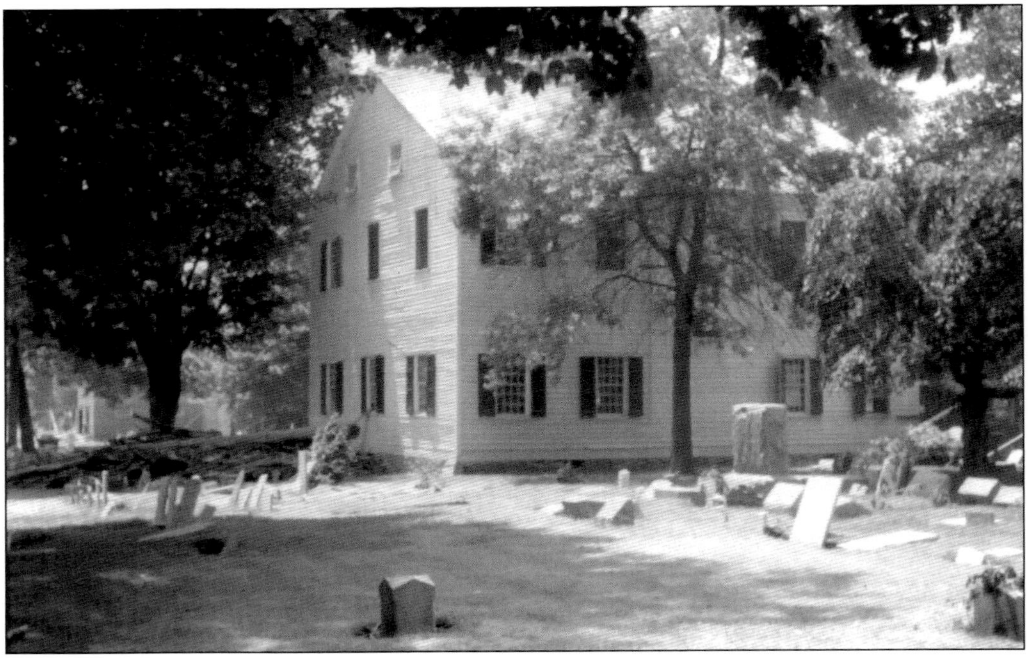

In this picture, the Susquehanna River still runs through part of the Forty Fort Cemetery. Residents were simply stunned at how effortlessly these massive stones and monuments were lifted and hurled throughout the grounds. First the levy was breached, then the treacherous waters ran roughshod over the burial plots of thousands of graves. (Courtesy of Forty Fort Cemetery Association.)

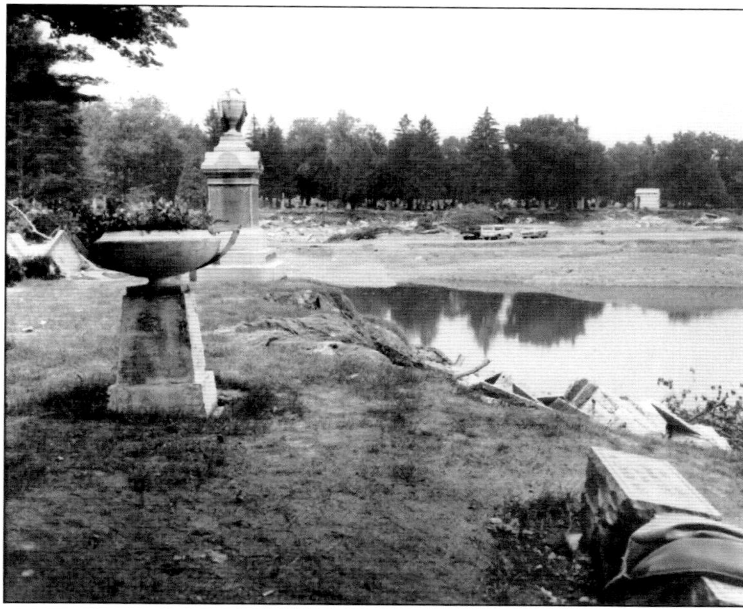

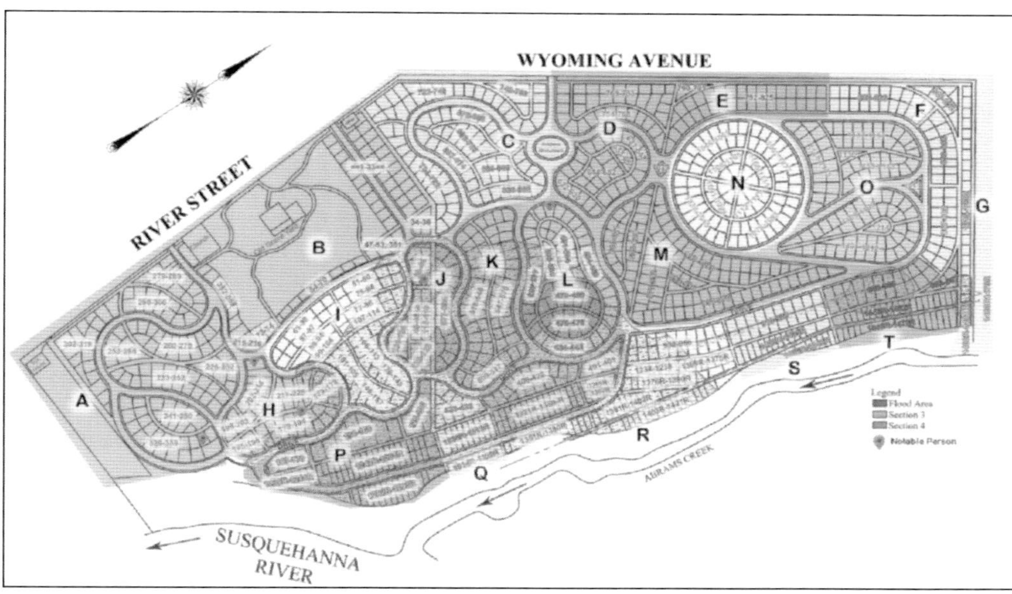

This map shows the layout of the Forty Fort Cemetery, as well as areas struck by the rushing waters of the river. Floodwaters initially reamed the graves out from underneath, though eventually the area was inundated completely. A year after the flood of 1972, a church service was held to honor those who had their eternal resting places disturbed by Hurricane Agnes. (Courtesy of Forty Fort Cemetery Association.)

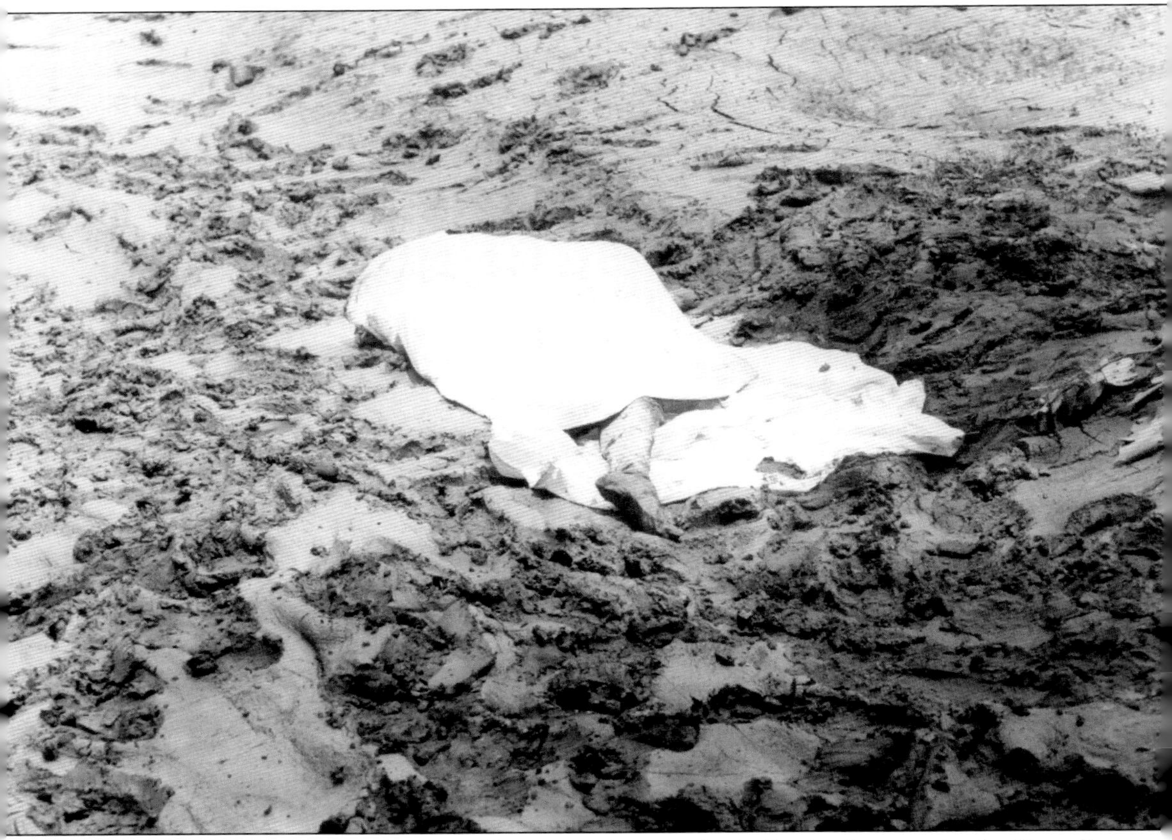

In one of the grisliest scenes from Hurricane Agnes, a body lies in the open in the Forty Fort Cemetery, covered from view by a blanket. Hundreds of caskets were exhumed by the rushing water. Many opened, revealing decomposing bodies, which would have to be laid to rest again. Human remains were scattered throughout the region. One resident, fully aware of the proper protocol for disposing of human remains, found a human bone during cleanup. With a quick toss, the body part went into the trash, and the homeowner continued cleaning up. Most of the corpses, or what was left of them, were never found. (Courtesy of Forty Fort Cemetery Association.)

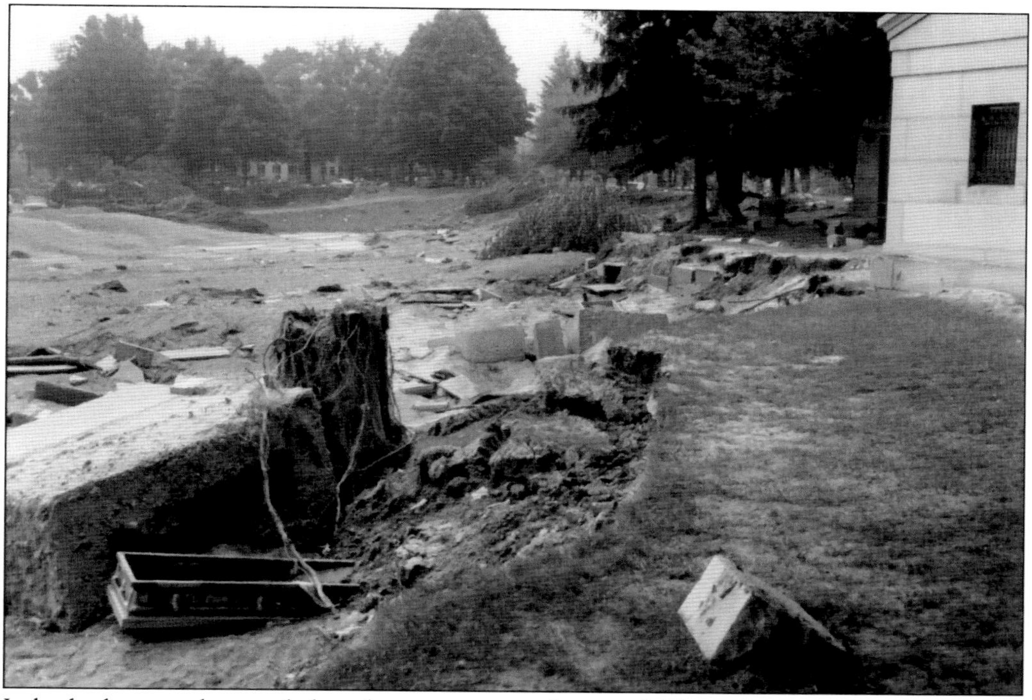

In both photographs, toppled tombstones, open caskets, and debris are strewn throughout what used to be the Forty Fort Cemetery. Despite the levy system, the waters of the Susquehanna River tore through the area, leaving the cemetery in her wake. Since the 1800s, the Forty Fort Cemetery stood as a final resting place for many community members. In the haste to leave the rising waters, records were left behind, only to be destroyed. The majority of the deceased could not be placed in their original graves, if they could even be located. They were memorialized in a monument when the cemetery was rebuilt. (Both, courtesy of Forty Fort Cemetery Association.)

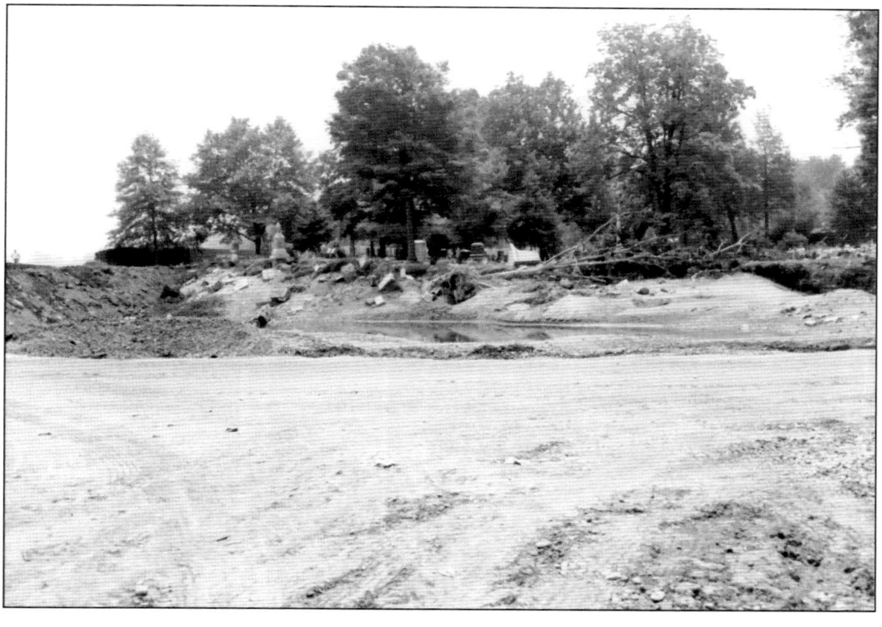

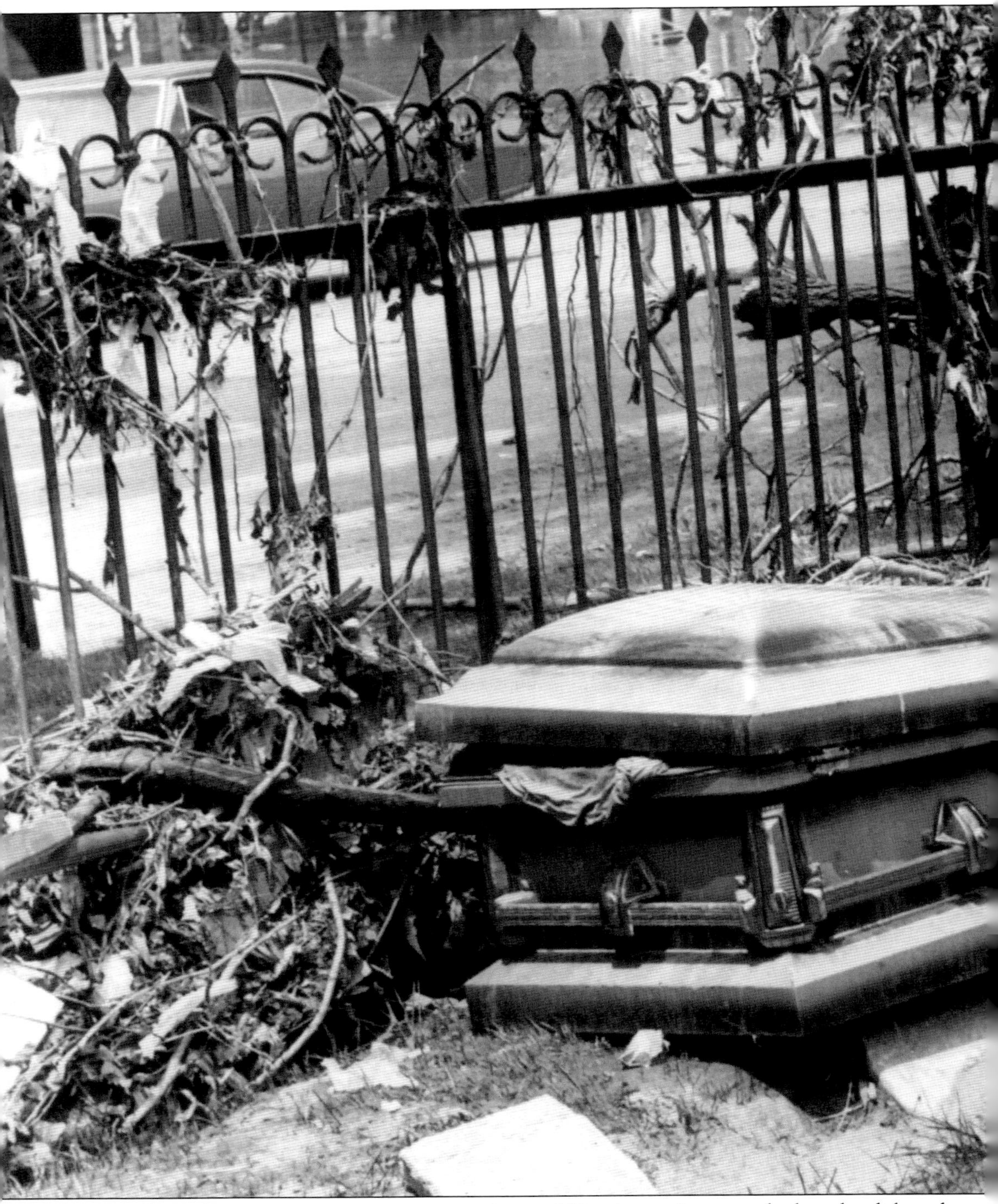

In perhaps the most iconic memory many have of Hurricane Agnes and what she did to the Wyoming Valley, a damaged casket lies above ground, having been uprooted and displaced by the raging waters of the Susquehanna River. Although the statistics of the flood—billions of dollars in damage, thousands displaced, a ruined infrastructure—are often cited, this picture

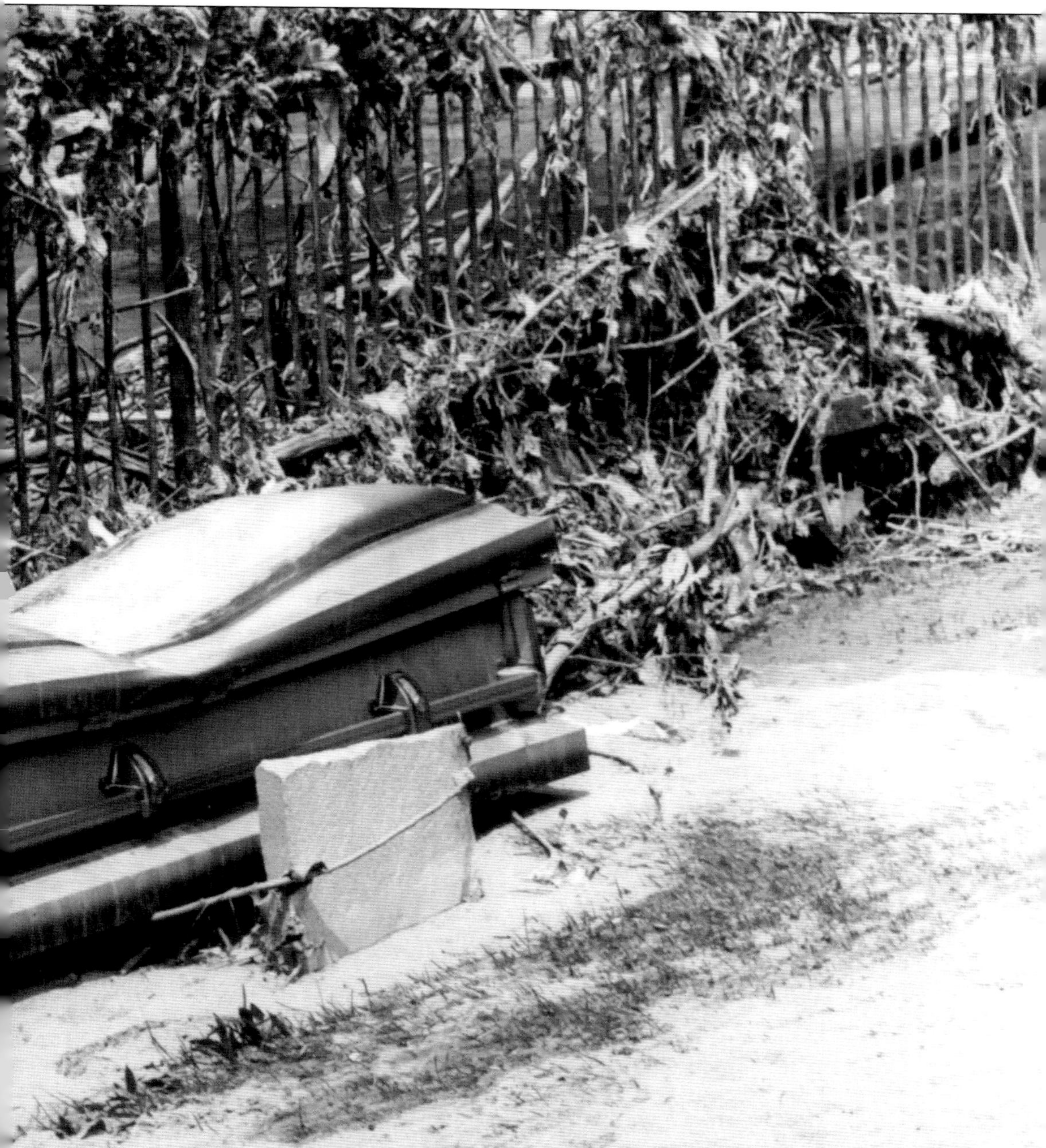

tells a human story that cannot be measured in mere finance. A loved one, placed for eternal rest in the Forty Fort Cemetery, is missing, their casket broken open. For many residents, the memories of this image lasted long after they rebuilt their homes and lives. (Courtesy of Forty Fort Cemetery Association.)

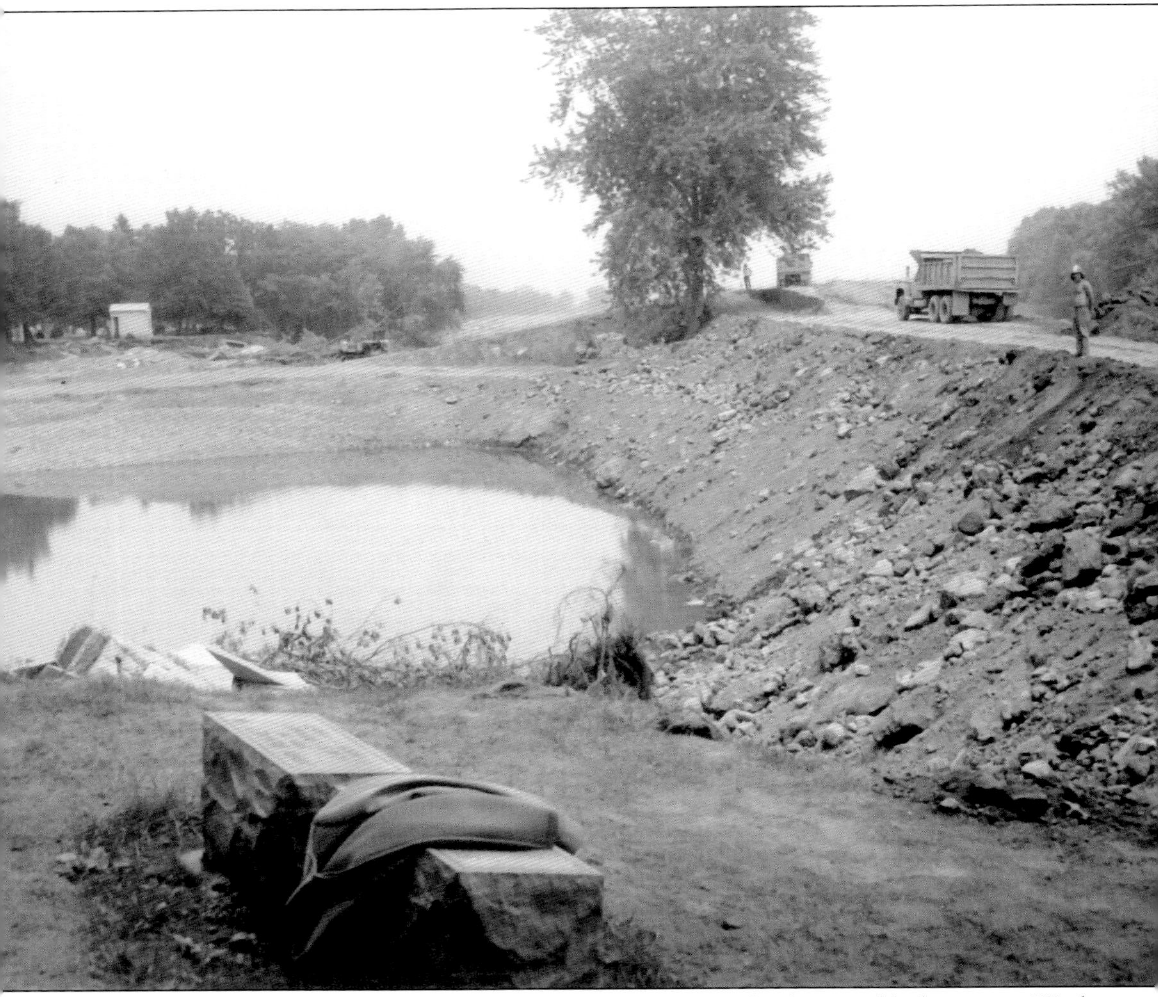

A worker looks on during the rebuilding of the cemetery, with a large sinkhole in view. Workers had been sandbagging the area until 10:30 p.m. Realizing their efforts were in vain, they left, not to their homes, but to go sandbag another vulnerable area. Before, after, and during the storm, one positive of Hurricane Agnes was that the community came together, first to halt the waters, then to rebuild what was destroyed. Although many stood and took pictures of the cemetery and the rising water, they soon put their cameras down and tried to outrun the Susquehanna River as it began its conquest of Forty Fort. (Courtesy of Forty Fort Cemetery Association.)

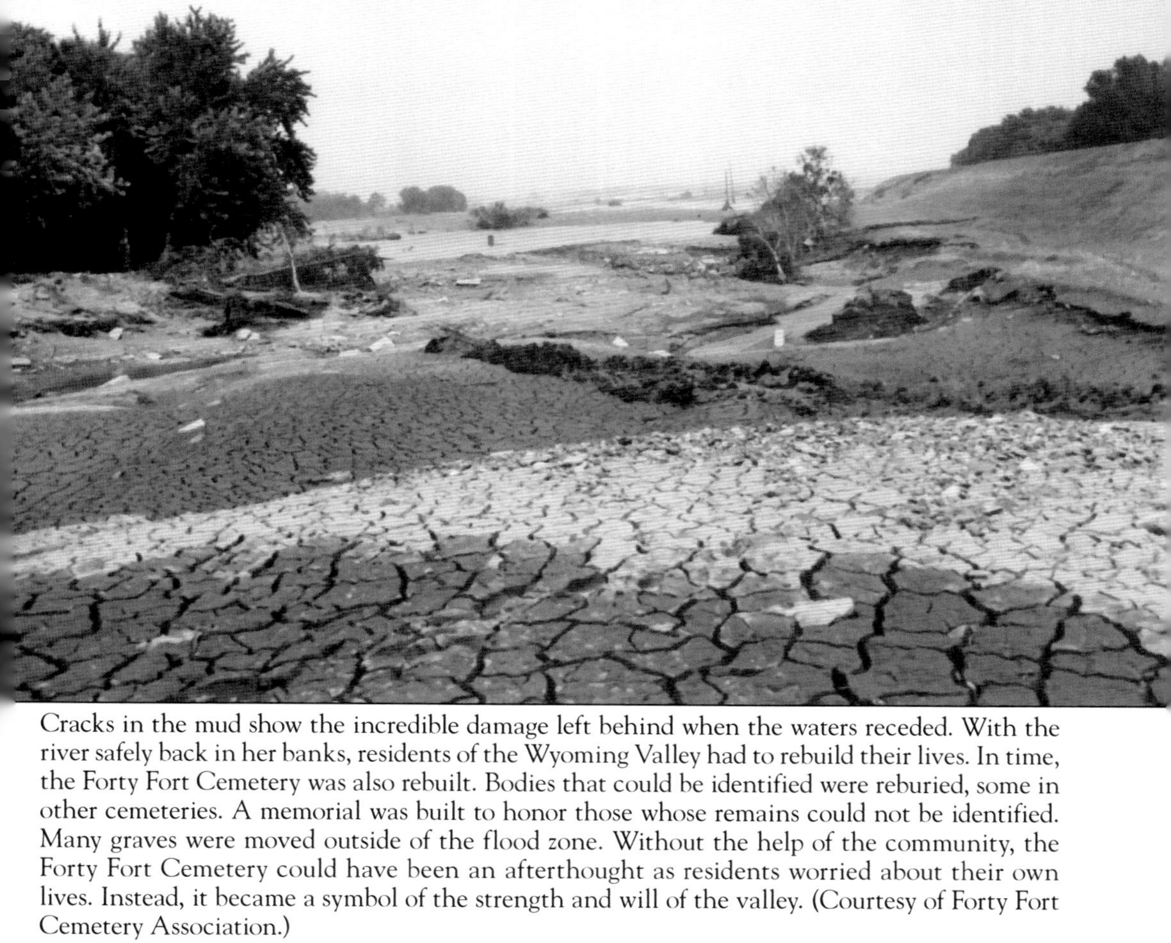

Cracks in the mud show the incredible damage left behind when the waters receded. With the river safely back in her banks, residents of the Wyoming Valley had to rebuild their lives. In time, the Forty Fort Cemetery was also rebuilt. Bodies that could be identified were reburied, some in other cemeteries. A memorial was built to honor those whose remains could not be identified. Many graves were moved outside of the flood zone. Without the help of the community, the Forty Fort Cemetery could have been an afterthought as residents worried about their own lives. Instead, it became a symbol of the strength and will of the valley. (Courtesy of Forty Fort Cemetery Association.)

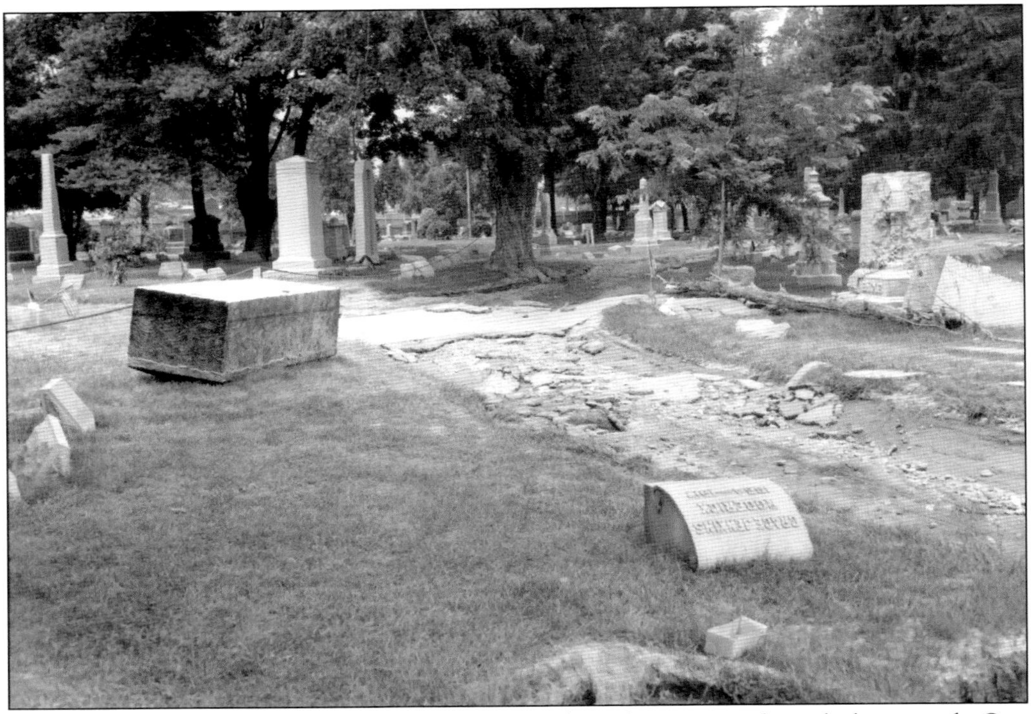

The path in the middle of both photographs shows where the river cut through the grounds. One resident recalled an 8- to 10-foot high torrent of water coming towards him, throwing gravestones "like matchboxes." Even large, granite mausoleums were knocked off their foundations. Many prominent members of society, such as Lazarus Denison, Rev. George Peck, Henry Hoyt, Charles Turpin, and even a famous poet, Elinor Morton Wylie, were buried at the Forty Fort Cemetery. Their contributions ranged from serving in the Civil War to politics to law and the ministry. Many of the notables were buried in the same section, which was close to the river and hammered by the rising water. (Both, courtesy of Forty Fort Cemetery Association.)

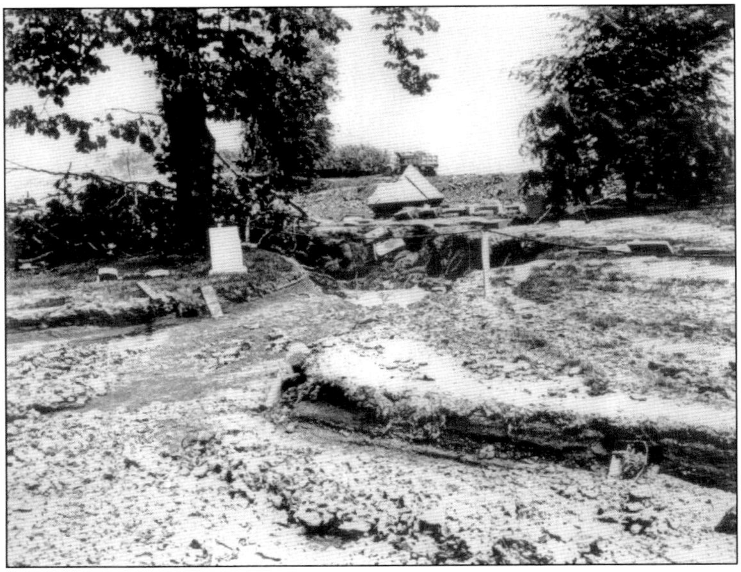

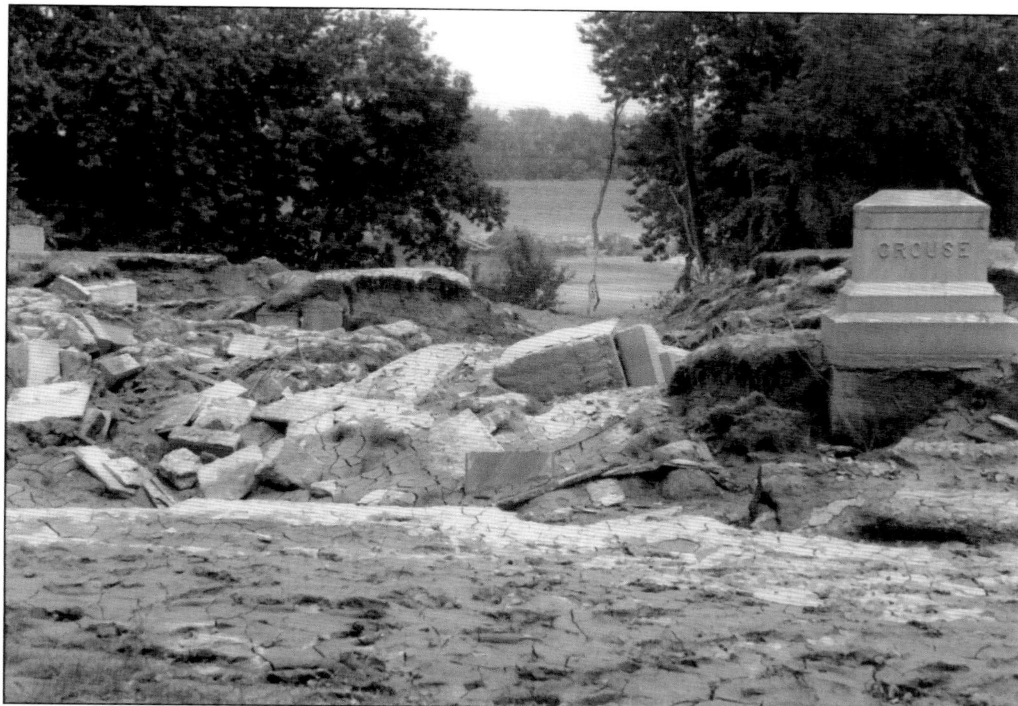

Above, the Susquehanna River lies in her banks behind the damaged cemetery. At 40 feet, the river had been a monster only days before. Now, it is the calm, placid river that seems so familiar. Yet the damage outside of her banks was a reminder of the power of moving water. Below, a worker stands next to a tombstone. It may have been the damage to the cemetery that spared Forty Fort and Swoyersville from more. Had the cemetery not taken the brunt of the blow, the water would have had a clear path to the homes and businesses in the area. (Both, courtesy of Forty Fort Cemetery Association.)

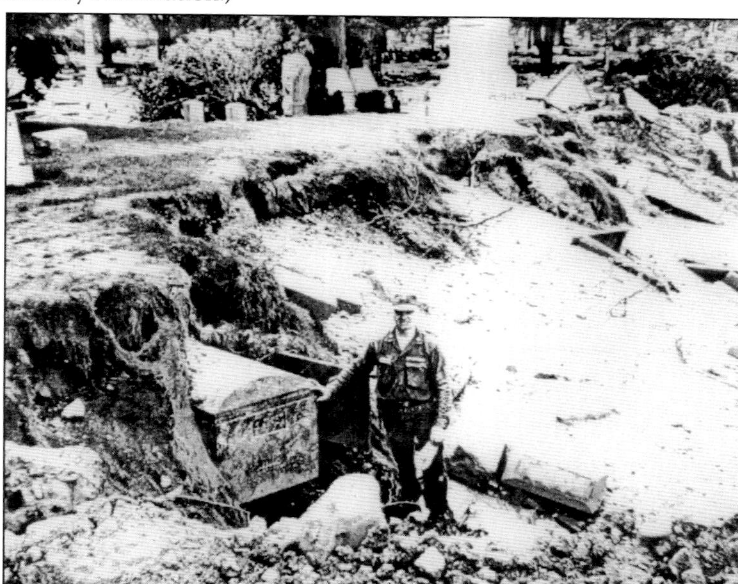

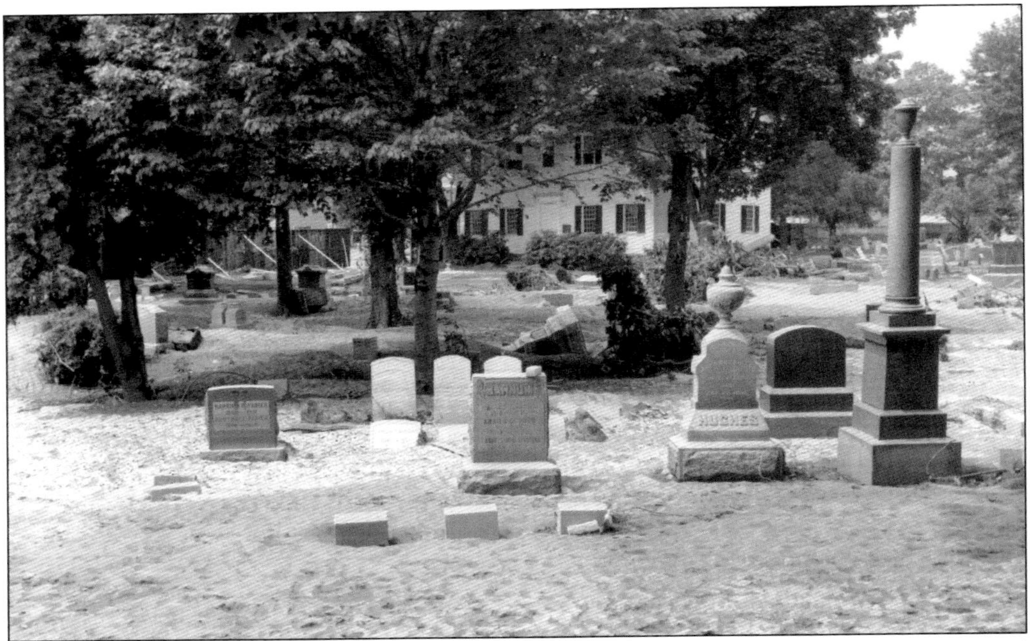

Fortunately, not every gravestone was toppled, as these two photographs show. The waters seemed to strike at random, with no rhyme or reason as to what was spared and what was destroyed. Geologists stated after the flood that the water bubbled underneath the dike system, essentially creating whirlpools that dug out large chunks of the ground. Despite this, initial river watchers were for the most part unconcerned. "It's been like this before," one stated. Curious onlookers were too busy snapping photographs to worry about evacuating. Eventually, those who chose to stay were too late and were caught trying to outrun floodwaters to save as many of their possessions as possible before the river, having taken her wrath out on the cemetery, moved into the borough to look for new targets. (Both, courtesy of Forty Fort Cemetery Association.)

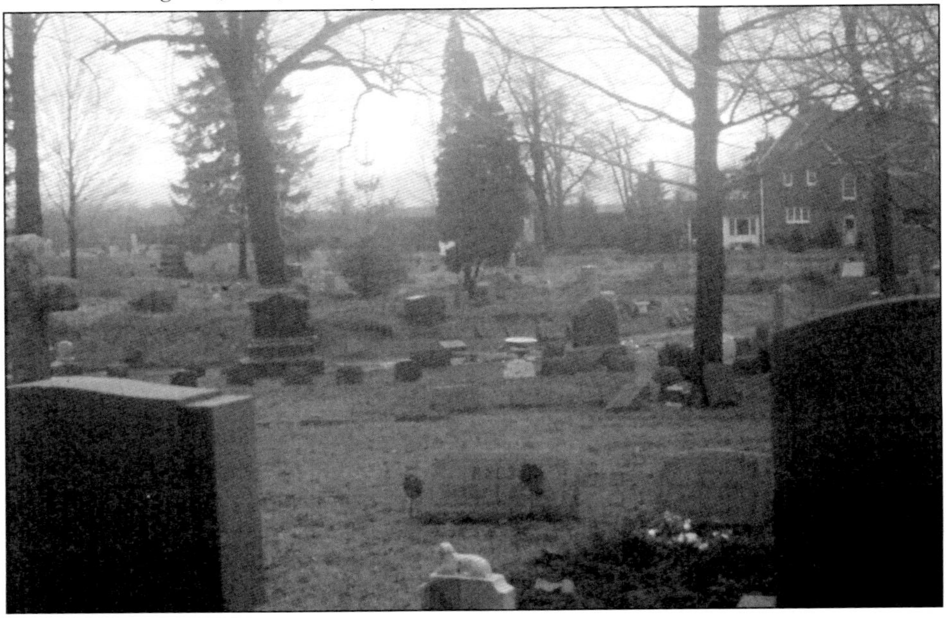

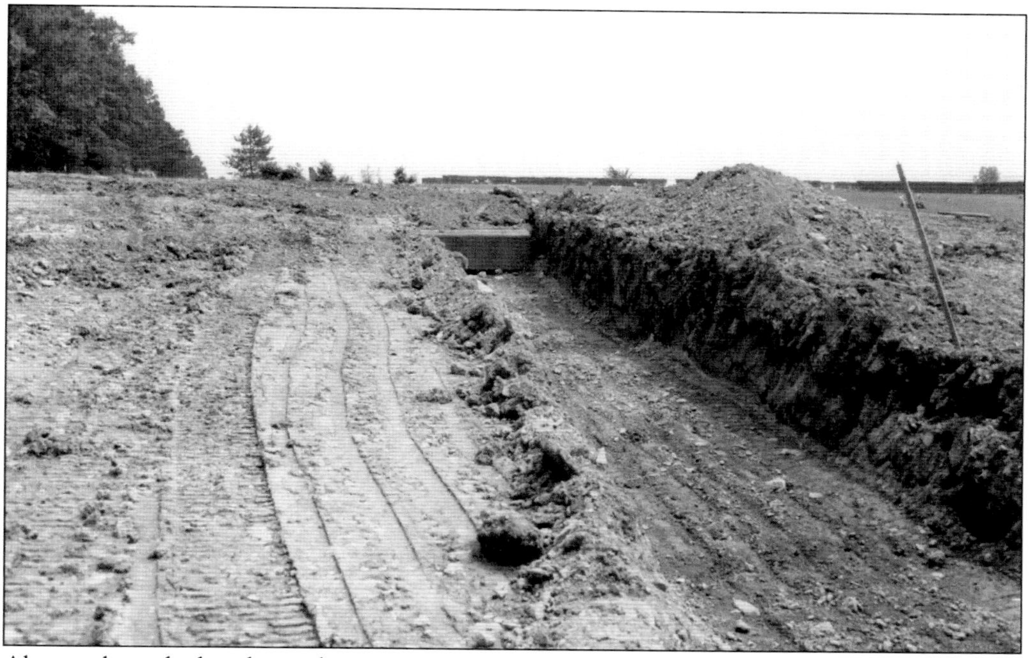

Above, a large ditch is dug as the cemetery is slowly put back together. Below, grass is growing near an area of ground that heavy machinery has attempted to level. It took over two years for workers to bring the cemetery as close as they could to the way it was before June 23, 1972. A year after the flood, a touching memorial service was held. With a theme of gathering and rebuilding, hymns were sung and residents prayed together to celebrate what was spared and mourn what would never be regained. Despite the damage, the outpouring of togetherness allowed the citizens of Forty Fort to appreciate each other as they rebuilt. (Both, courtesy of Forty Fort Cemetery Association.)

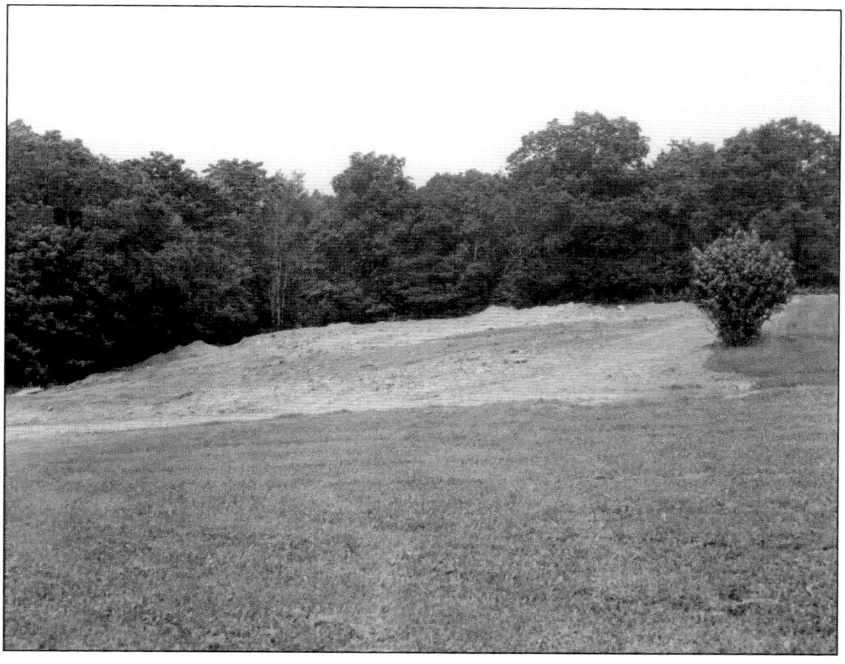

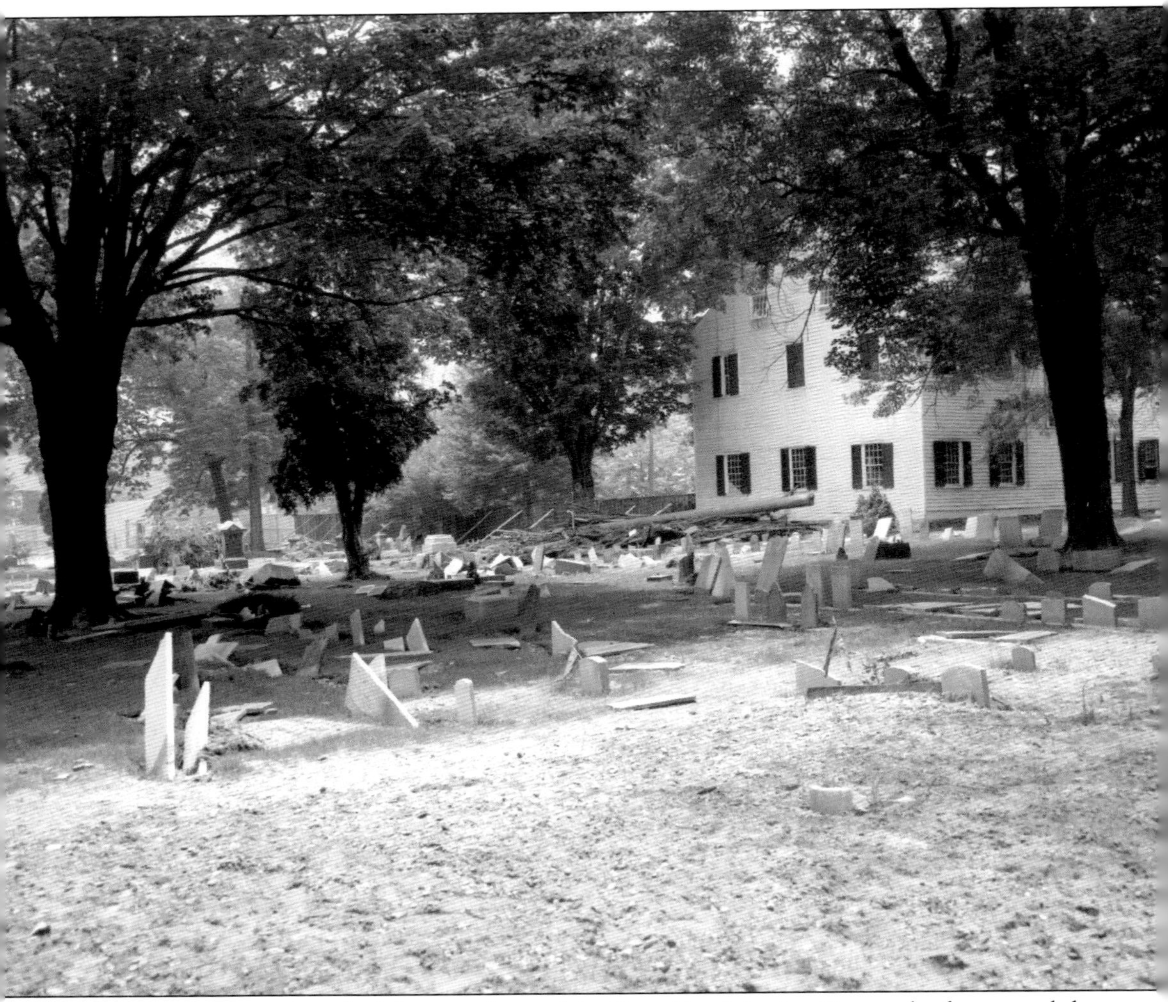

With a large tree knocked down in front of the Forty Fort Meeting House, the foreground shows tombstones buried in several inches of mud. Despite water going to the top of the pews inside the building, the damage was mostly limited to the outside. All the meetinghouse required was a good cleaning. A year after the flood, a church bulletin stated, "It was one year ago today at this hour that the waters broke through the dike . . . we shall continue to rebuild our homes, our community, our valley, and our lives." (Courtesy of Forty Fort Cemetery Association.)

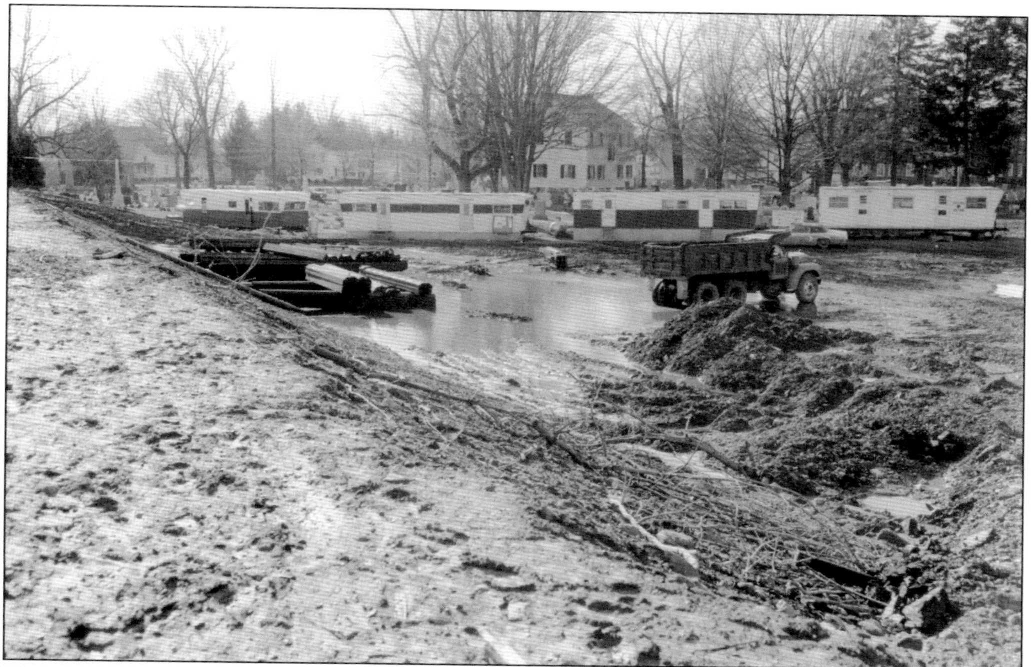

The cleanup of the Forty Fort Cemetery was an immense undertaking, as seen in these images. Some 40 volunteers, many of whom had never seen a corpse, would be charged with locating, retrieving, and identifying bodies for reburial. Despite the stench, workers did their best to complete their task. Of the over 2,500 bodies disturbed, only 36 were identified. Workers felt a sense of duty, despite the ghastly task for which they signed up. "Thank God for the hippies," one man declared. Economic status, age, or ethnicity did not seem to matter. People came down to help because it was the right thing to do. (Courtesy of Forty Fort Cemetery Association.)

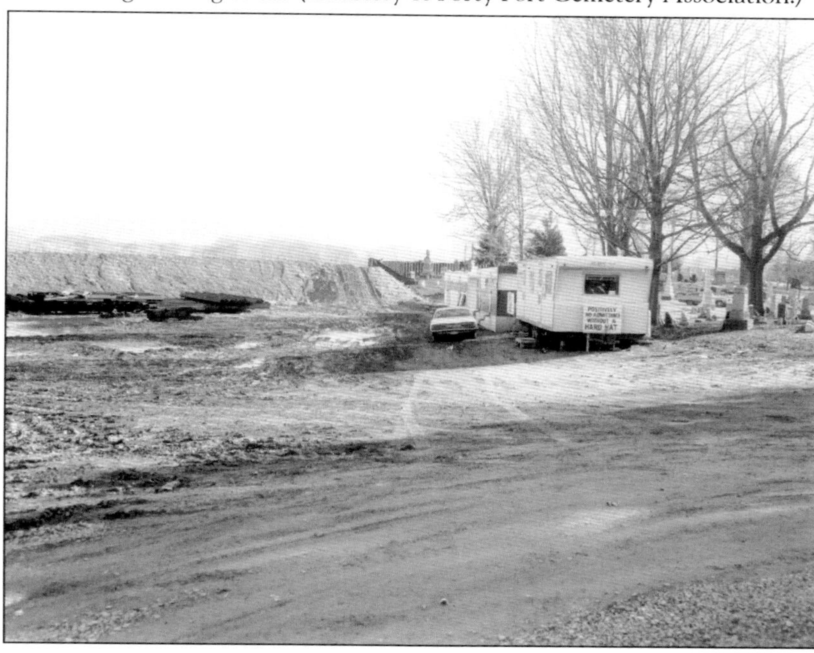

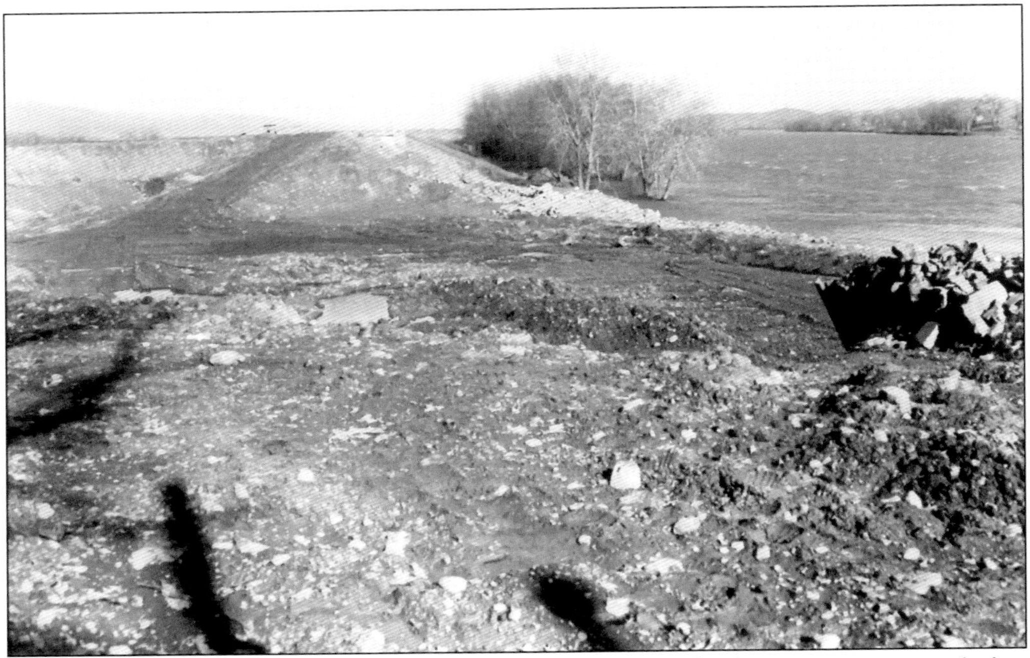

In the photographs above and below, the Forty Fort Cemetery slowly returns to its state before the flood. Deputy coroner Joseph Shaver noted that as he and his staff worked, family members with relatives buried in the cemetery would stop to ask if they had found "my mother" or "my brother." "It was sad," Shaver recalled. The flood of 1972 exposed the faults of the levy system designed to protect the cemetery from the unpredictable river. Although it was physically and financially impossible to rebuild the cemetery as it was, officials did the best they could to put the cemetery back together. (Courtesy of Forty Fort Cemetery.)

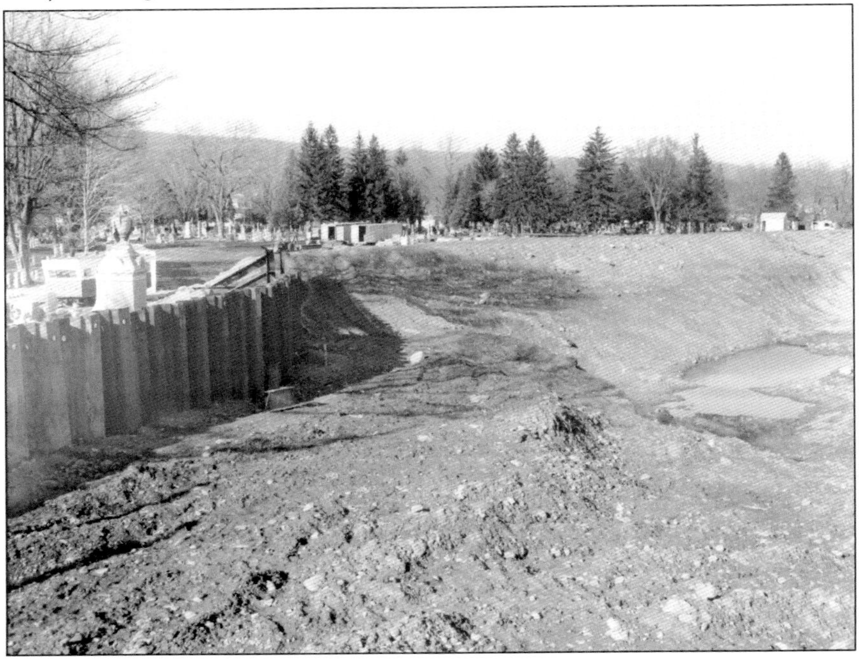

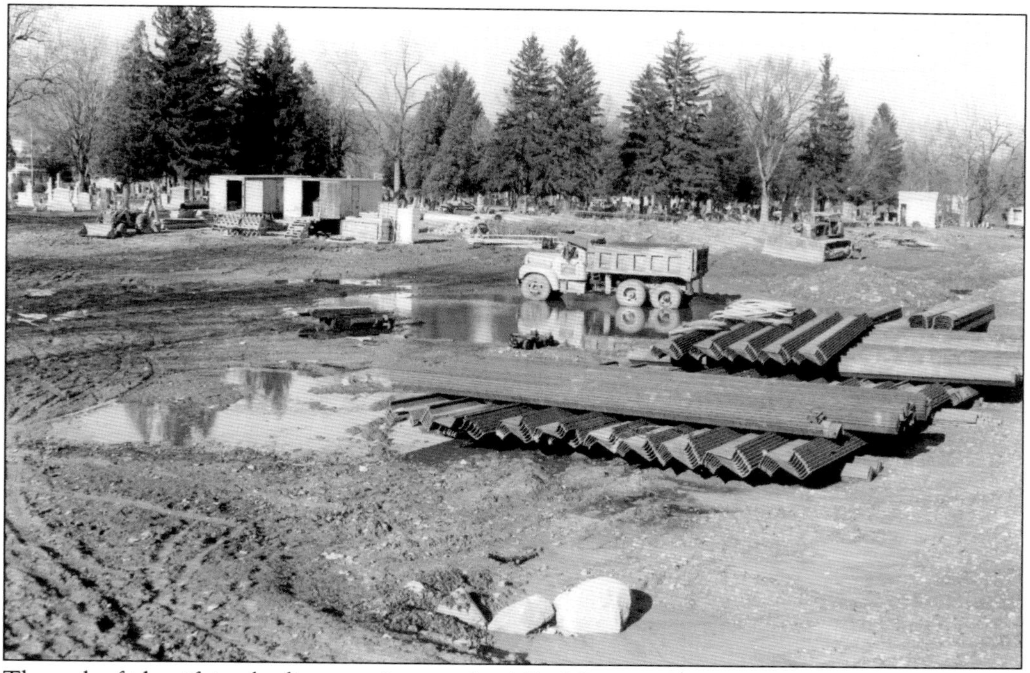

The task of identifying bodies was given to the 442nd Service Company of the US Army Graves Registration Department, out of Bellefonte, Pennsylvania. With their headquarters set up at the Swetland Homestead, they worked closely with local officials. They were joined by Marines and volunteers from the Trucksville Junior Volunteer Fire Department. Though not pleasant, it was necessary work. The Forty Fort Cemetery is an area of great local fame. To see it so damaged by the flood was difficult for not only those with loved ones buried there, but residents who appreciated the historical significance of the grounds. (Both, courtesy of Forty Fort Cemetery Association.)

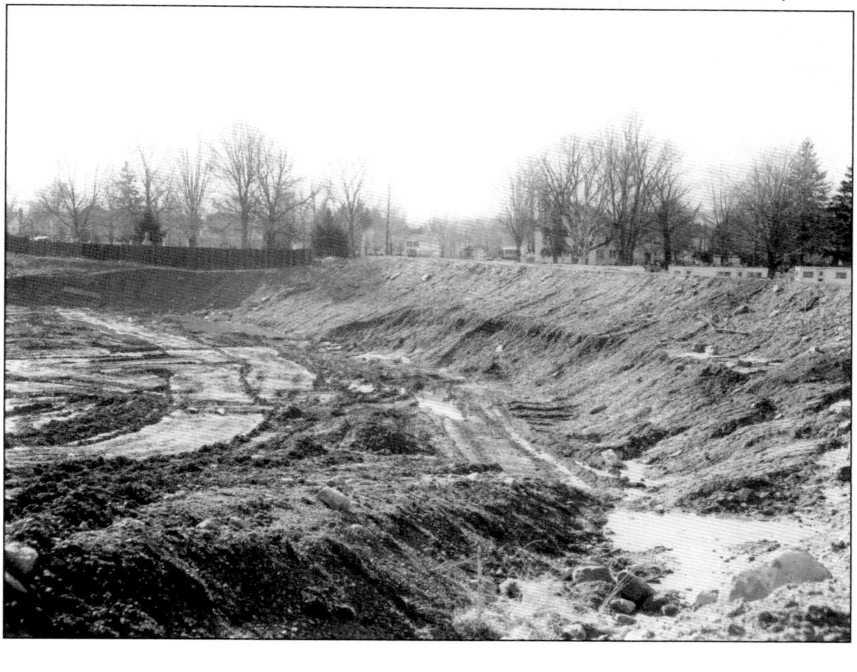

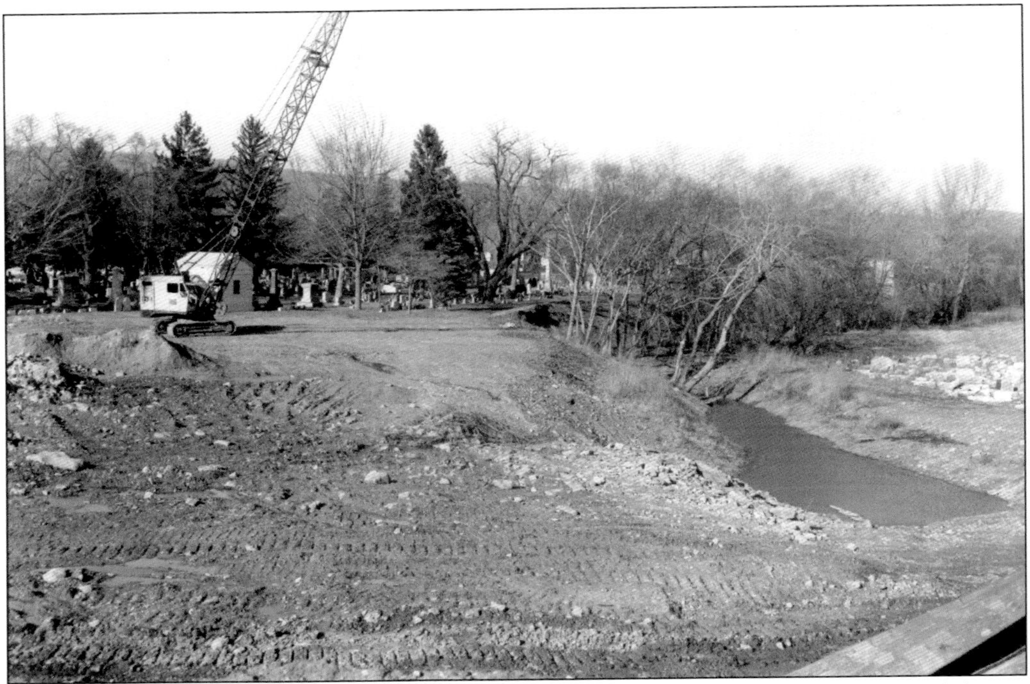

Heavy equipment was used to reconstruct the dike and the surrounding area. With such heavy damage, a burial site would be needed; thus, many bodies were relocated to the Memorial Shine Cemetery in Dallas, Pennsylvania. When not working, volunteers ate their meals at the Wyoming Methodist Church, often with the smell of decay still in their minds. Between 1973 and 1975, workers did their best to rebuild the Forty Fort Cemetery. Local organizations that donated items such as flagpoles and monuments, especially the Veterans of Foreign Wars Post 283, recognized the lack of respect Hurricane Agnes showed to the dead and did their part to bring the Forty Fort Cemetery back to a respectful state to honor them. Below, some new flowers on graves show the cemetery is beginning to look the way it did before the flood. (Both, courtesy of Forty Fort Cemetery Association.)

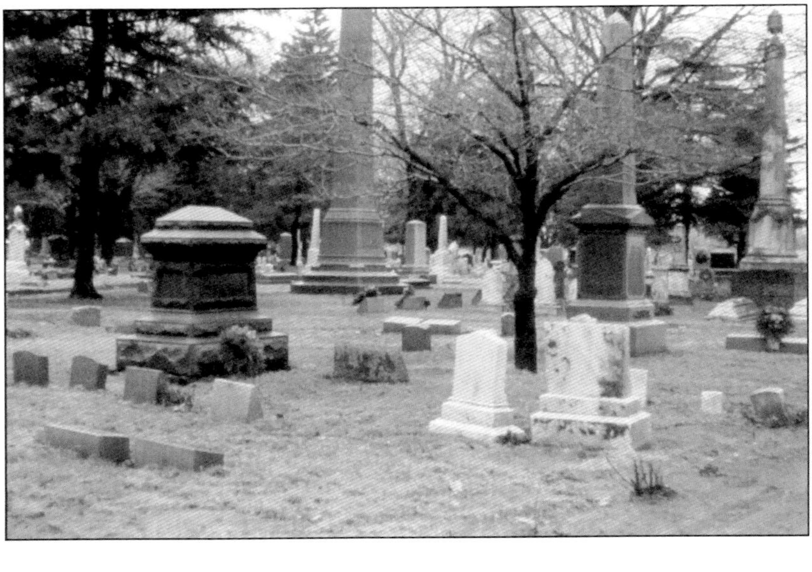

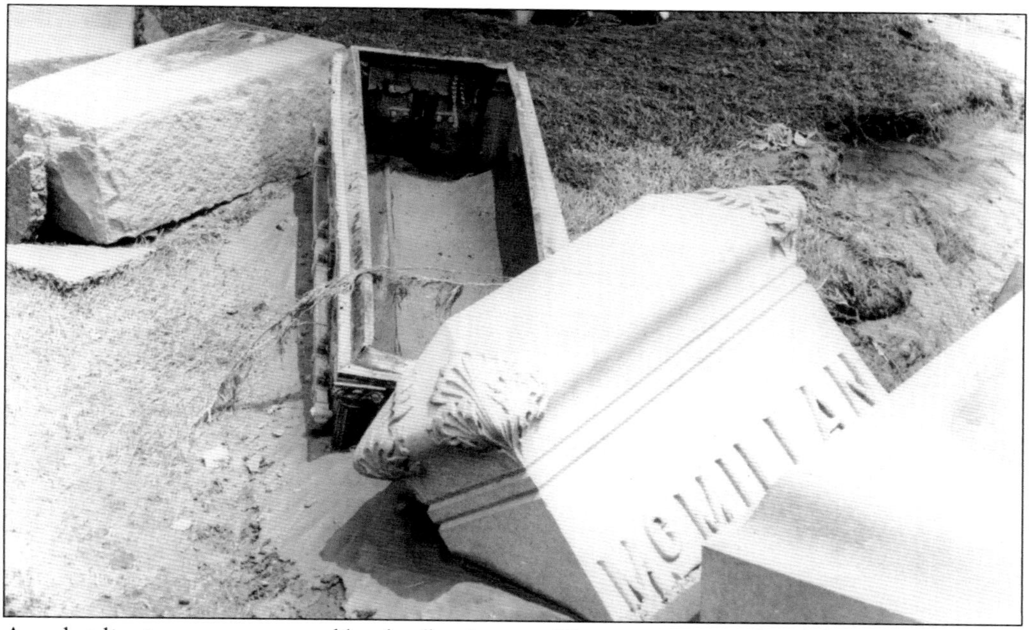

A casket lies in a grave, opened by the floodwaters. The immense weight of the stone structures meant nothing to the rising river. Although most caskets were empty, some trespassing residents claimed, as they explored the cemetery after the flood, that they witnessed open caskets with decomposing bodies in them. Many complained of the stench. For those who chose to ignore warnings and venture into the off-limits area, few would forget the sight of bodies thrown everywhere, in various states of decomposition. (Courtesy of Forty Fort Cemetery Association.)

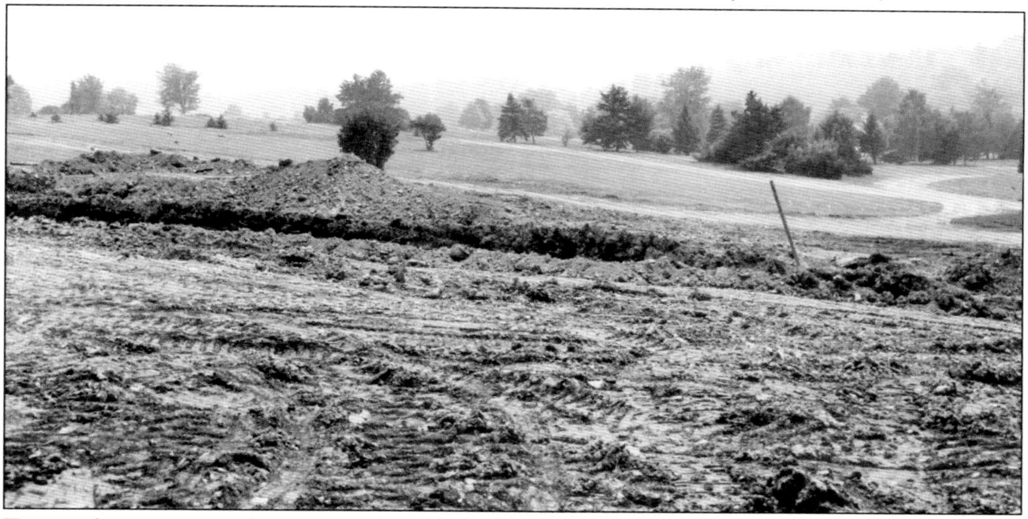

Tire tracks are seen in the mud in what is left of the cemetery. As the river retreated to her natural banks, the cemetery was closed off and work began to rebuild. Since the mid-1800s, the Forty Fort Cemetery has been a prominent local feature. Officials were grateful for the outpouring of support and help they received to rebuild the grounds. With trees hundreds of years old, along with the meetinghouse and graves, the Forty Fort Cemetery once again takes its place as a major historical feature residents pass on their way up and down Route 11. (Courtesy of Forty Fort Cemetery Association.)

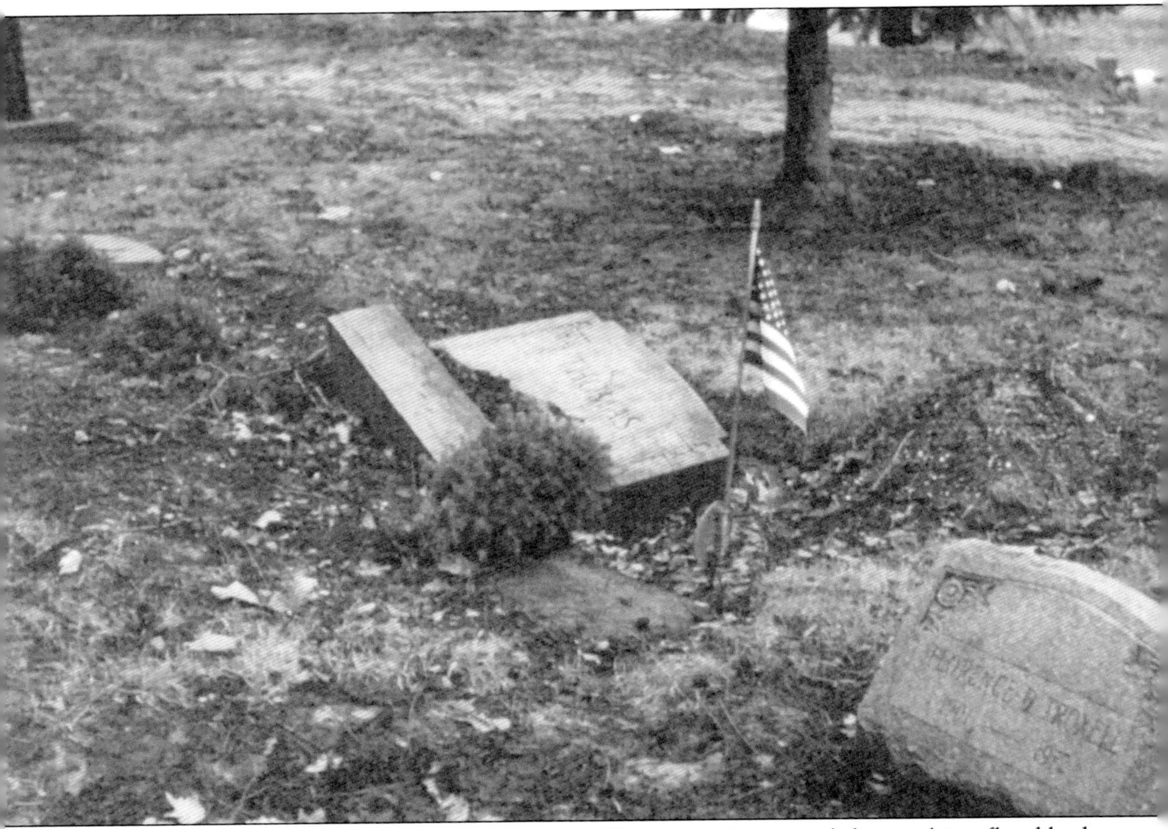

Once again, the sheer devastation and impact Hurricane Agnes and the resulting flood had on the Forty Fort Cemetery is seen in this photograph. Over 2,700 graves and tombs were destroyed, of which only 1,410 were recovered. Only a handful of bodies could be identified. The remaining ones were never found, having been washed away, disintegrated, or buried under flood debris. Deputy coroner Joseph Shaver recalled, "First there were 90 bodies, then 150, then 500, by the time we were through." Many of the bodies were moved to other locations throughout the valley, or just outside of it, with the hope they would not be disturbed again. (Courtesy of Forty Fort Cemetery Association.)

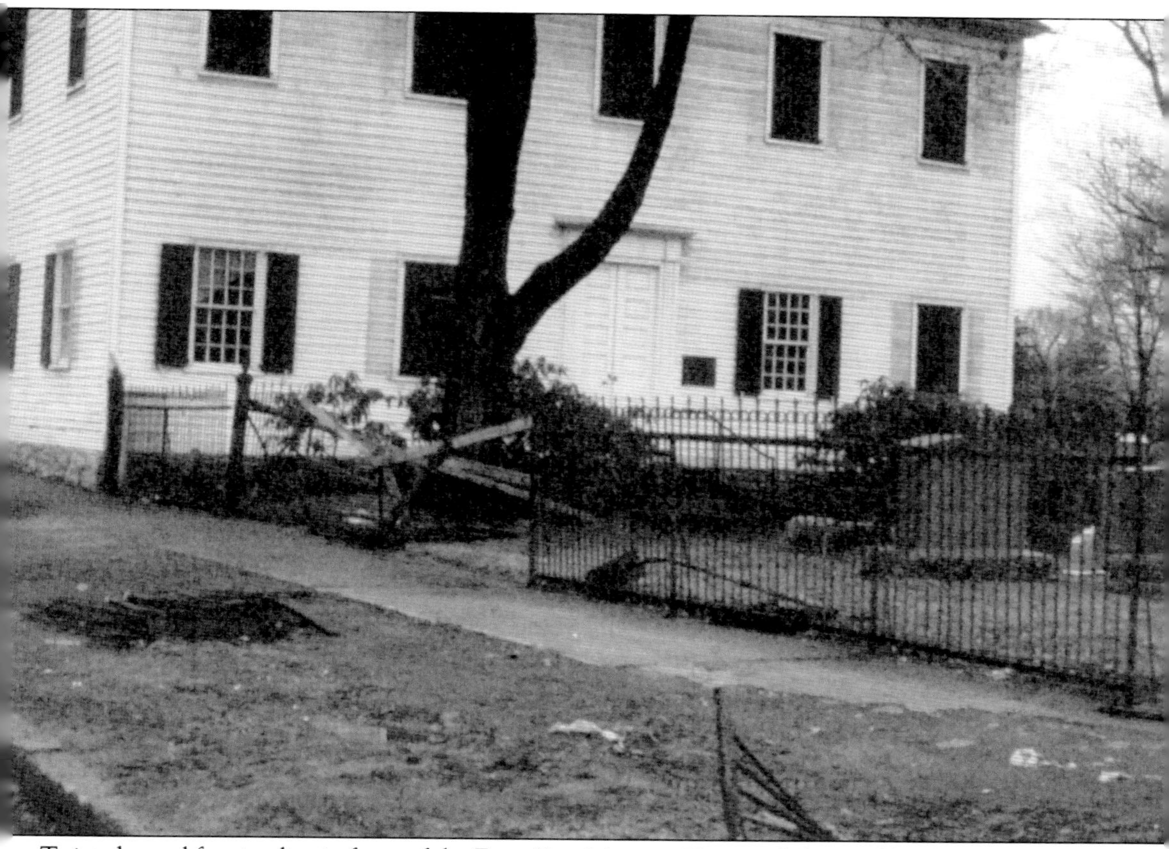

Twisted metal fencing lies in front of the Forty Fort Meeting House, while wood has been hastily placed to block the gate, hoping to keep trespassers and curious onlookers out of the site. With its first church service dating to 1807, the Forty Fort Meeting House has been a major part of the area for over 200 years. The Susquehanna River has flooded dozens of times since the structure was built, yet it has withstood them all. For many residents, the building is a symbol of strength and pride. It is amazing that the building survived the flood of 1972 essentially intact. (Courtesy of Forty Fort Cemetery Association.)

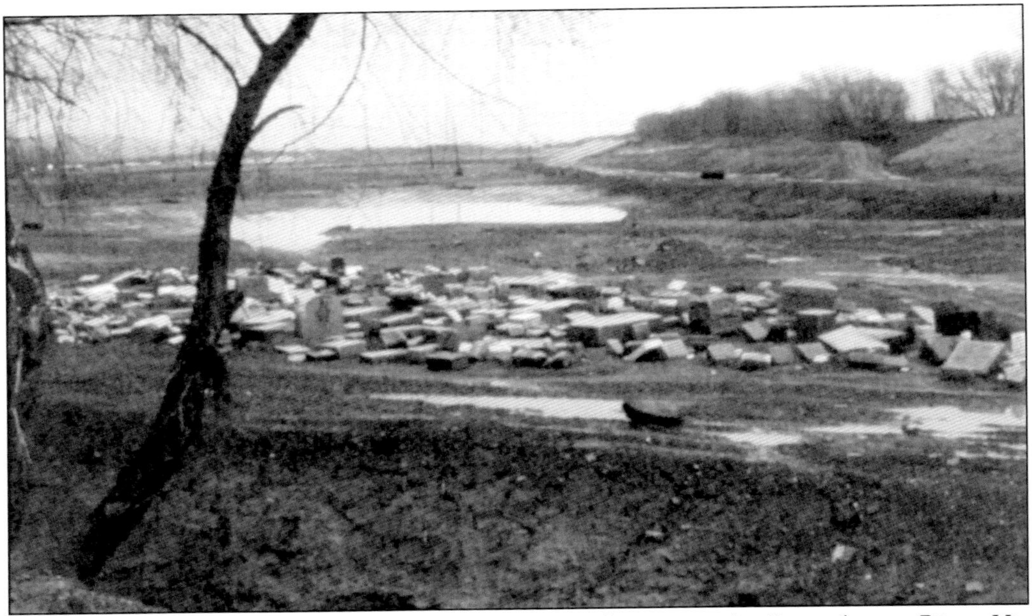

A helicopter pilot from the Navy recalled seeing logs floating in the Susquehanna River. His passenger, not a fan of flying to begin with, realized they were not logs but bodies from the Forty Fort Cemetery. As deputy coroner Joseph Shaver flew over Forty Fort, barely recognizing streets now covered in water, his focus was on his family. Soon, however, he knew someone would have to clean up the corpses strewn about by the flood. These pictures show the collection of tombstones that were found. "We just lined them up," Shaver recalled. Officials had an enormous mess on their hands, with bodies and cemetery structures thrown as far as the eye could see. (Both, courtesy of Forty Fort Cemetery Association.)

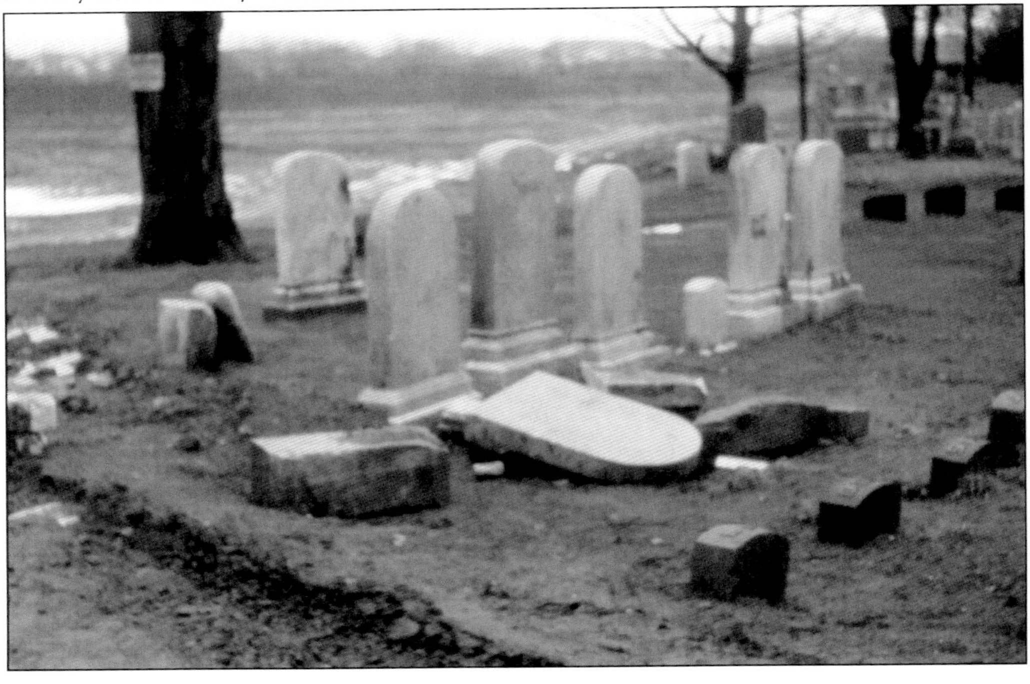

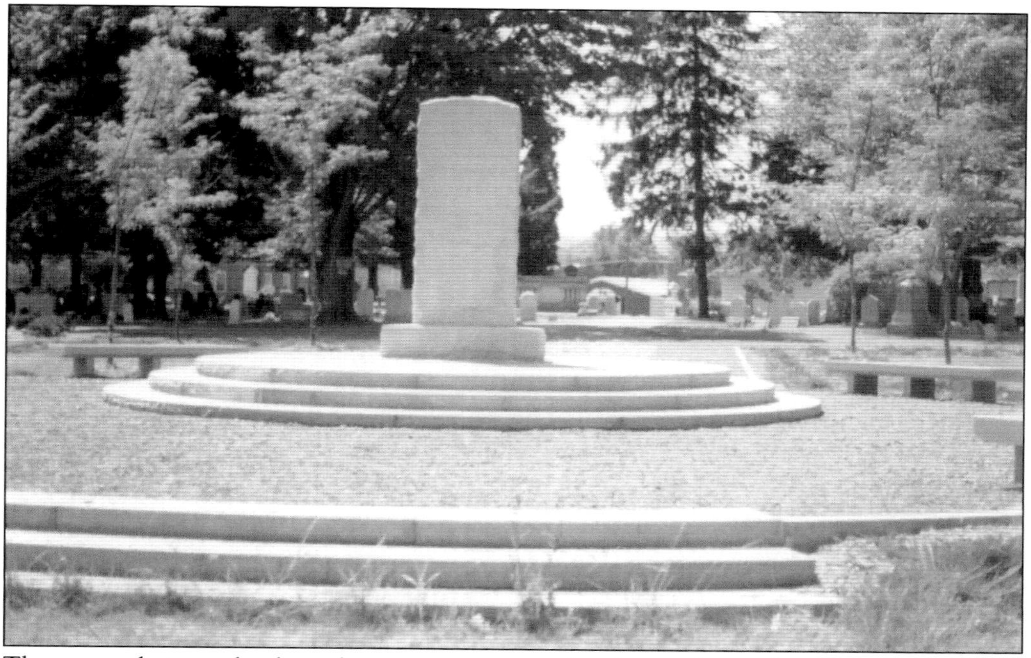

These two photographs show the monument erected to honor those whose final resting place was disturbed by the floodwaters. Located in the Forty Fort Cemetery, a granite marker in the middle of a circular bed of crushed stone serves as a reminder of what was lost that day. It would have been impossible to plot out the cemetery as it had been before the flood, so this memorial was built to honor those unearthed by Hurricane Agnes. It is a simple yet touching reminder of those who were buried and lost here. Graves that had been at rest for hundreds of years are again at rest. (Both, courtesy of Forty Fort Cemetery Association.)

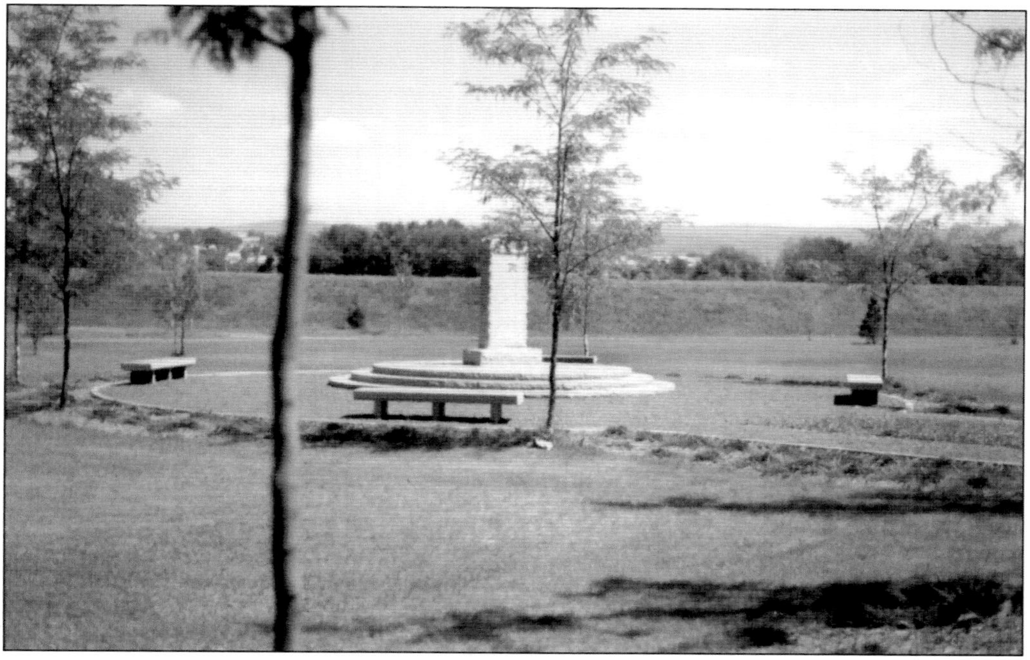

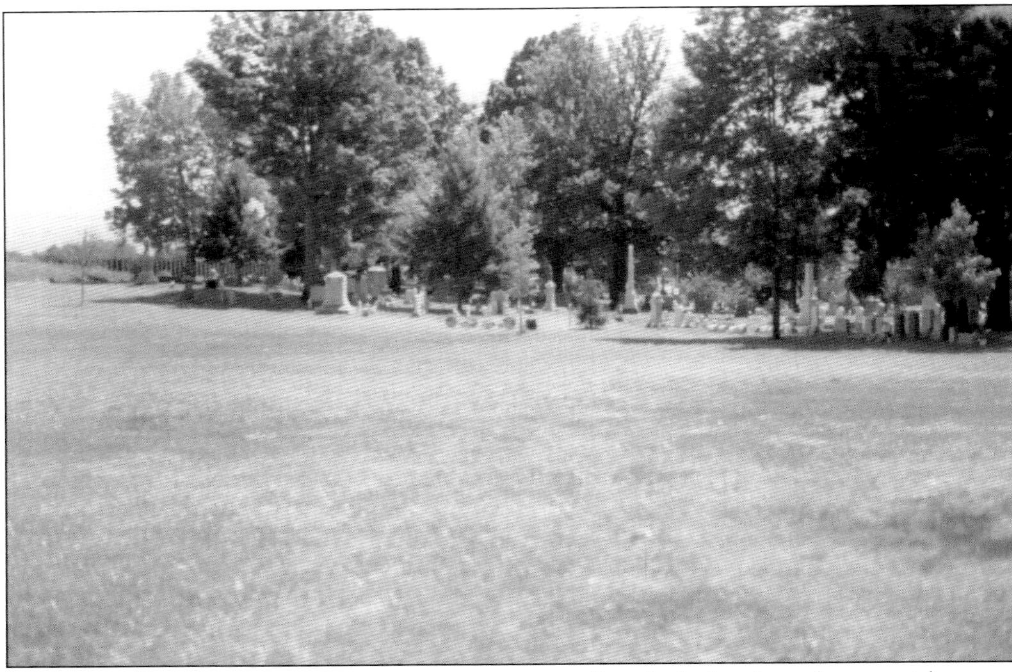

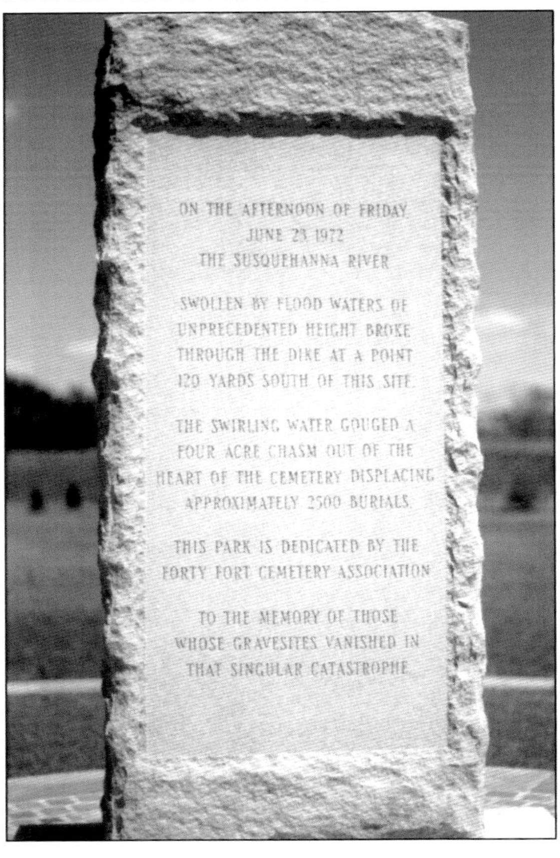

On a bed of replanted grass, with a new flood wall visible in the background, the Forty Fort Cemetery is seen as it was rebuilt. It is hard to imagine, from this peaceful photograph, what Hurricane Agnes did to the cemetery. Despite being rebuilt, residents often cite the destruction at the Forty Fort Cemetery as their most vivid memory of June 1972. (Courtesy of Forty Fort Cemetery Association.)

A somber tribute to those displaced by the flood can be found in the cemetery: "On the afternoon of Friday, June 23, 1972, the Susquehanna River, swollen by floodwaters of unprecedented height, broke through the dike at a point 120 yards south of this site. The swirling water gouged a four acre chasm out of the heart of the cemetery displacing approximately 2,500 burials. This park is dedicated by the Forty Fort Cemetery Association to the memory of those whose grave sites vanished in that singular catastrophe." (Courtesy of Forty Fort Cemetery Association.)

Three

A Valley under Water

Agnes Delivers the First Blow

"It was only the second time in my life I saw my father cry," Sheldon E. Glahn recalled. His late father, A. Sheldon Glahn, was the local disaster chairman for the Red Cross, having received the letter of his appointment the day of the flood. As was the case with many families, the Glahns were told if they did not get water in "36," they would not in "72." Ruth Glahn was preparing dinner on June 23, 1972, when her husband came home and said they had to evacuate. A single pot, along with ingredients for that night's meal, was hastily thrown into the back of a station wagon and off the family went to a small cabin at North Lake, joined by several more relatives in the three-room cottage. The pot was the only item they took from their home. As the senior Glahn did his duty by boat in the streets of Forty Fort and Swoyersville, the family anxiously awaited any news. Contact was nonexistent, and they had no way of knowing how he, or their home, was doing. While using his son's Glastron boat, a submerged fence punctured a hole in the hull, and errant wires, which he had to duck to avoid, smashed the windshield. Breaking the news of the damage to his son's boat was the final straw for A. Sheldon, as the family cried together.

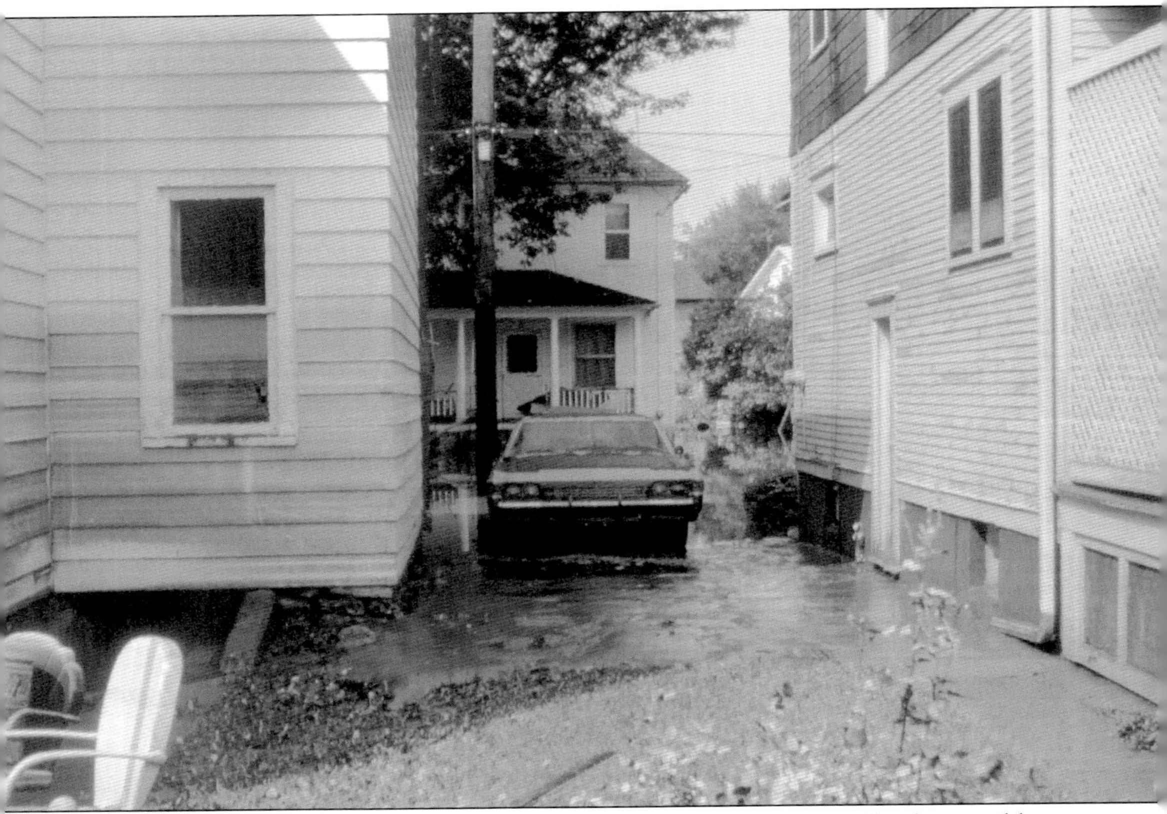

A 1968 Chevrolet Impala belonging to Jack Hessler sits between two flood-ravaged homes on Bidlack Street in Forty Fort. The waterline is clearly visible on the homes, showing just how high the floodwaters got. Although not visible in the picture, the car received a dent in the roof when a rescue motorboat's propeller struck it. Riding around the street in a boat was not as casual an activity as one might imagine. Live wires were a constant threat, as was the danger of a dead battery or engine. Debris just under the water did damage to many boats. Losing power in the powerful current could be fatal. (Courtesy of Sheldon Glahn.)

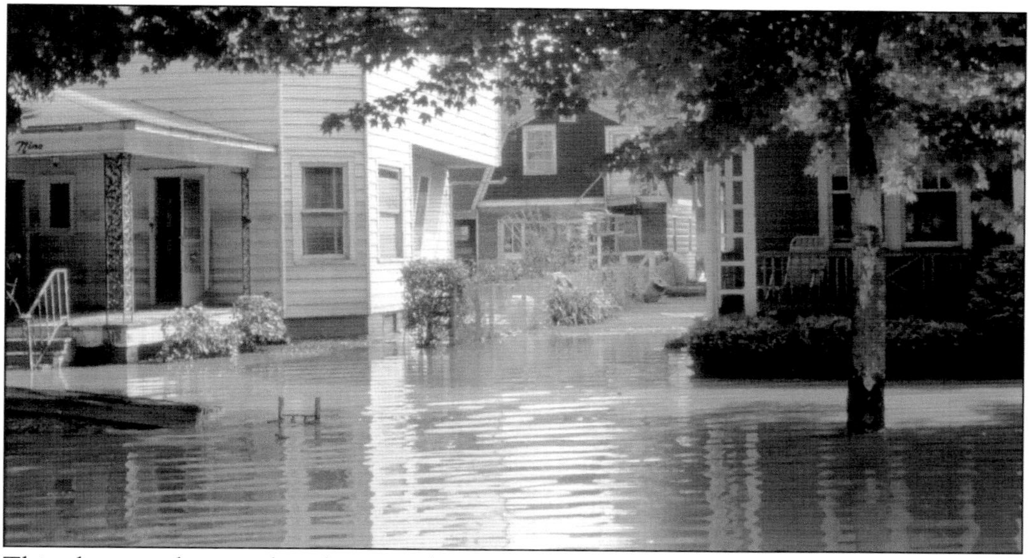

This photograph was taken from an aluminum boat before the floodwaters had completely receded. In the foreground is the home of Sheldon and Ruth Glahn, with the detached garage and workshop visible in the back. The boat was tied down before the water got too high and was used during the flood. In one of the more harrowing flood stories, Glahn recalled rescuing a neighbor and her husband who were stranded, the latter in a wheelchair. Somehow, the wife had managed to drag her husband in his wheelchair up the stairs, and the Glahns pulled him off the roof to safety as floodwaters raged inches away. (Courtesy of Sheldon Glahn.)

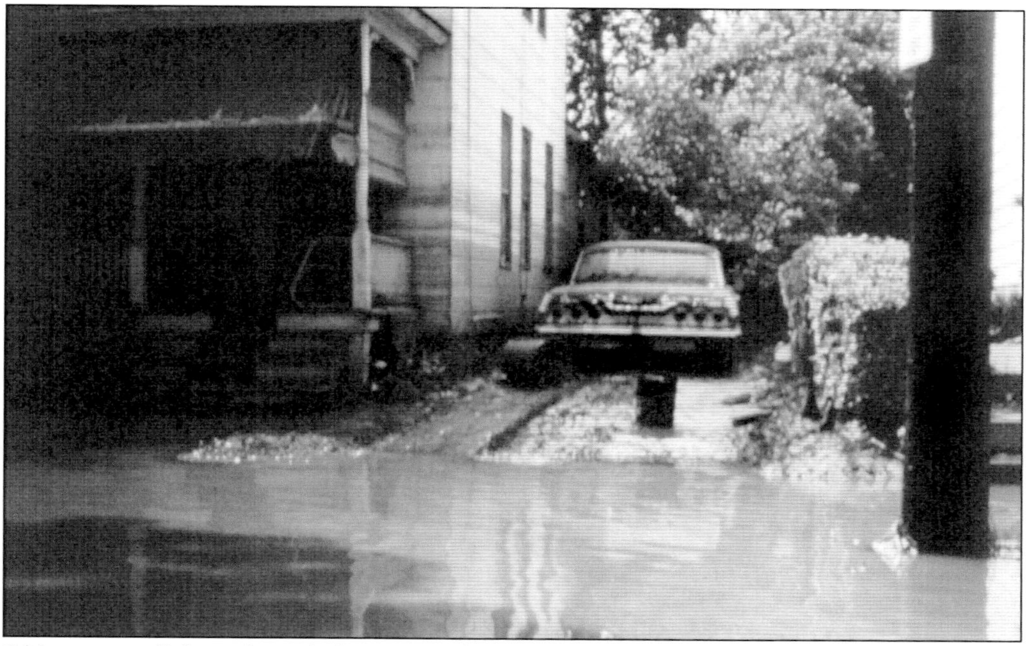

Filthy water still flows through the streets of Forty Fort in this photograph. Although many recall the mud, the water carried many other toxins, including sewage, waste, and fuel. It was a cesspool of filth, and care was required during cleanup to make sure one washed properly after spending a day covered in the polluted water. (Courtesy of Sheldon Glahn.)

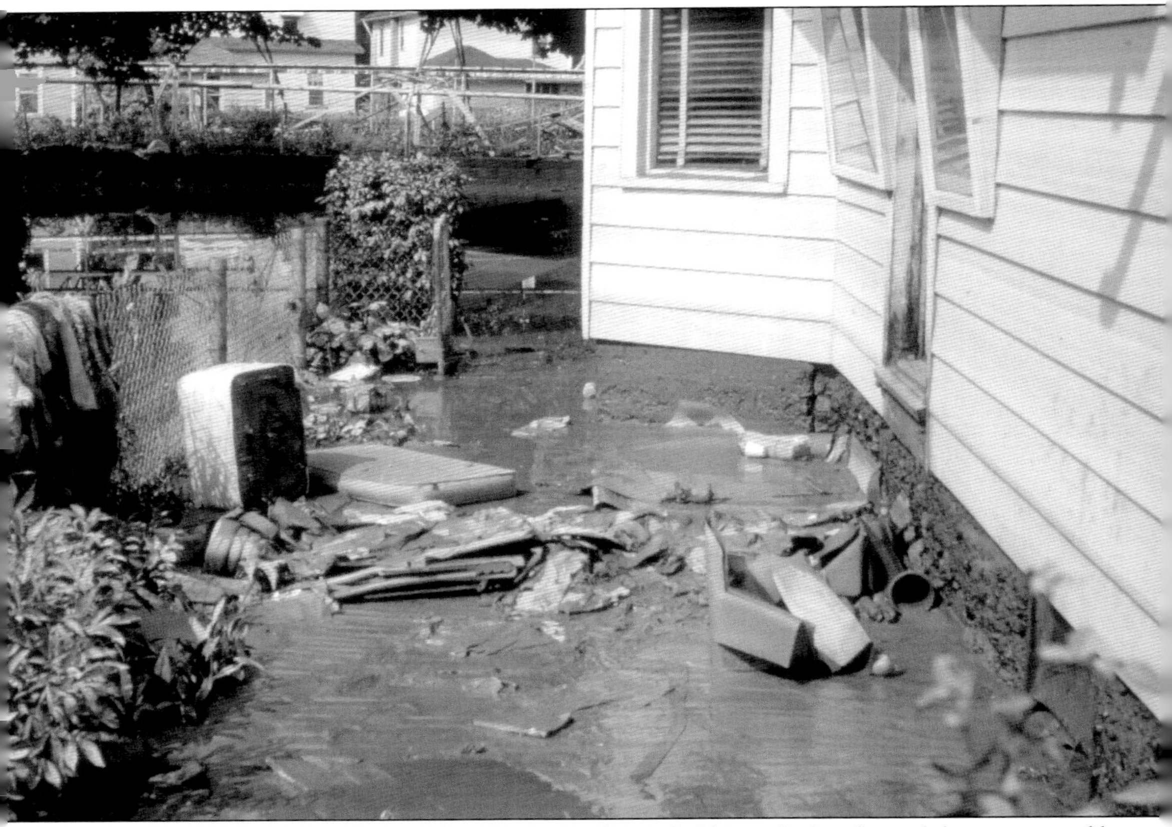

Debris from a flooded home is thrown out for disposal. Although the physical damage caused by Hurricane Agnes totaled over $2 billion, the emotional toll on the residents was further reaching. Few forgot the traumatic experience of returning to their homes to find their possessions and family heirlooms gone forever. Photo albums seemed to be the item that caused the most heartache; mementos of weddings, birthdays, and other events were gone forever. Despite the items being discarded, many residents went door to door, or rather curb to curb, trying to find anything they could use from another neighbor's trash heap. (Courtesy of Sheldon Glahn.)

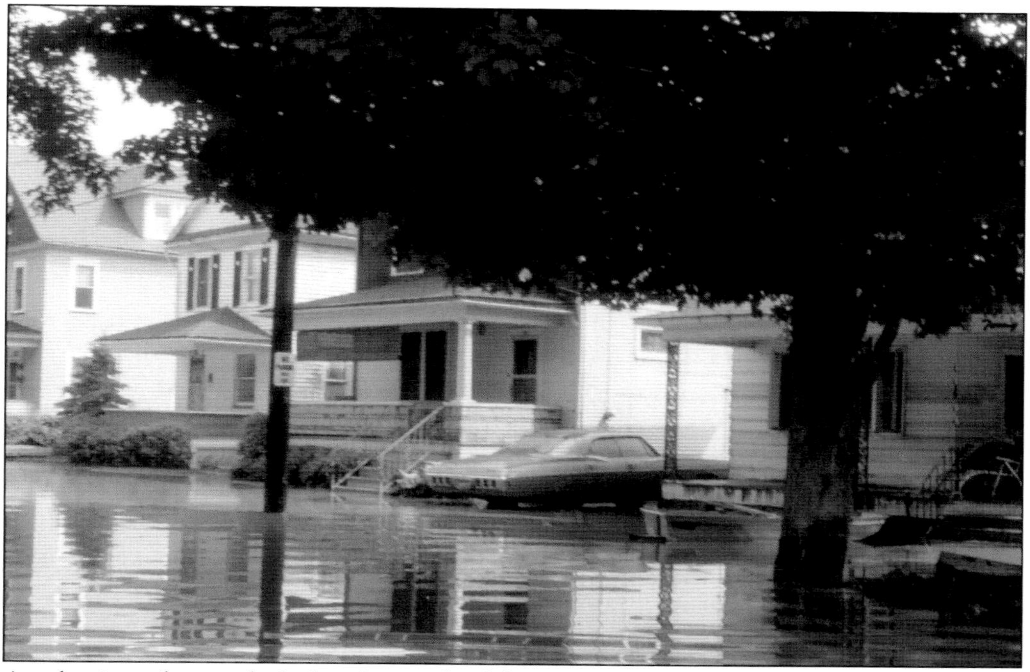

An aluminum boat is docked at the porch of the Glahn home. Utter devastation was the only way to describe what homeowners saw upon their return. In addition to furniture and family heirlooms that were lost forever, the mud was the most frequent complaint cited by citizens. If the mud was still wet, one had a fighting chance of cleaning it. But once it was dry, "it seemed to seep into the pores of everything," a homeowner recalled. Many homes to this day still have flood mud in cracks and crevices. (Courtesy of Sheldon Glahn.)

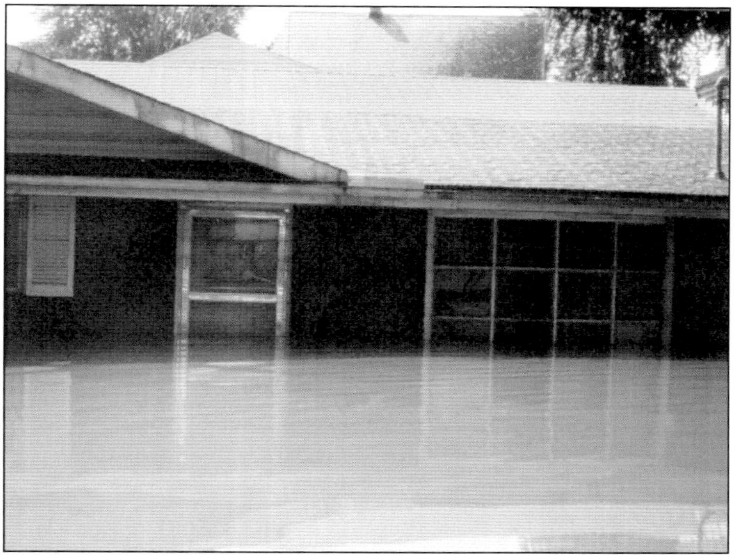

This one-story ranch home was nearly completely covered by the waters of the flood. Note the waterline that goes halfway up the roof. Although many homeowners decided to stay after the flood, it took years and tens of thousands of dollars to fix such damage. In a home such as this, the only option was to completely strip the house down to bare studs and replace almost everything. (Courtesy of Sheldon Glahn.)

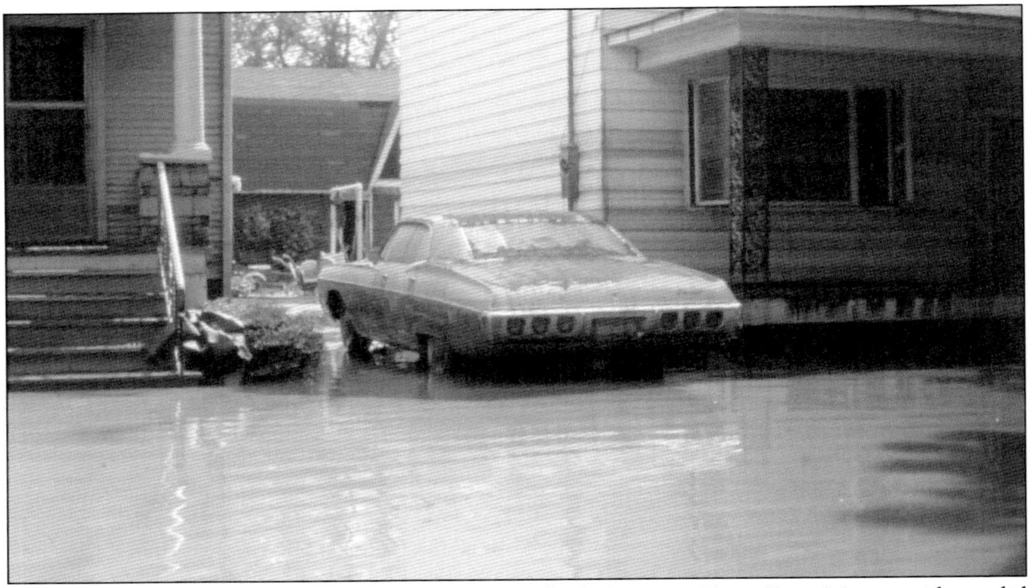

A mud-covered vehicle sits between 29 and 31 Bidlack Street in Forty Fort. Many residents did not feel Agnes would be such a disaster. On June 21, 1972, the river depth read 4.30 feet at 10:00 p.m. By 7:00 p.m. on June 24, it would crest at over 40 feet. Few residents could prepare for the incredible destruction that awaited them upon their return. Although some had the foresight to move cars to high spots and move property to the second floor, most just never thought the floodwaters could get so high. (Courtesy of Sheldon Glahn.)

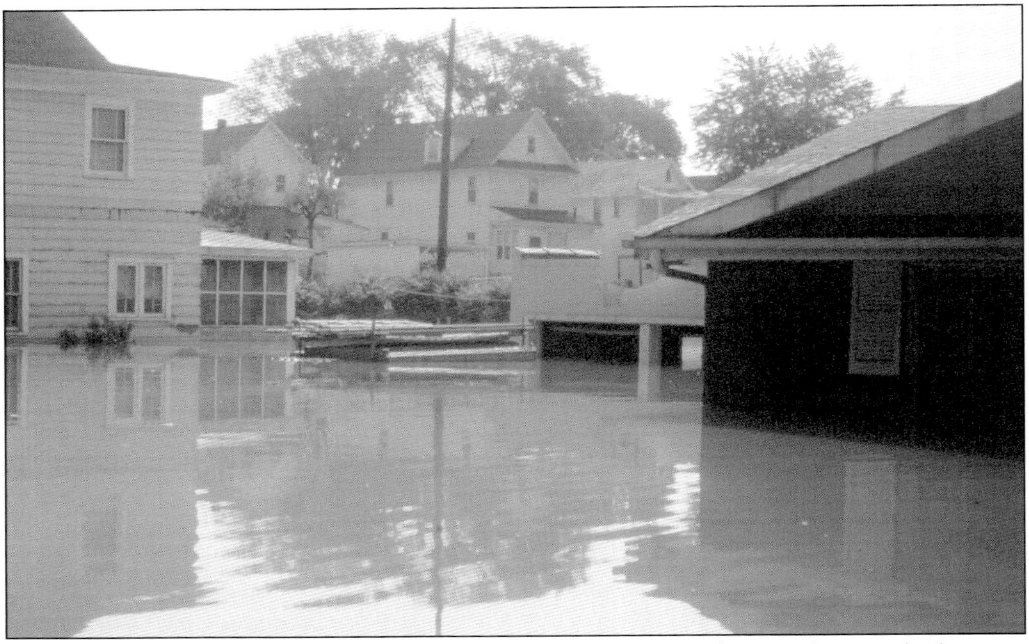

A damaged garage and homes stand in over eight feet of water. The waterline on the home at right shows that floodwaters touched the second floor in some areas. For many who failed to leave in time, rescues were made out of second-floor windows and from rooftops. (Courtesy of Sheldon Glahn.)

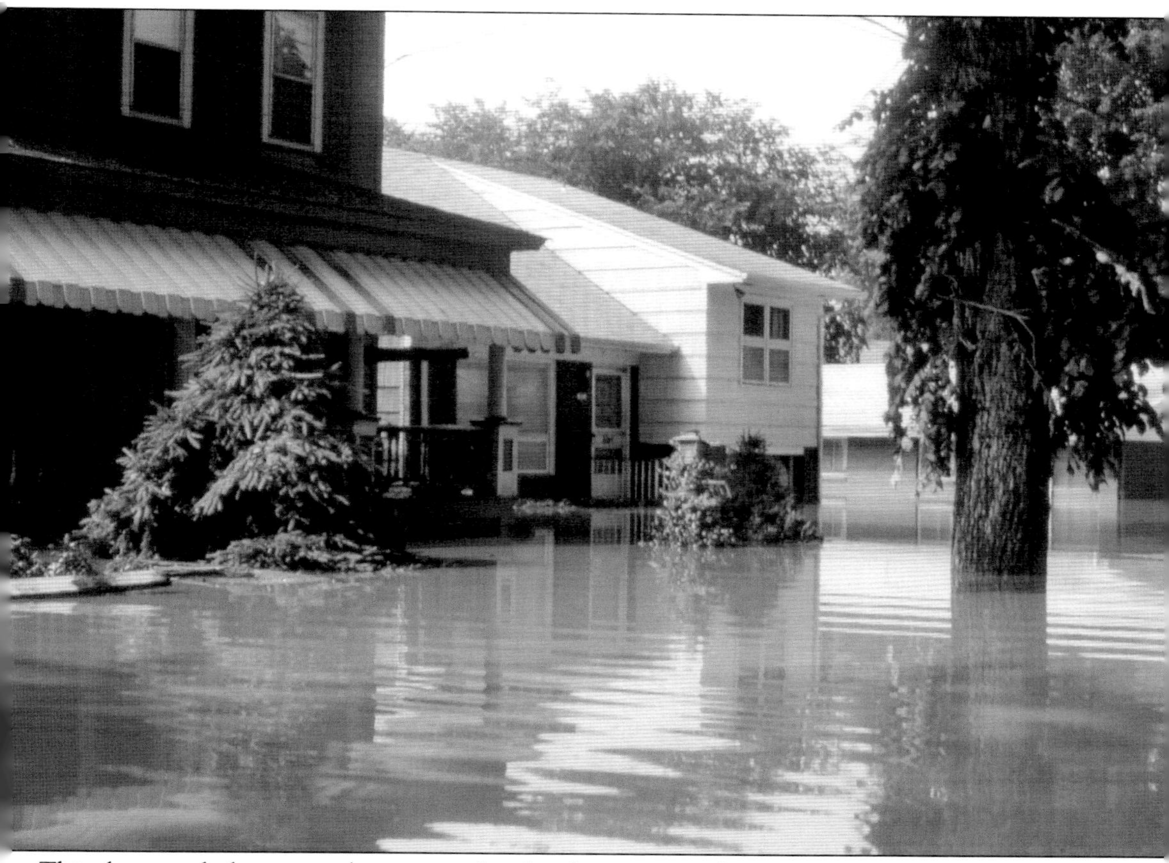

This photograph shows more homes inundated with water, near the corner of Bidlack and Murray Streets in Forty Fort. Due to the drop in the road, floodwaters were deeper at this end of the street. Many people who failed to leave had to anxiously wait for rescue, often on the second stories of their homes. "Why didn't you leave" was the most common question asked, and the answer for most was, "We didn't think we were going to get it." Residents learned the hard way not to take warnings so lightly. (Courtesy of Sheldon Glahn.)

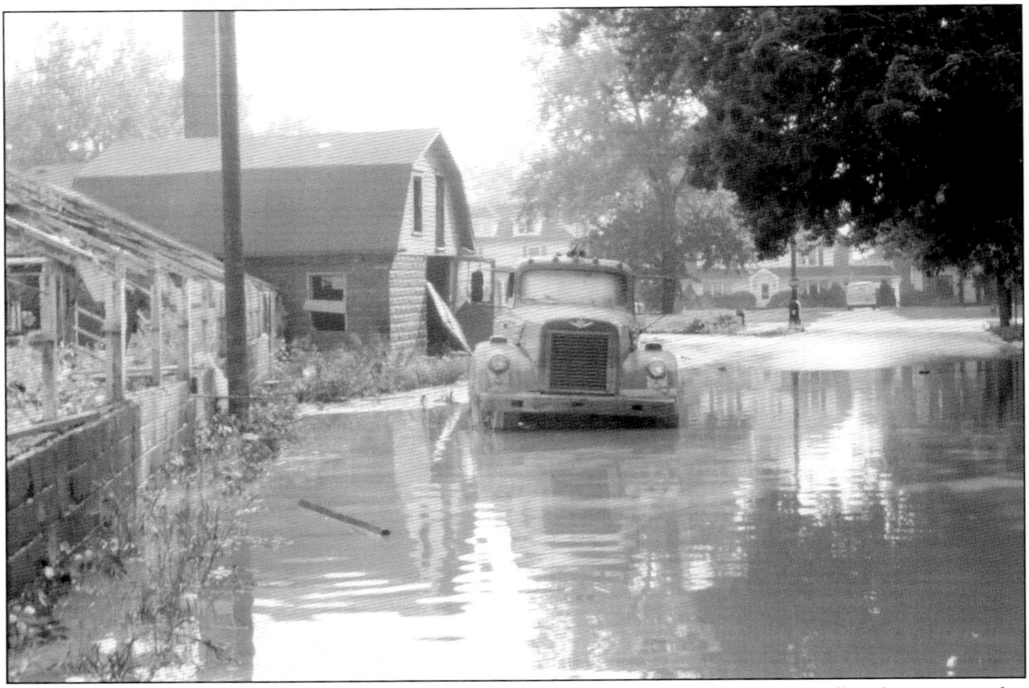

In the above photograph, damaged property and an old truck lie in stagnant floodwaters in the borough of Forty Fort, with this view looking toward Wyoming Avenue. At left are the remains of Tobin's Greenhouse, which was actually in the process of being torn down before the flood. The truck was originally there to remove boilers; however, it was left behind when the owner was unable to make it back into the flooded area to retrieve it. Below, two vehicles sit, never to run again, with mud around them. Many residents had to leave vehicles behind because of limited means to move them. (Both, courtesy of Sheldon Glahn.)

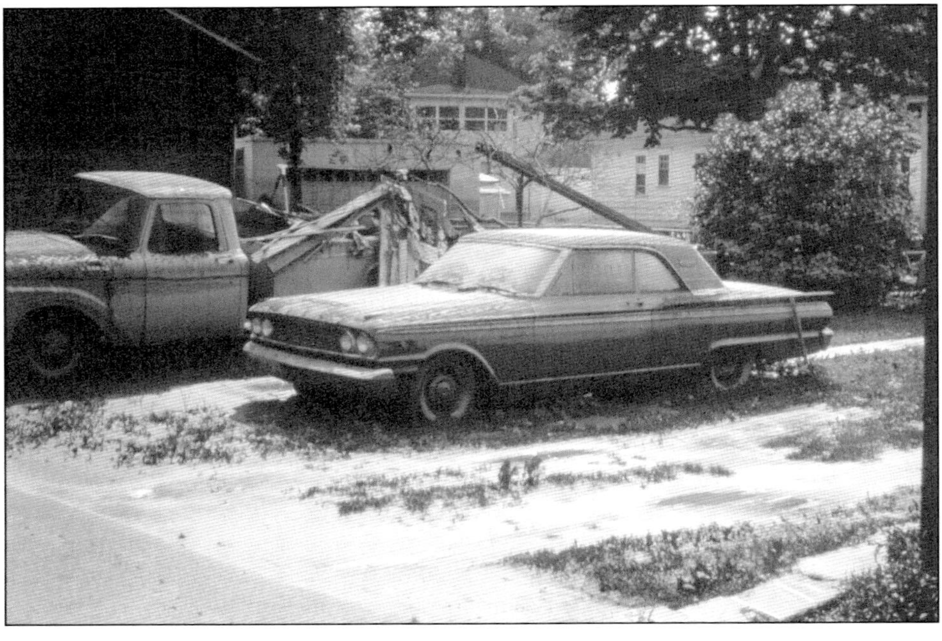

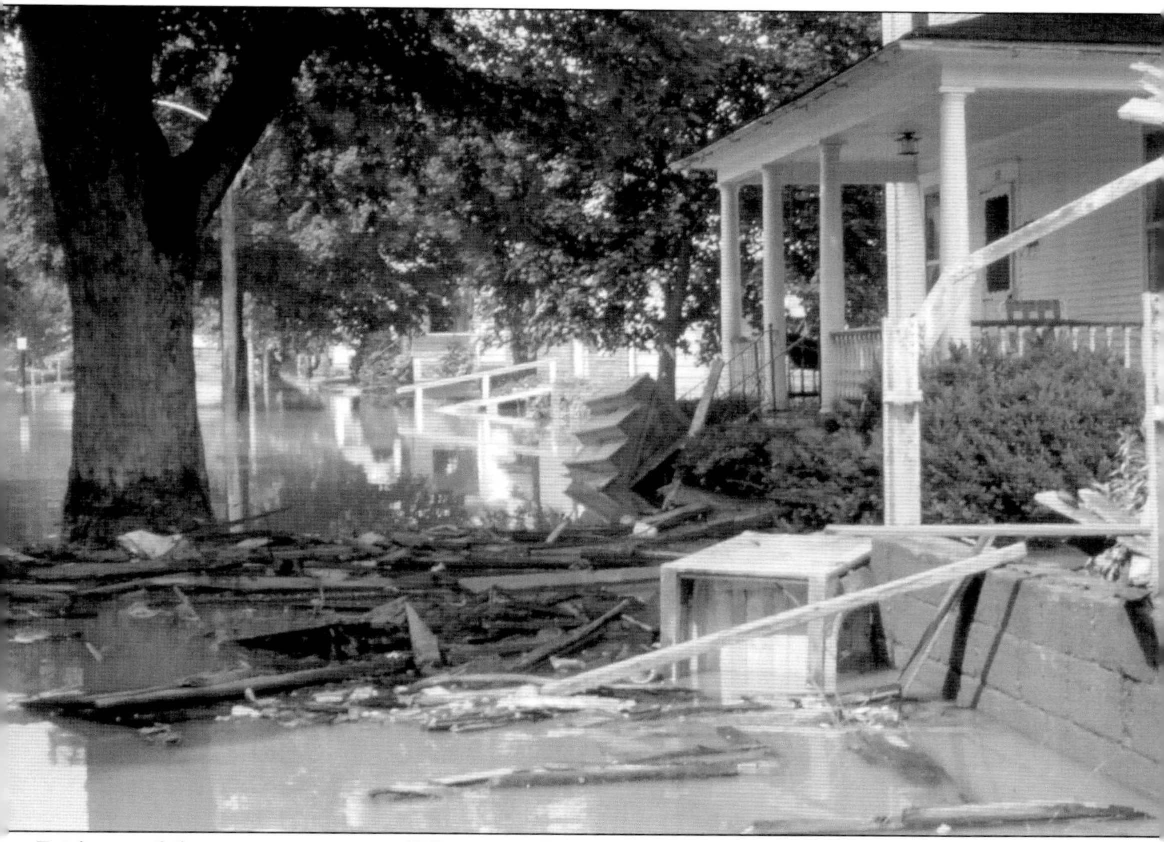

Evidence of the immense power of Hurricane Agnes is seen in this photograph. Front porches were ripped right off of homes, often taking the roof with them. Structures were knocked off their foundations, with debris often found several blocks from their original location. For many residents, it was a total loss. Many times, the damage to their homes cost two to three times as much as they paid for them. Many allowed themselves a moment of self pity before digging in and beginning the slow process of putting their houses back together in the hope of making them homes again. (Courtesy of Sheldon Glahn.)

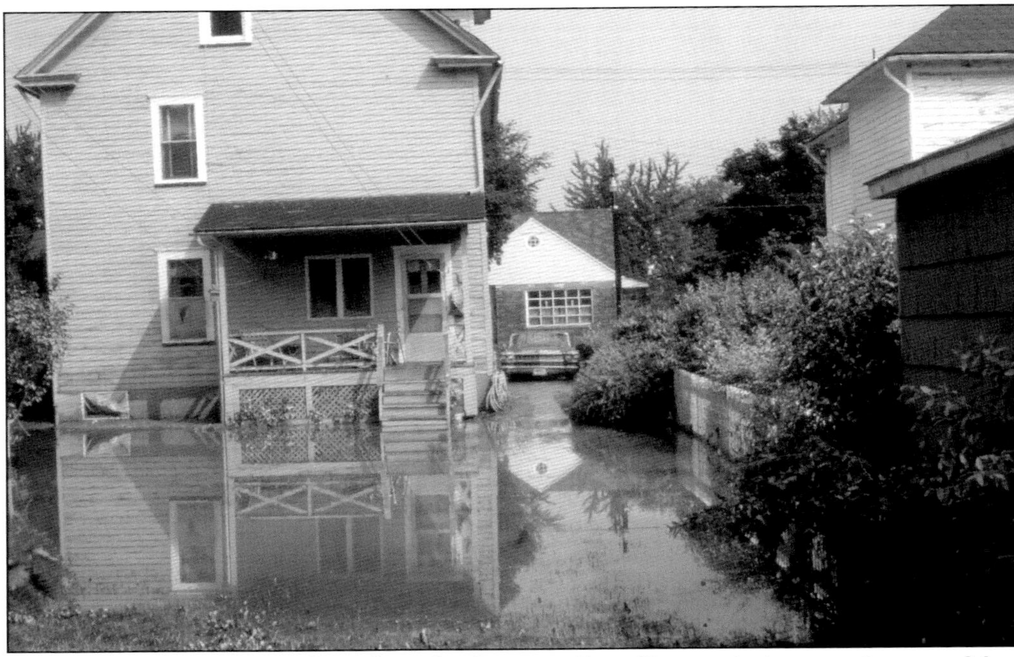

As water is in the process of receding, this house in Forty Fort awaits its owner's return. Many citizens did not believe Agnes would inflict the damage she did, so residents were late to leave or left behind objects that, in hindsight, could have been saved. Little of what was touched by water was salvageable. (Courtesy of Sheldon Glahn.)

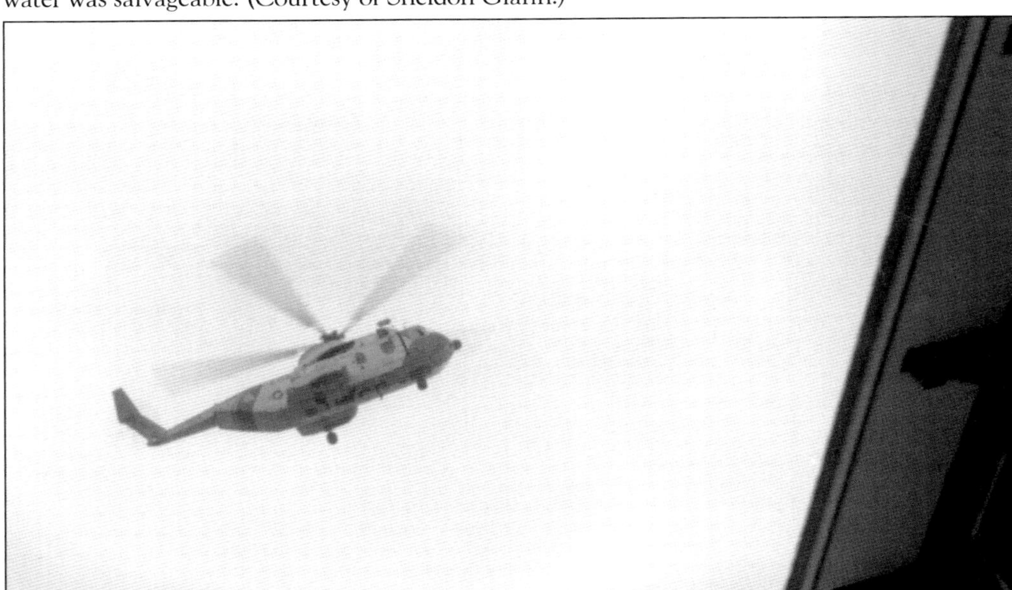

A US Coast Guard helicopter prepares to land at College Misericordia after flying over flood-ravaged cities. While volunteers and officials motored a variety of watercraft through the streets to help victims, pilots flew over the area to drop supplies, look for people who needed help, or provide tours to politicians who needed to see the damage for themselves. (Courtesy of Sister Mary Carmel McGarigle University Archives, Misericordia University.)

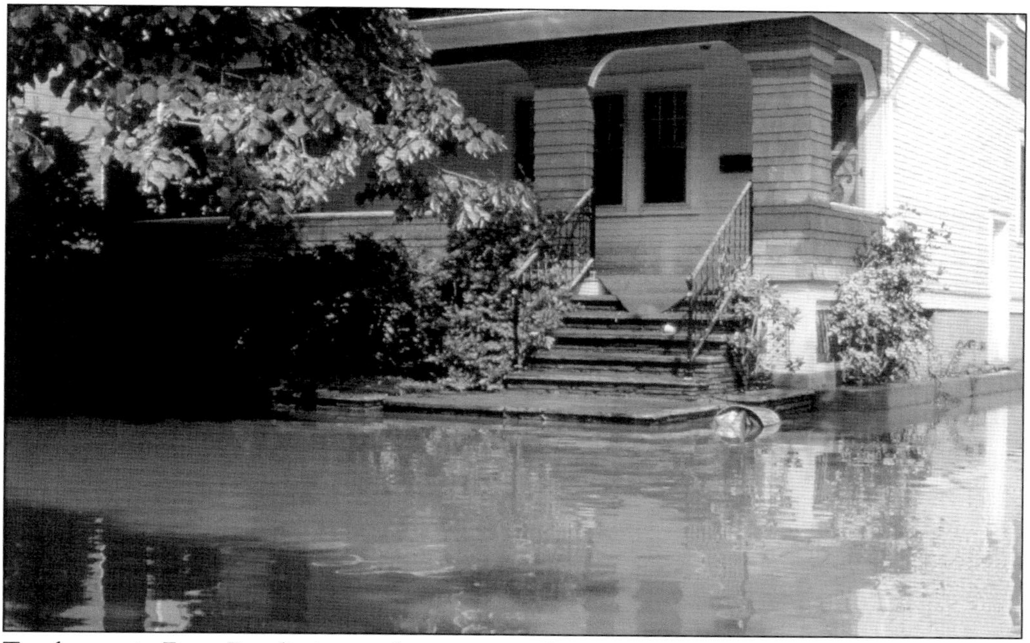

Two homes in Forty Fort lie in receding water in these pictures. An estimated 1,600 homes in the small borough were damaged. Many residents refused to leave until the last second, which resulted in them frantically taking as many personal items as they could to the higher floors of their homes. Despite the calamity, some were able to keep a sense of humor. When asked how the water got in, one resident quipped, "It came in through the chimney." Another warned a rescuer in a boat to "watch the lawn," as he had just had it landscaped. Some citizens hung American flags from their homes as a show of pride during cleanup. (Both, courtesy of Sheldon Glahn.)

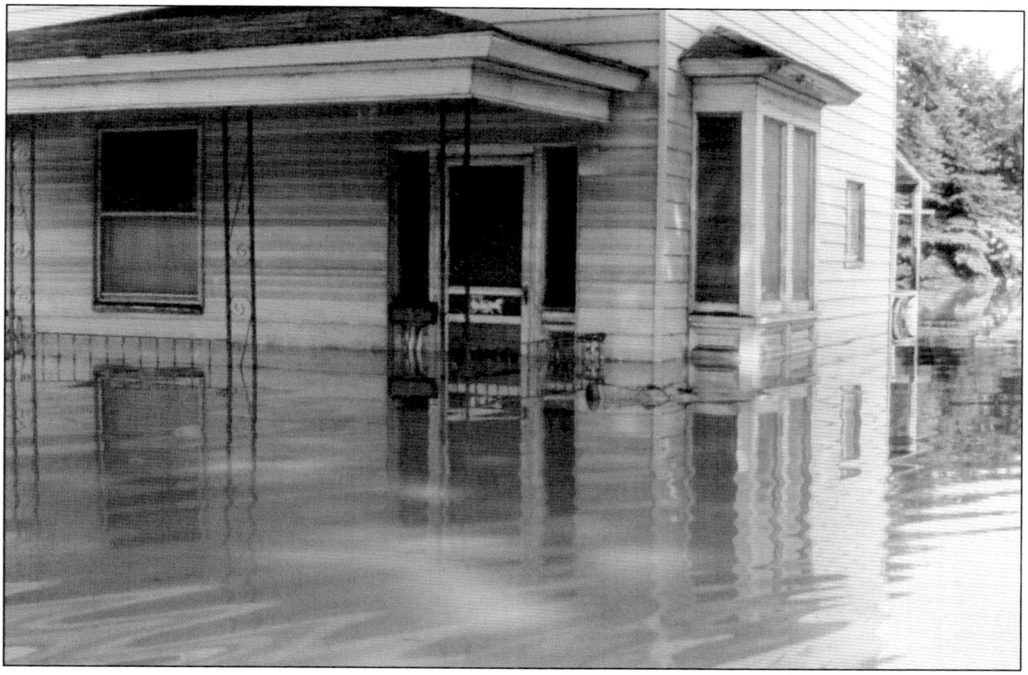

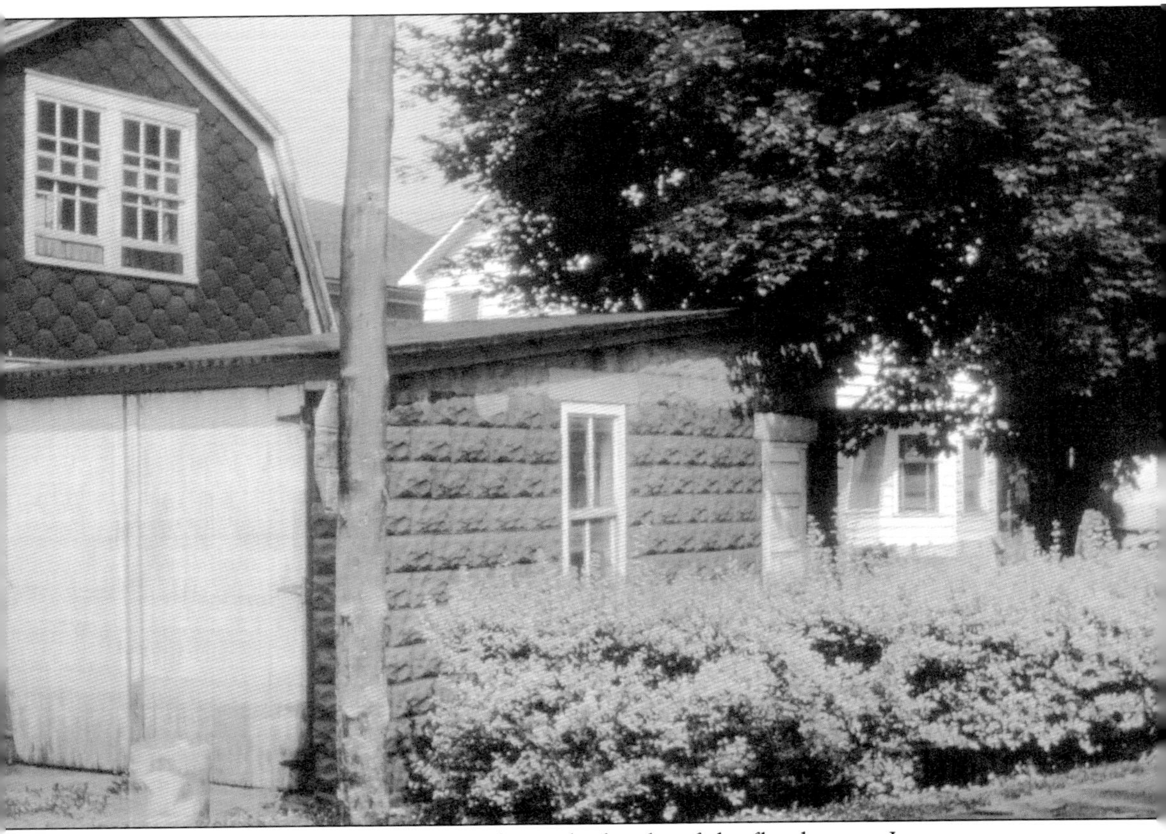

The waterline on this garage again shows the height of the floodwaters. In many areas, waters were 8 to 10 feet high. Had the water gone higher, it is likely the roof of this structure would have come off. One strange aspect of the flood was, due to the topography of the area, a house could have water touching the second floor while one a few doors down only had water in the basement. Electricity was a huge risk. Aluminum siding jolted more than one homeowner who made the mistake of touching it, not realizing it was touching a live wire. Some homes in fact burned to the ground. (Courtesy of Sheldon Glahn.)

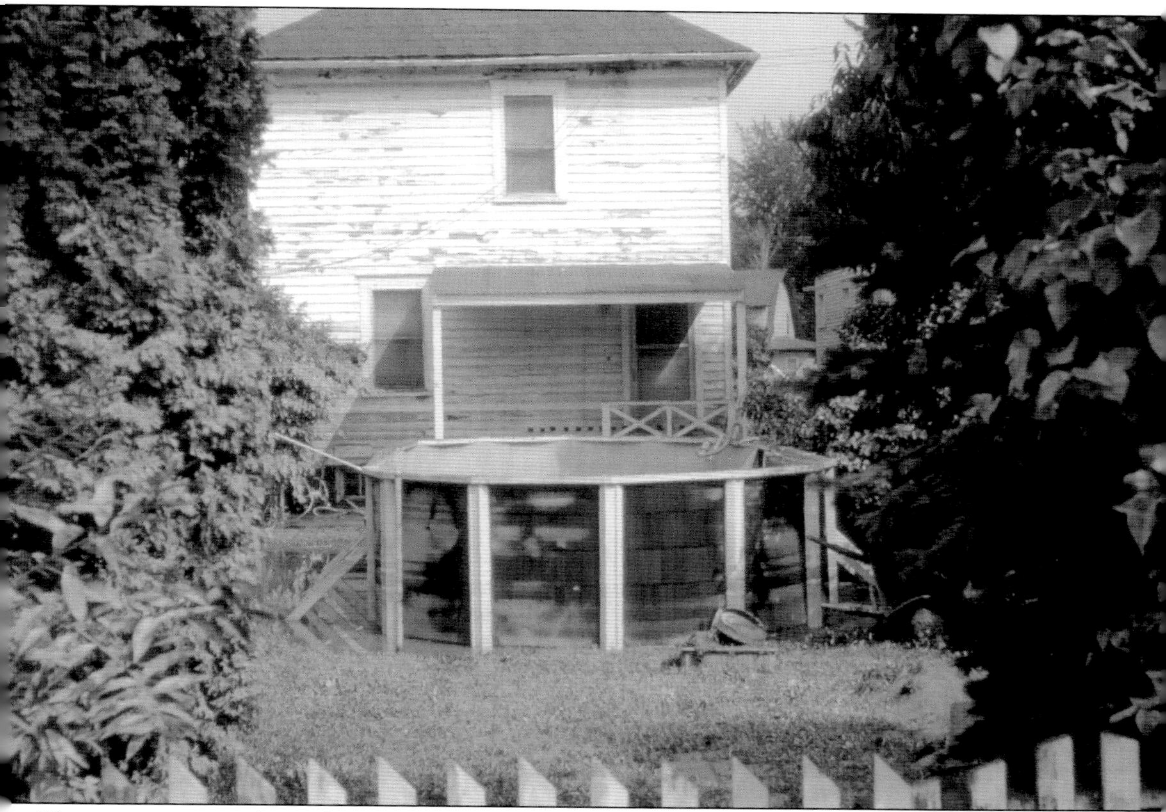

This swimming pool somehow survived the torrent. Originally thinking the water would stay relatively low, A. Sheldon Glahn had planned to use the pool as a source for drinking water. However, the river rose, the pool filled with mud, and the liner expanded like a balloon and burst. Despite the emotional lift many felt from their family and friends, not everyone was so fortunate. The suicide rate rose dramatically in 1972, perhaps as the result of the hopelessness many felt in losing everything. (Courtesy of Sheldon Glahn.)

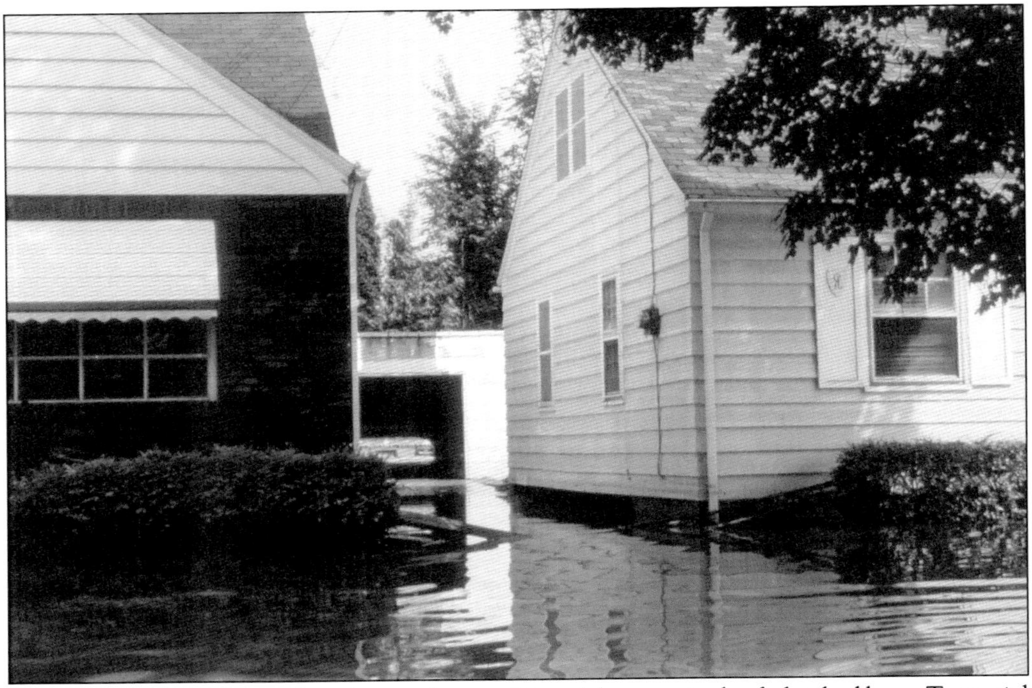

The receding waters among these homes show nothing of the magnitude of what had been. Torrential rain in early spring had already contributed to a swelling water table. As Hurricane Agnes set her eyes on the Wyoming Valley, what Pres. Richard Nixon called the greatest national disaster to hit the United States would soon unleash its fury on the residents along the Susquehanna River. Above, a car sits in a garage, left behind in haste. Below, a garage in Kingston sits on a car, having been moved by the powerful current of the river. (Both, courtesy of Sheldon Glahn.)

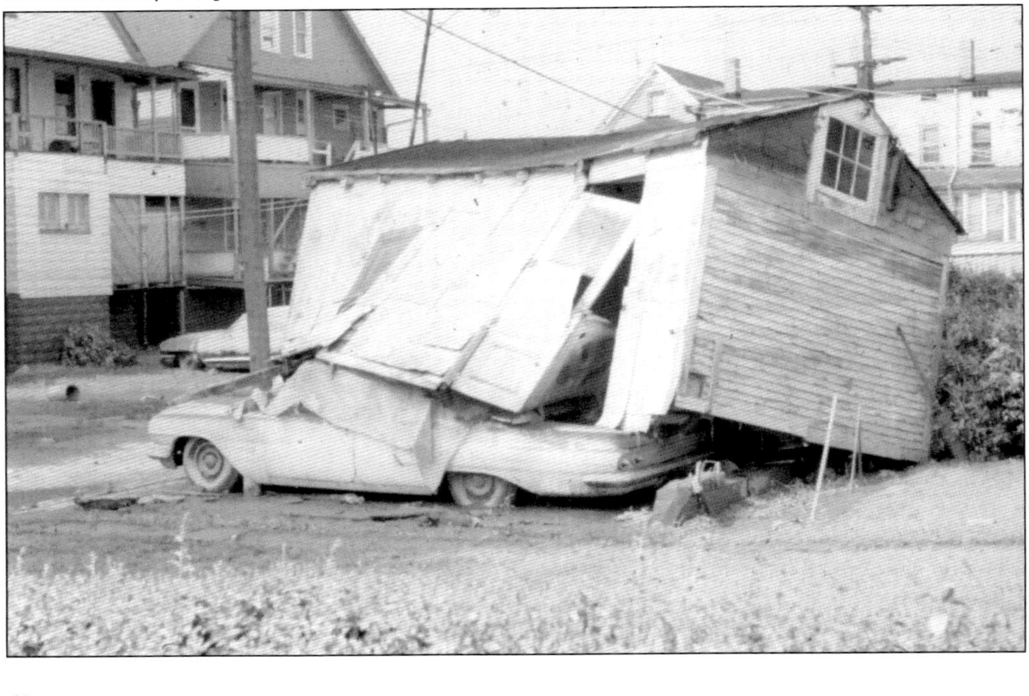

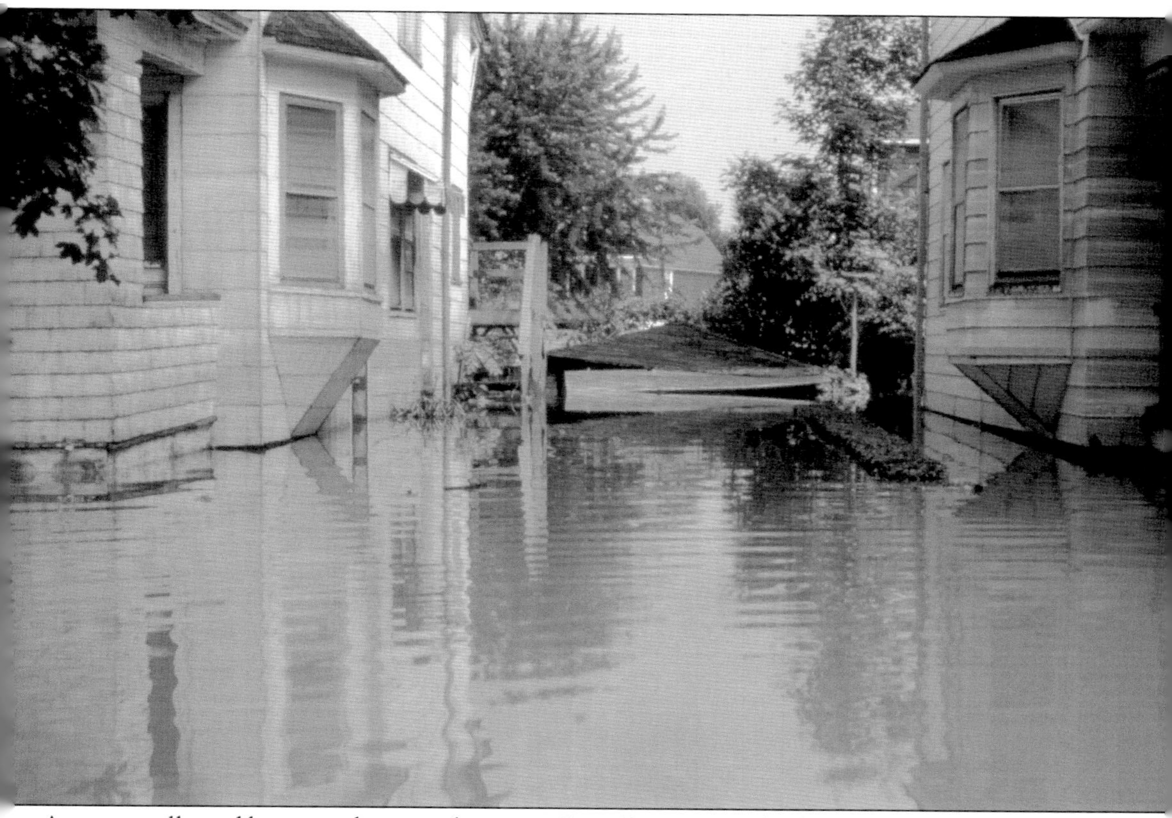

A garage collapsed between these two homes in Forty Fort as a result of the raging waters of the Susquehanna River. Although most people from the communities affected did not believe the flood would turn into the disaster it became, many were even less prepared for their reaction to it upon their return. A. Sheldon Glahn recalled parking his boat on his front porch, wading through his home, then returning to the front steps to sob. (Courtesy of Sheldon Glahn.)

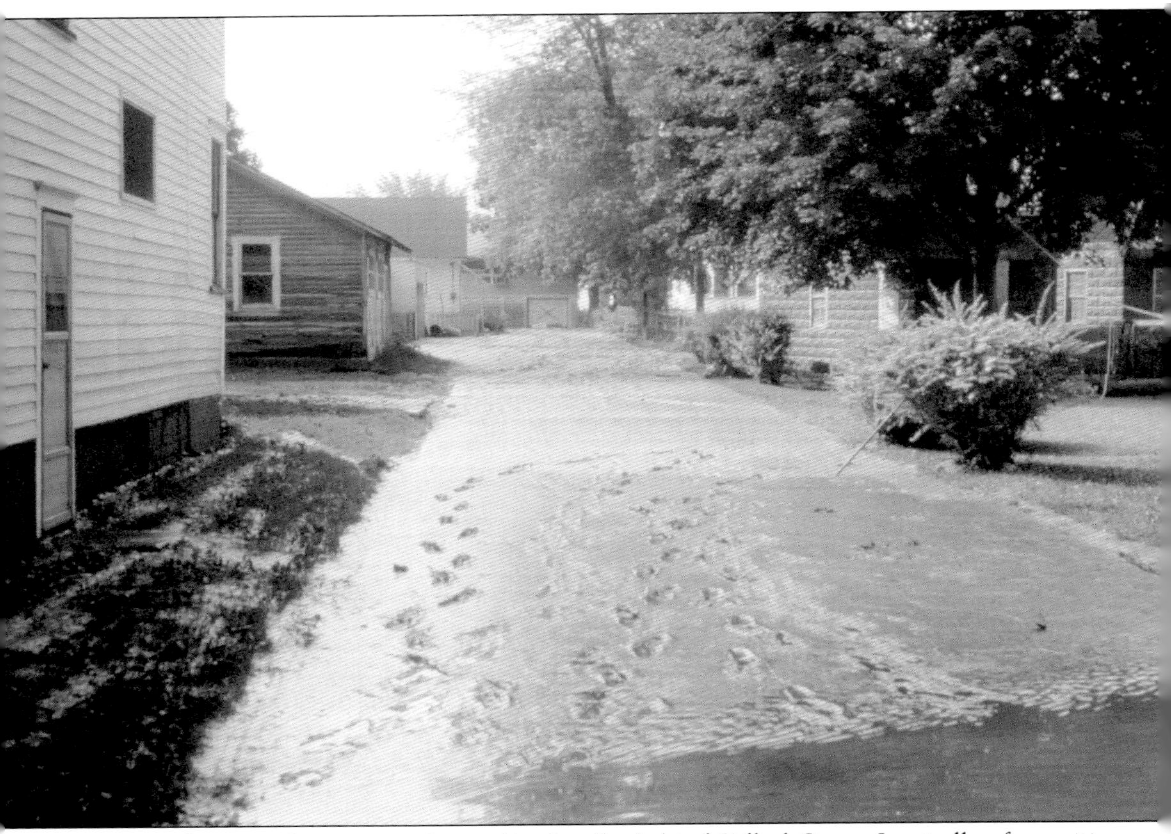

"Lunar footprints" are seen in the mud in the alley behind Bidlack Street. Ironically, after waiting for 50 years, this road had just been paved, only to have the flood strike. As the water receded, residents were slowly coming back to the area to check on their homes and businesses. On Tuesday, June 27, authorized military personnel were the first to see the damage firsthand. Some residents were able to sneak past checkpoints, while others were surprised how stubborn the guards could be. One Forty Fort man recalled asking, begging, and then demanding with a hurl of insults to be allowed in to find his father, all to no avail. (Courtesy of Sheldon Glahn.)

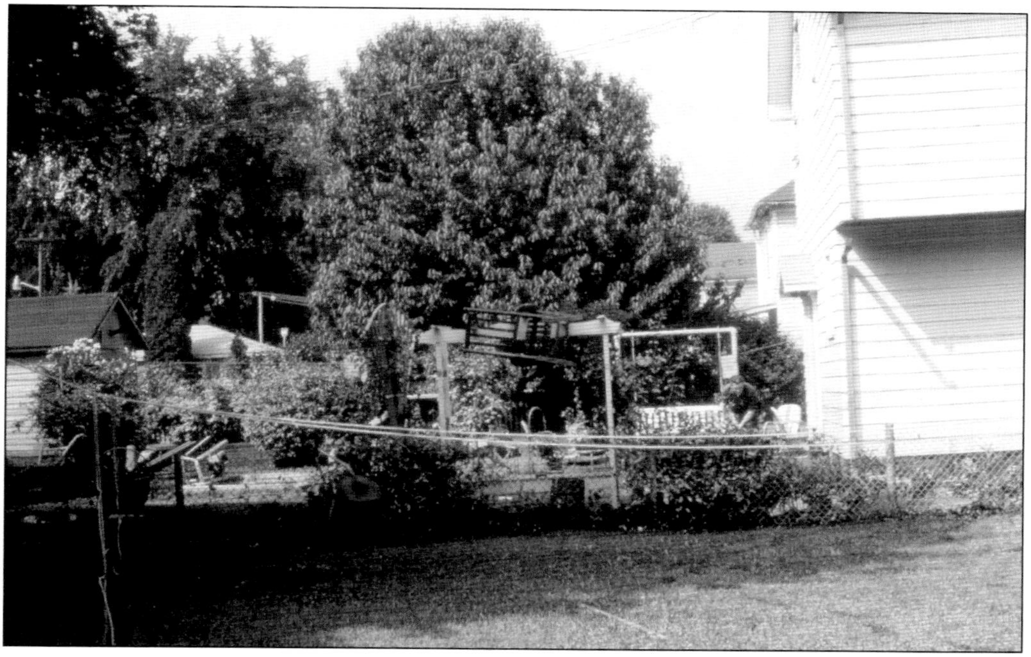

In the center of the above photograph, a wooden chair sits atop a trellis, having been deposited there by floodwaters. This is the rear yard of the Walters family home on Bidlack Street in Forty Fort. Below, a picnic table has been transplanted to the front yard from its previous resting place in the backyard of this Forty Fort residence. The Wyoming Valley was described by one homeowner as looking like a European war zone from World War II. Windows were blown out, and debris was everywhere. The magnitude of the disaster and the enormous cleanup awaiting everyone was incredible. (Both, courtesy of Sheldon Glahn.)

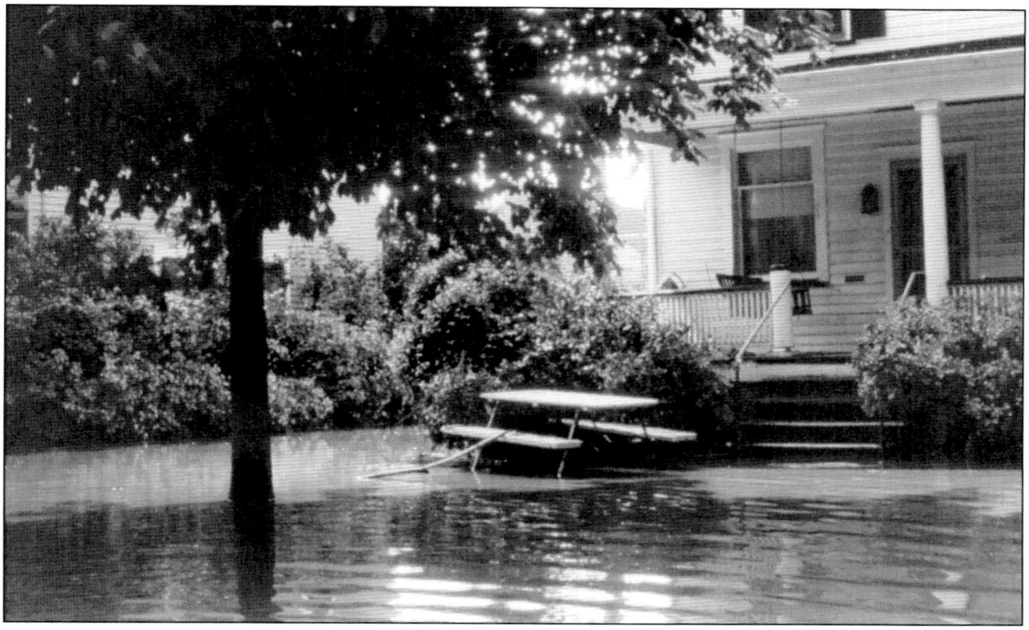

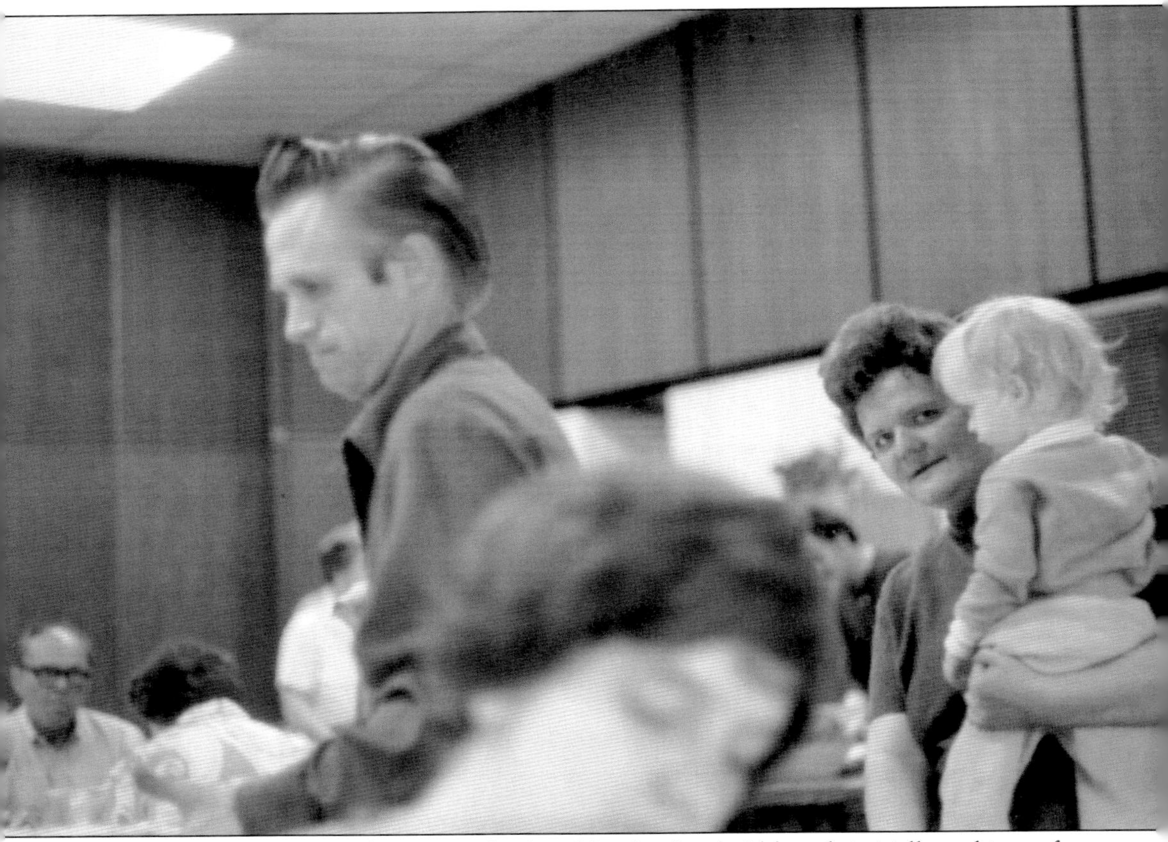

Many residents such as these were displaced by the flood. Although initially seeking refuge at public sites, such as Dallas High School, Lake-Lehman, or College Misericordia, many with young children were placed with complete strangers who were kind enough to open their homes to them. The threat of illness was high, so many left shelters to go stay with families instead. (Courtesy of Sister Mary Carmel McGarigle University Archives, Misericordia University.)

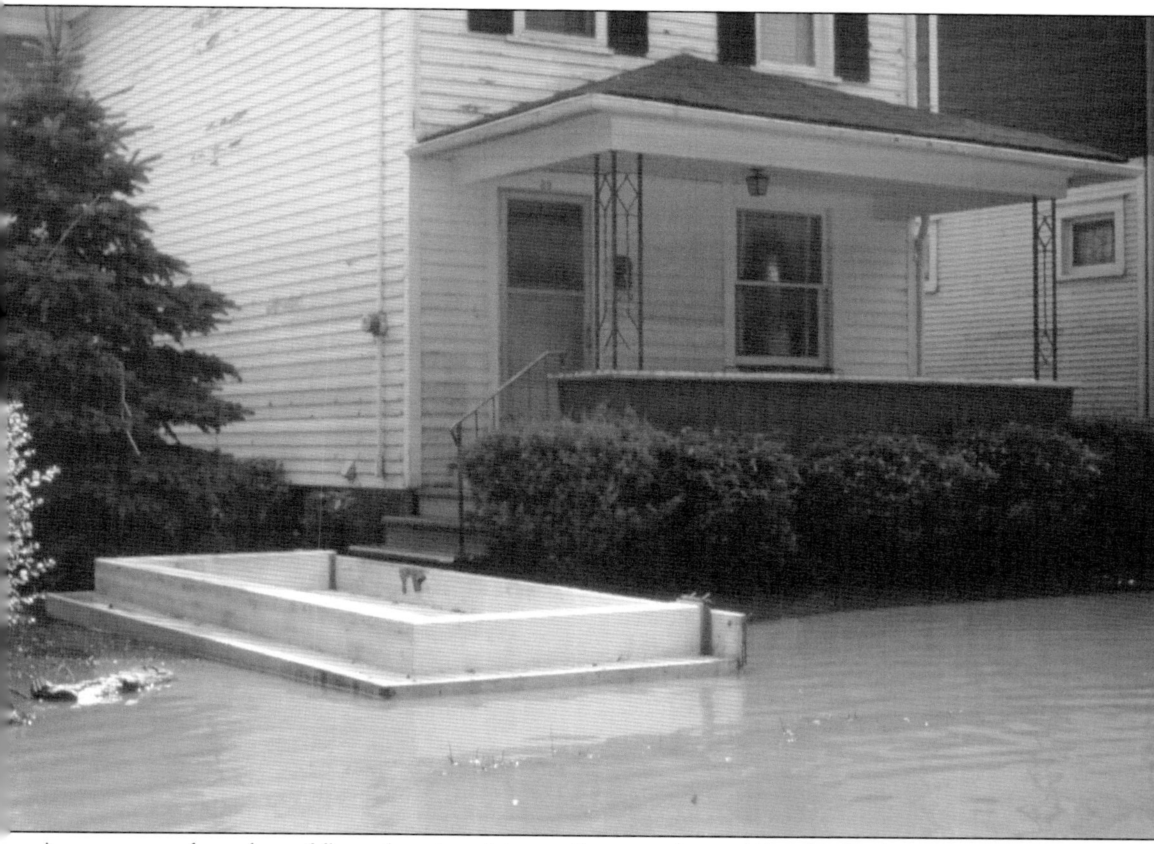

An overturned porch roof floated up from Murray Street to the middle of Bidlack Street in Forty Fort. Many residents returned to their homes not only to find familiar items gone, but to discover new structures and debris on their property. These structures could be hazardous to those in boats. A. Sheldon Glahn had gone over to a neighbor's house to feed her cat during the high water. As he was trying to fight the current to anchor his son's boat, he hit a fence and punctured the bottom. Thinking quickly, he plugged the hole with a foam flotation device. He then used supplies from his place of employment to repair the hull. (Courtesy of Sheldon Glahn.)

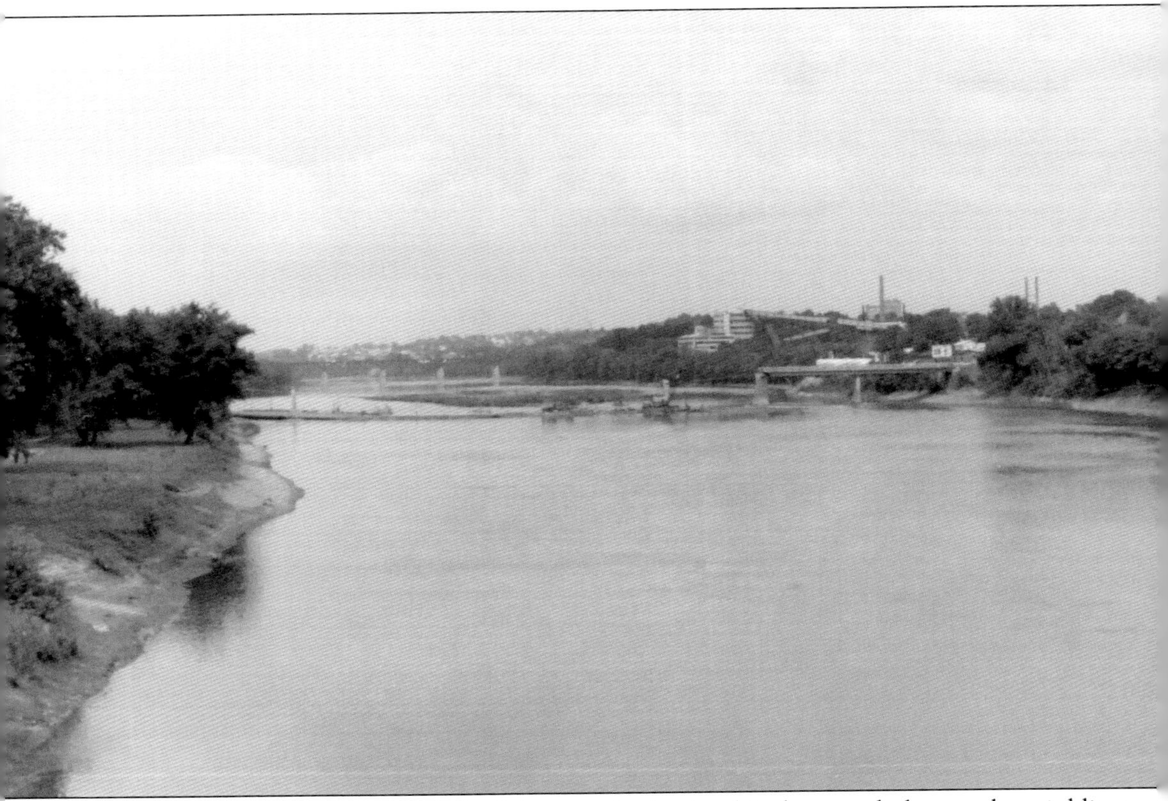

As the mighty Susquehanna slides back between her banks, this photograph shows only an inkling of the destruction that waited for residents' return. In the middle of the picture, the Pierce Street Bridge, connecting Kingston and Wilkes-Barre, has been washed away. Bonnie Stinson recalled that her father was one of the last to drive over the bridge before it was closed, and water splashed his tires. She lamented that if her father had been more forthcoming about how high the river was, they would have started moving faster. In all likelihood, however, it would not have mattered, as the Stinsons had water on the first and second floor of their Sharpe Street home. Amazingly, the hutch opened and fell over and all the dishes were floating around their dining room with not a single one broken. The missing item that hurt the most, however, was the Bible of her late brother John, which was never found. (Courtesy of Sheldon Glahn.)

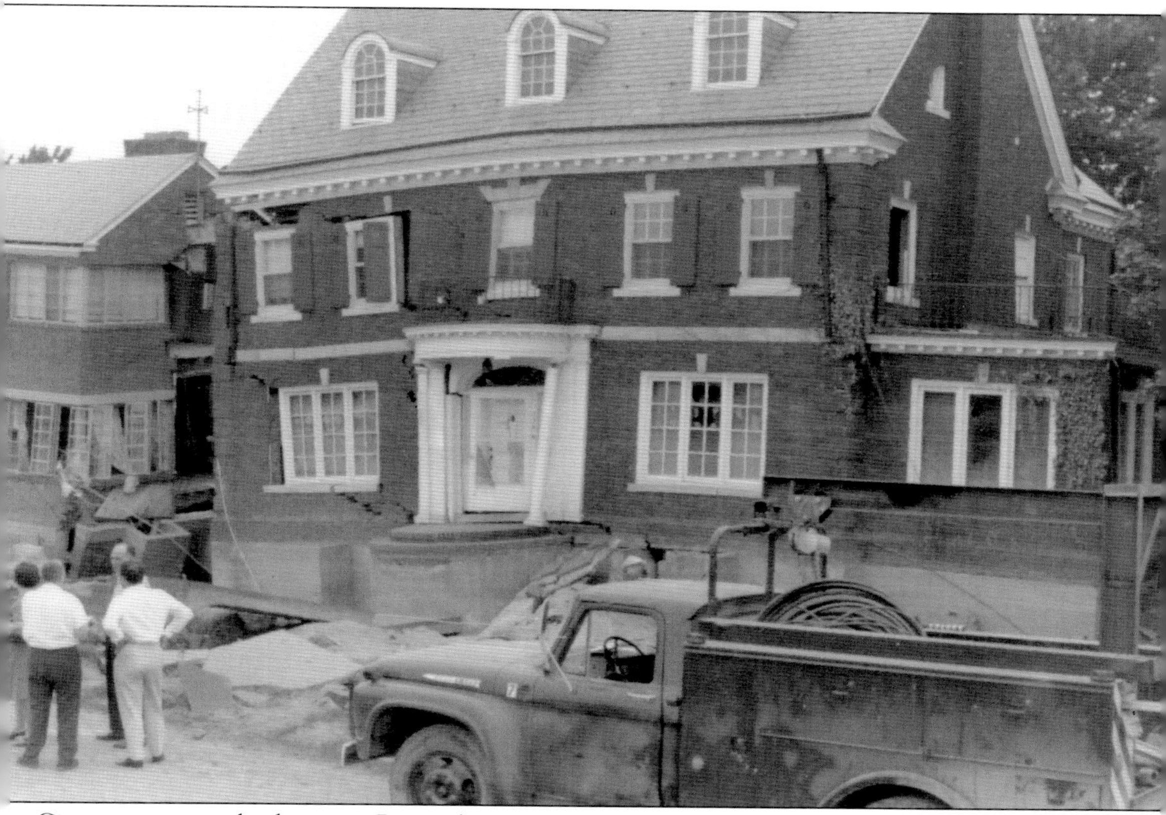

Citizens examine this home on Riverside Drive in Wilkes-Barre, another example of the flood's destruction. This gorgeous brick building had to be torn down. Repair was made impossible by the flood. Bulldozers tore down dozens of homes in this area due to the immense damage. The East Side Landfill Authority was responsible for handling the waste. Initially, debris was removed, followed by windows, doors, and other household materials that had to be discarded. As such a large city, the Wilkes-Barre cleanup was simply mammoth. In addition to homes, libraries, schools, universities, and hundreds of businesses were also affected. (Courtesy of Sheldon Glahn.)

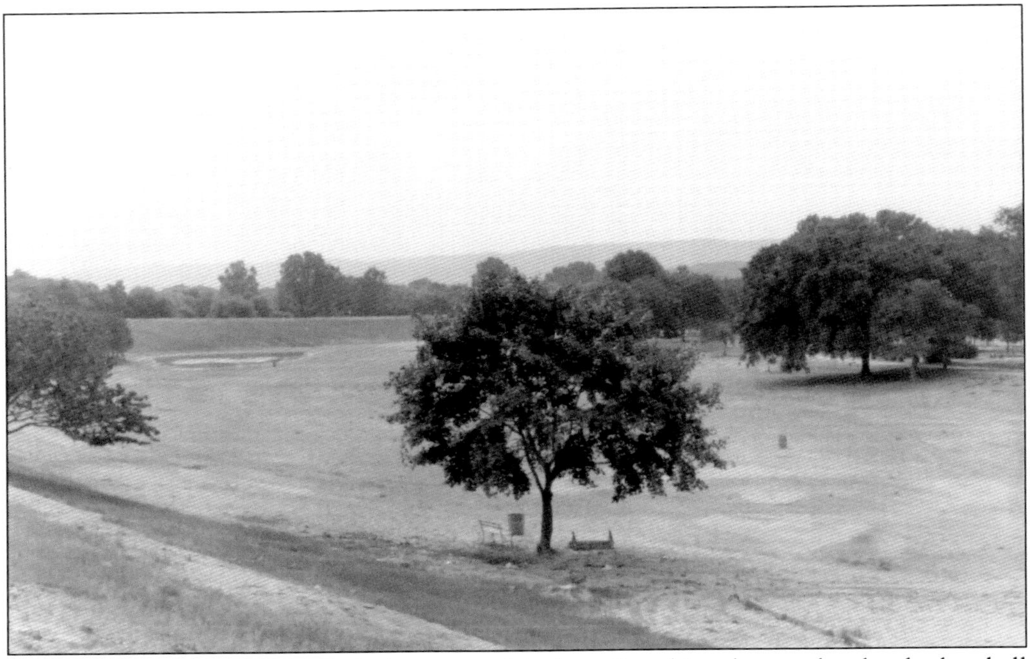

These photographs of Kirby Park show several inches of mud in what used to be the baseball fields, tennis courts, and playgrounds local residents enjoyed prior to the flood. The further south one traveled on Wyoming Avenue, the deeper the mud got. In the span of only a few miles, mud could be anywhere from an inch to several inches deep. Bordering Kirby Park is the levy system, built by the US Army Corps of Engineers. At 36 feet in 1972, the levy system was four feet too short to hold back the raging river. It has since been raised to over 40 feet. (Both, courtesy of Sheldon Glahn.)

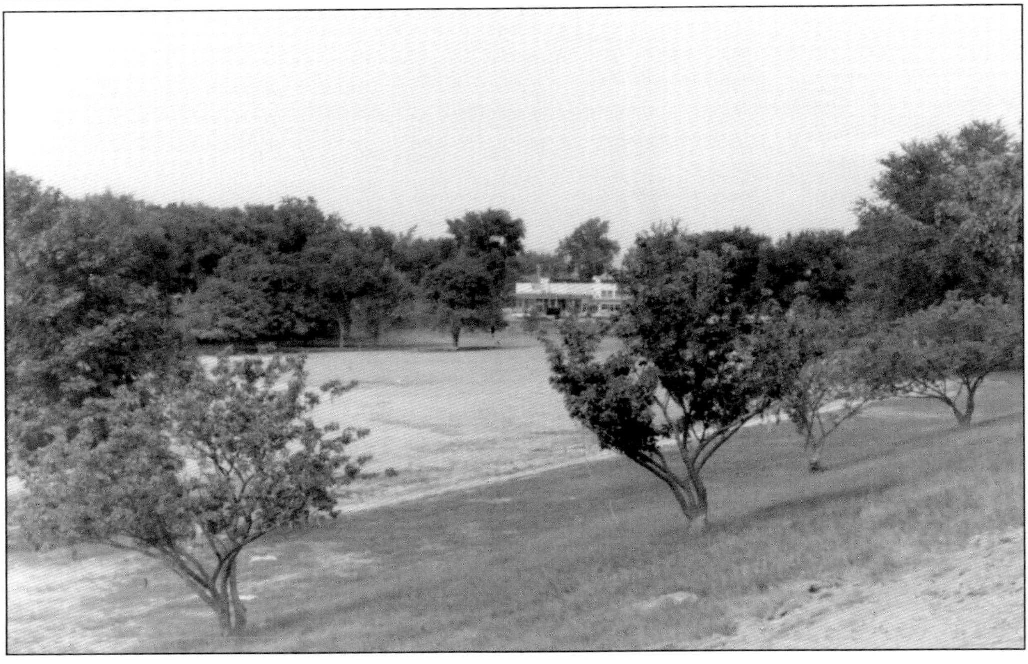

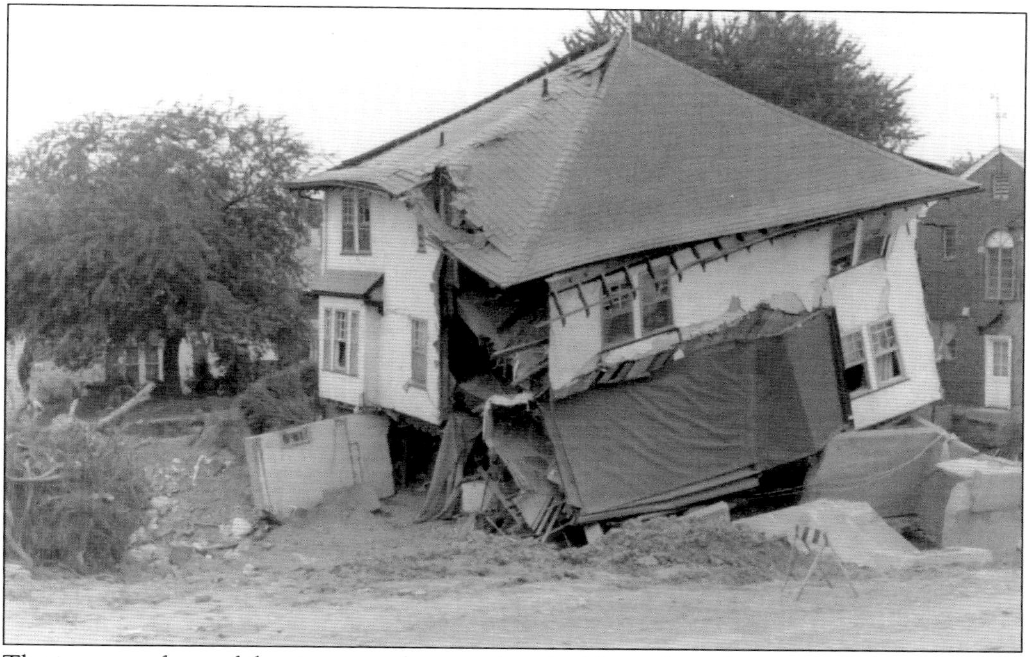

The immense force of the river was almost unimaginable until residents returned to see images such as this house in Wilkes-Barre knocked entirely off its foundation. The Riverside area of Wilkes-Barre was particularly ravaged by Agnes, with water levels reaching anywhere from 8 to 30 feet high. Many homes were practically brand new, but they could not be saved. It is incredible that the homes in these pictures are even standing. A worker recalled walking though one of them after the flood describing how the floors shook and creaked. Both homes were torn down by heavy machinery. (Both, courtesy of Sheldon Glahn.)

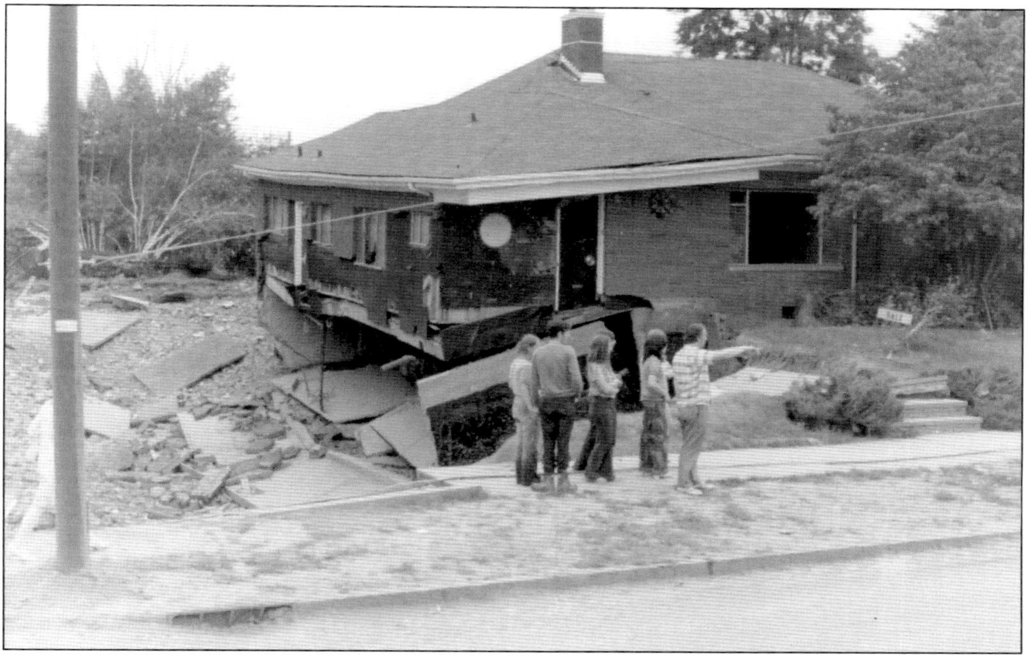

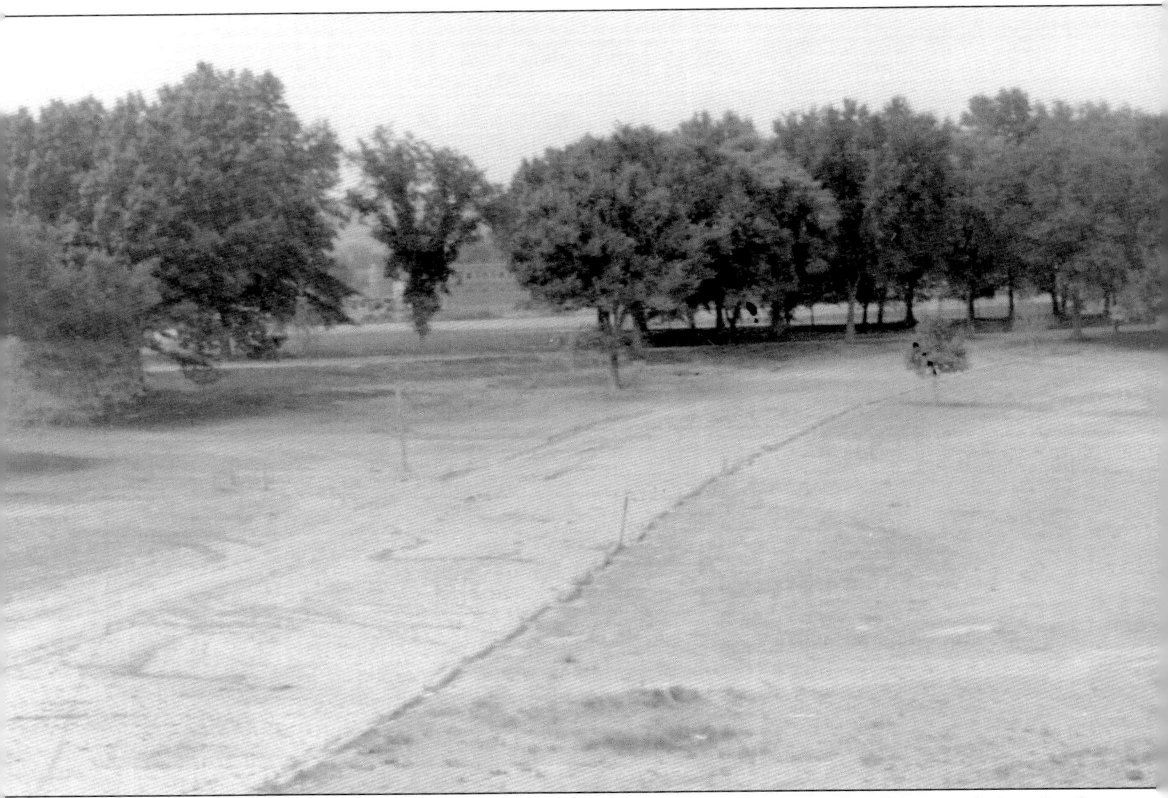

The Kingston Armory is visible in the background in this photograph of the road that leads to Kirby Park. The building is home to the 109th Field Artillery Battalion. Nearly 18 feet of floodwater infiltrated the armory. Radios, artillery, heavy equipment, and other supplies were taken from the building in the hours before the water hit. Three old cannons still stood on the front lawn, covered in mud after the water receded. The armory is only a short walk from the Susquehanna River near the Market Street Bridge, which connects Kingston and downtown Wilkes-Barre. (Courtesy of Sheldon Glahn.)

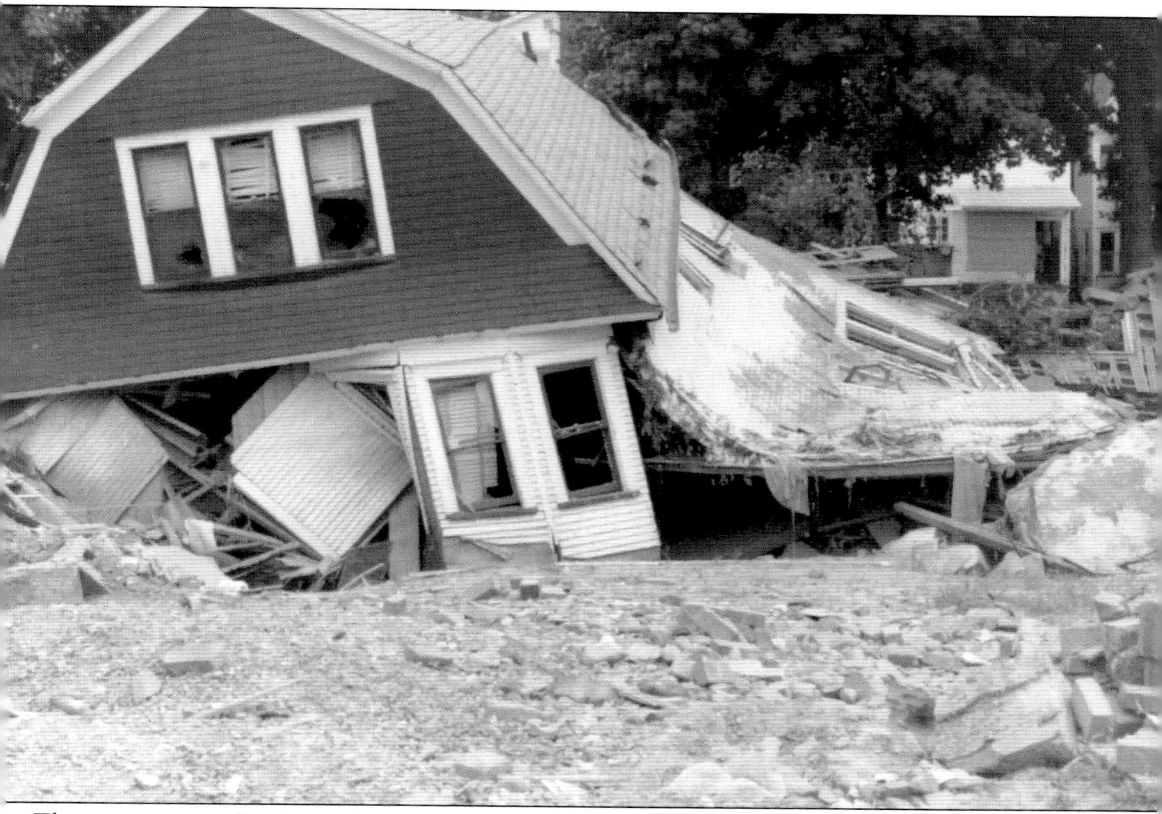

This picture actually shows the attic and second floor of a house in Wilkes-Barre. The entire first floor was washed away, leaving only the top levels. The right side shows the bent wall of the home. As a humorous aside, one young resident in his teens described how he and friends took cinder blocks from homes such as this and built makeshift party houses in the woods. One even bragged they had electricity in theirs. For many youth, the excitement and wonder of such an event were in contrast to the feelings of despair and financial ruin of their parents. (Courtesy of Sheldon Glahn.)

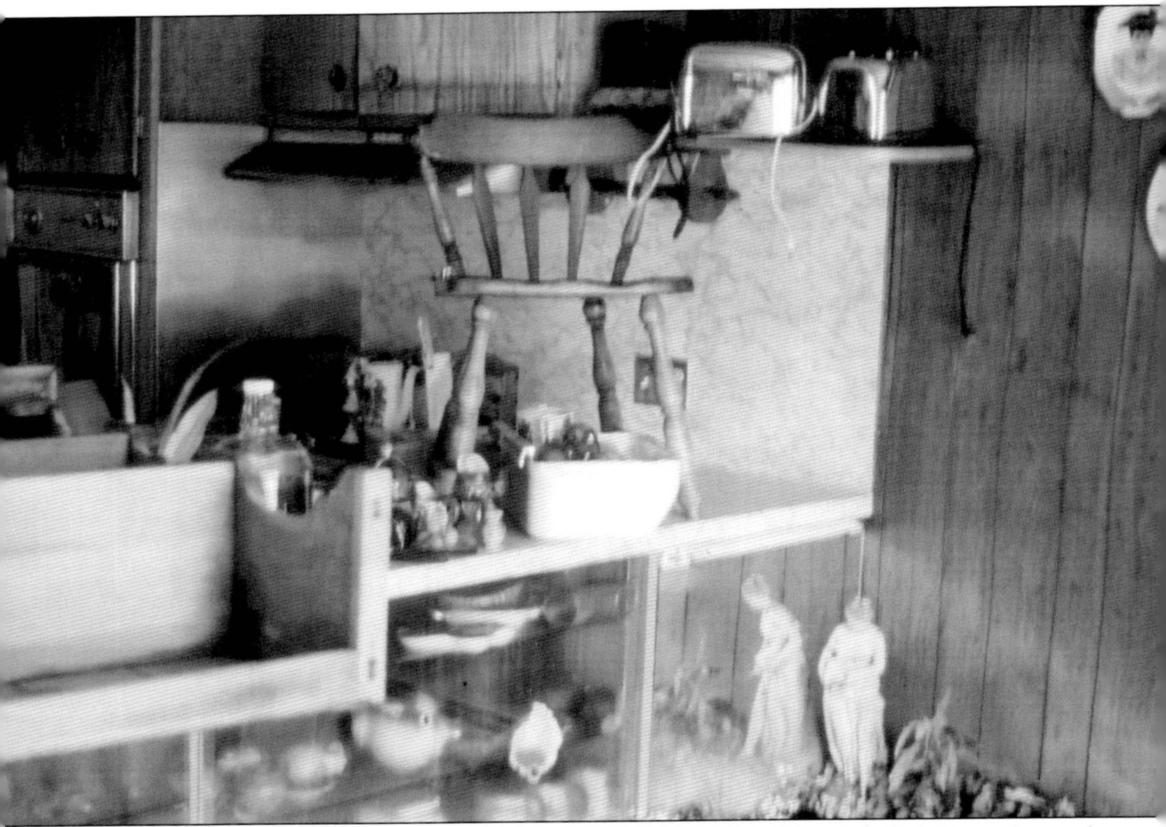

The kitchen of a home in Forty Fort is shown after the waters receded. Amazingly, neither the glass doors nor the glassware were damaged, except for mud. In the same home, the hutch, which held the fine china, was knocked over; again, nothing was broken because it landed in the water. One resident remarked that the only glass that broke in his home was what he stepped on, hidden under several inches of mud. All the other delicate china and glass was taken out back, hosed off, and used for generations to come. Not every homeowner was so lucky. (Courtesy of Sheldon Glahn.)

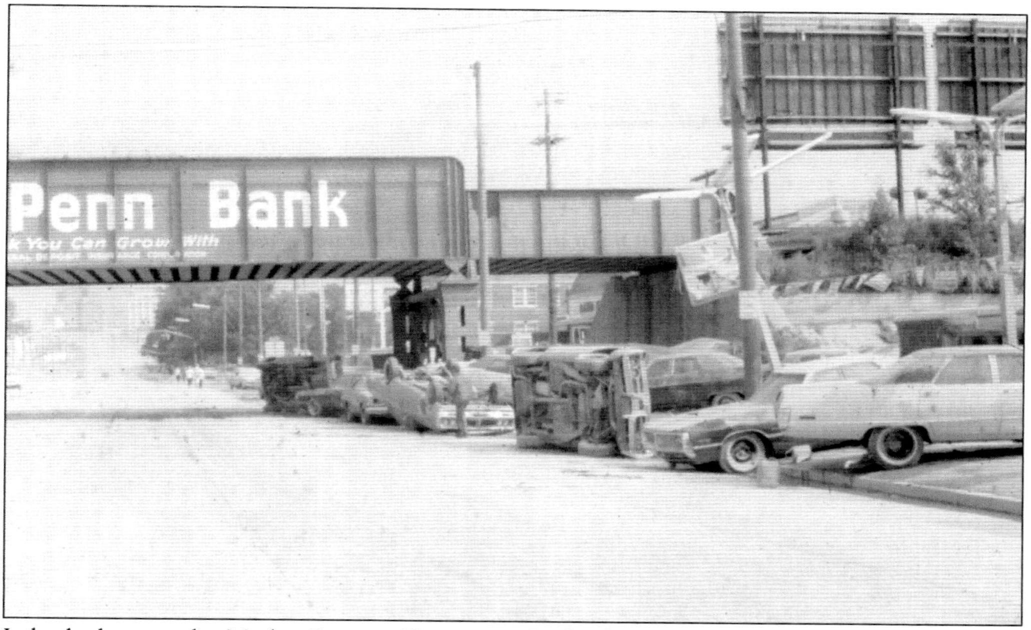

In both photographs, Market Street in Kingston is the final resting place for brand new automobiles from Superior Motors, destroyed by the flood. Many businesses simply did not have the manpower or personnel to remove all objects from harm's way. One boat rescuer recalled how, at first, he could not figure out what the grinding noise was coming from under his craft. When he got his bearings, he realized he was hitting cars in an automobile lot. Large dealerships had to leave most of their inventory behind, as they had nowhere to put the vehicles, and they had their own homes to worry about. (Both, courtesy of Sheldon Glahn.)

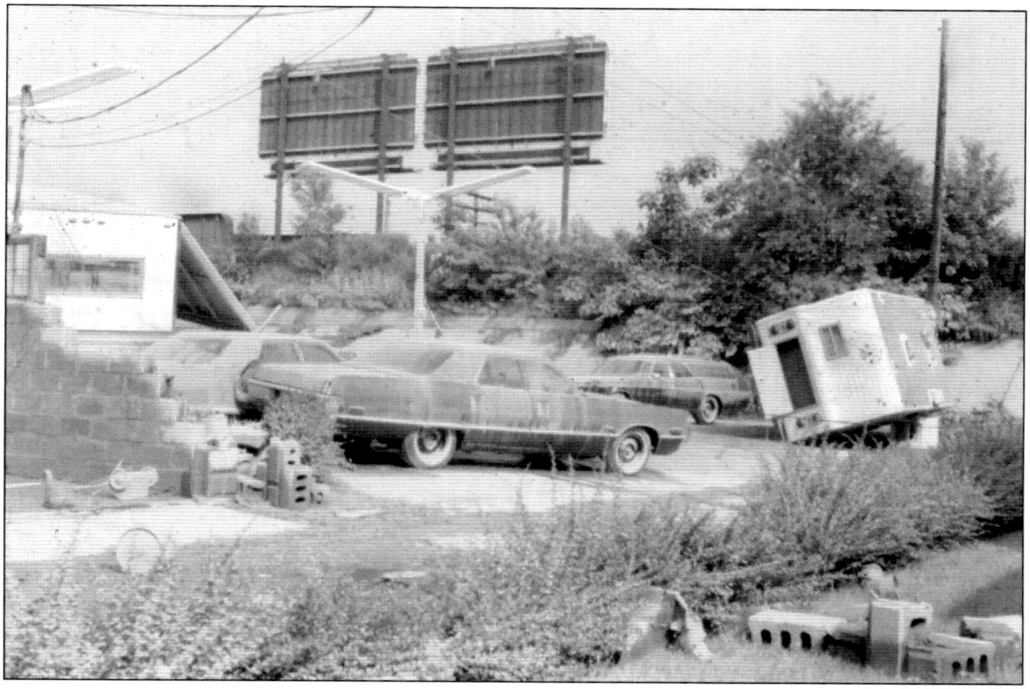

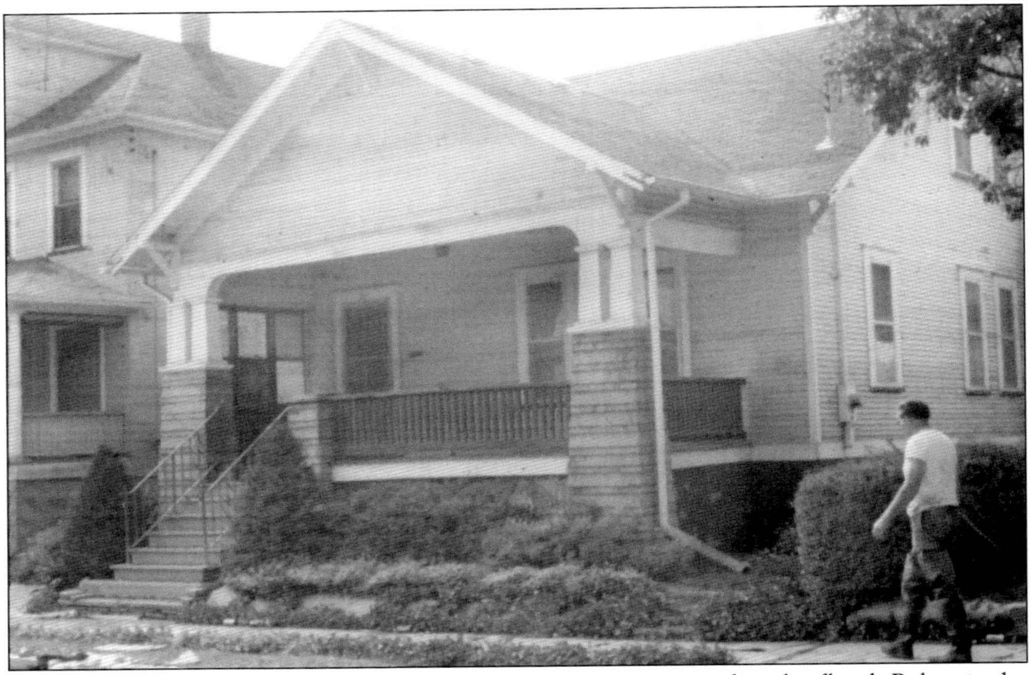

Pictured above is a home on South Gates Avenue in Kingston after the flood. Below is the backyard of the same home. The home had been through three floods since the 1920s, surviving them all. Fred Glahn, the owner, along with his brother and nephew, reinforced the building with structural steel to make it livable. To this day, the steel beams are in the basement, holding up the home. After the flood, the owner of this home told his wife that now was the chance to redo everything just as she wanted it. At the time, she demanded everything be made exactly as it was before. After the project, however, he said she constantly complained about the layout of the house. (Both, courtesy of Sheldon Glahn.)

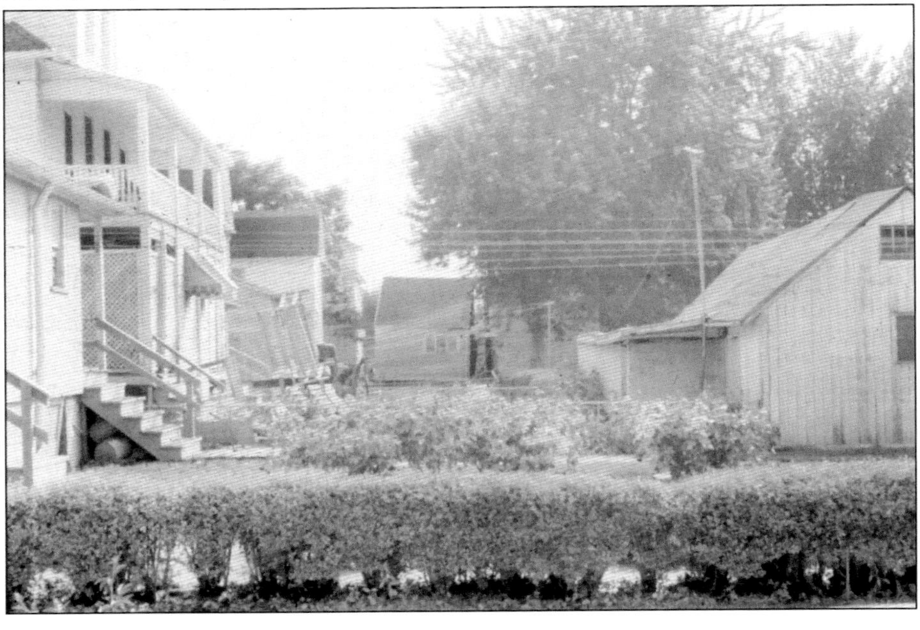

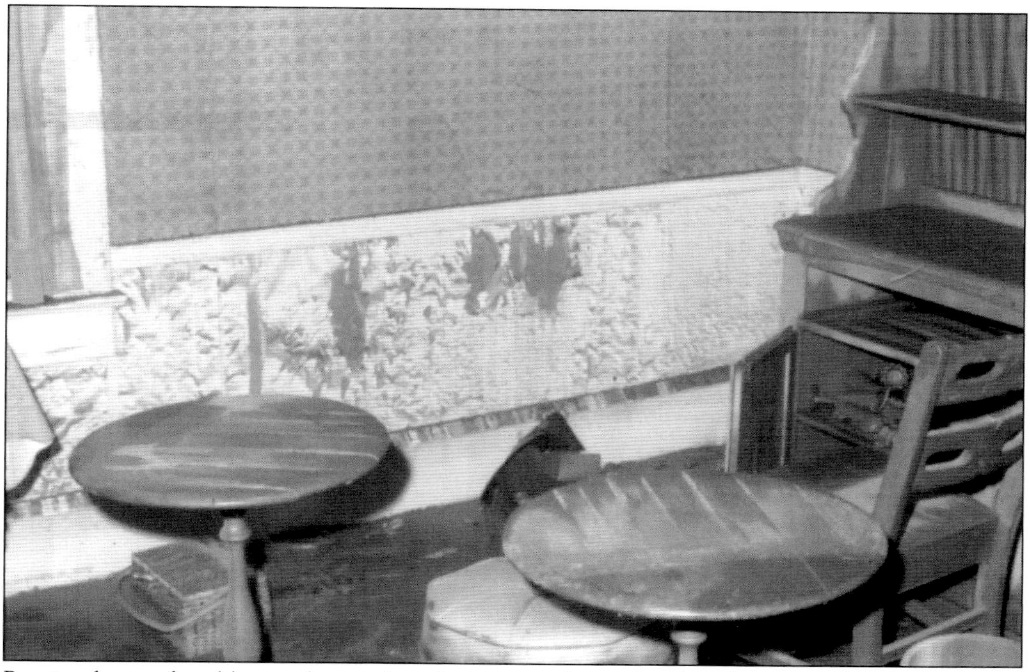

Previously comfortable couches and a television set lie with other furniture where floodwaters left them in the Walters home in Forty Fort. It was a shock to homeowners to see their houses at first. In many cases, the doors had swollen shut, so entry was difficult. When a group of workers was trying to use a rope to lift a heavy refrigerator out, the appliance fell, smashing on the ground and bursting open. The smell of the rotting food was too much for the men to bear. Over 1,600 homes in Forty Fort were destroyed by the river waters. (Both, courtesy of Sheldon Glahn.)

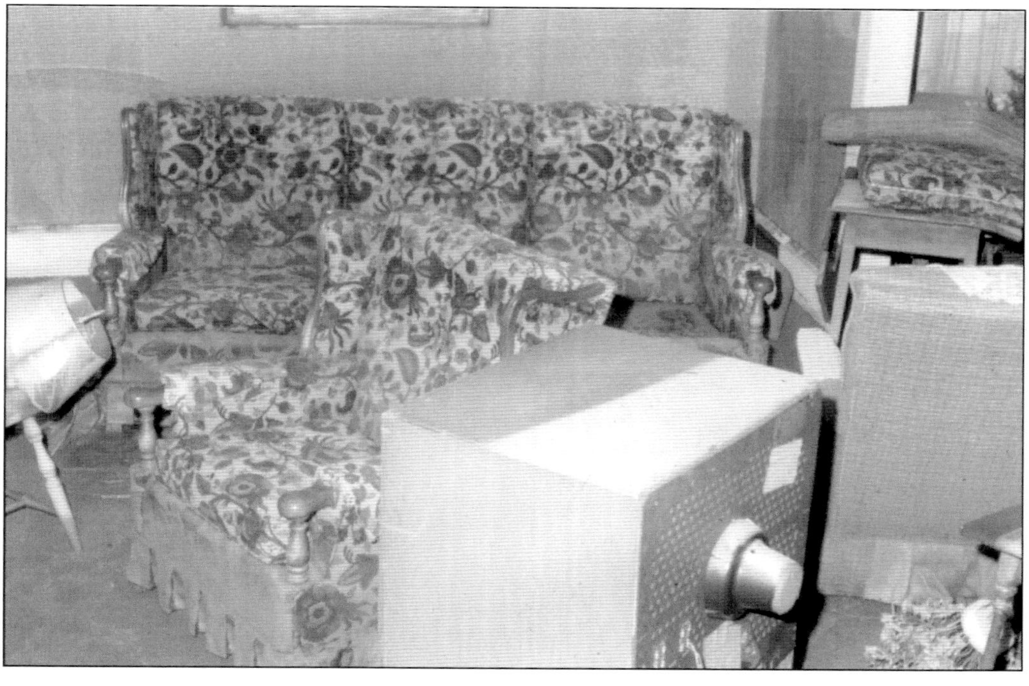

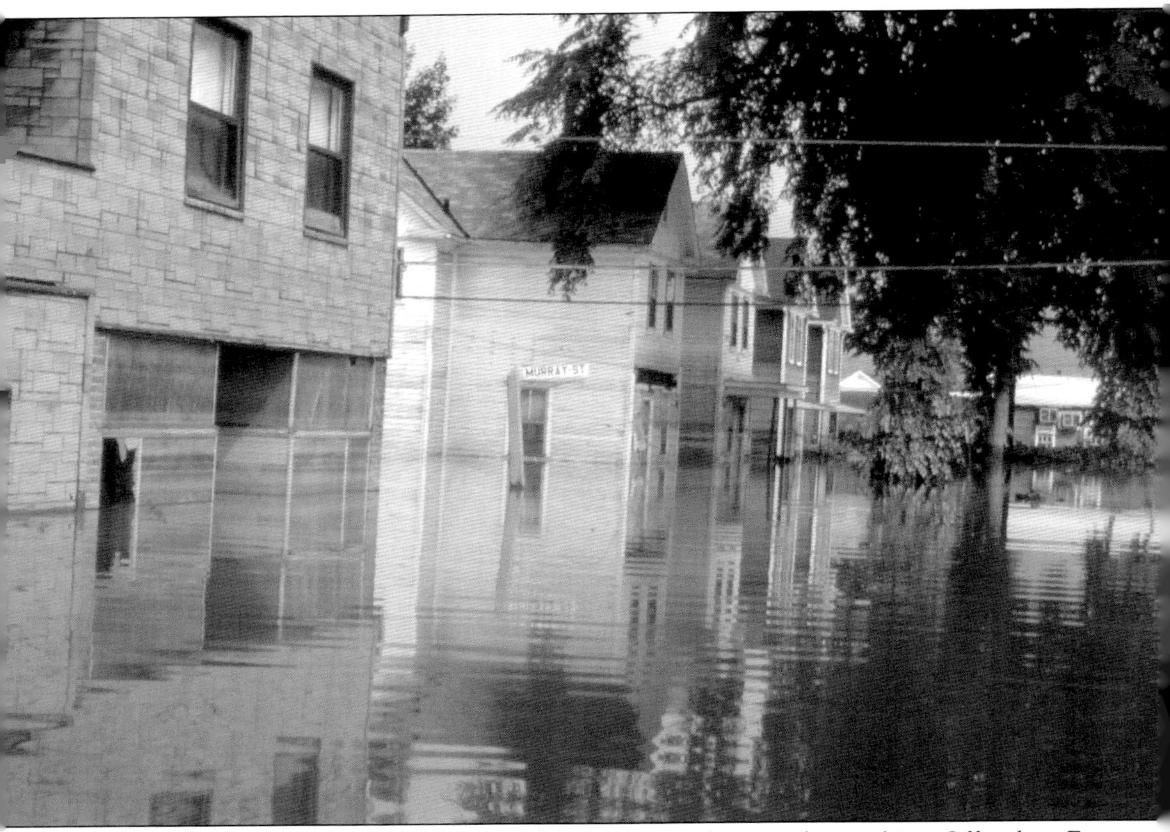

Taken from a boat, the depth of the floodwaters in this photograph is striking. Officials in Forty Fort were angered over residents taking photographs. In fact, one of them yelled at Sheldon Glahn while he was taking this photograph, to which he replied, "If you want to swim out and take my camera, you can have it." Many residents felt betrayed by local officials who left town during the flood. This photograph was taken near Slocum Street, which led to the "back road" in Swoyersville, where rescue operations were headquartered. Workers would get in boats and motor down into the valley to check damage and aid victims. (Courtesy of Sheldon Glahn.)

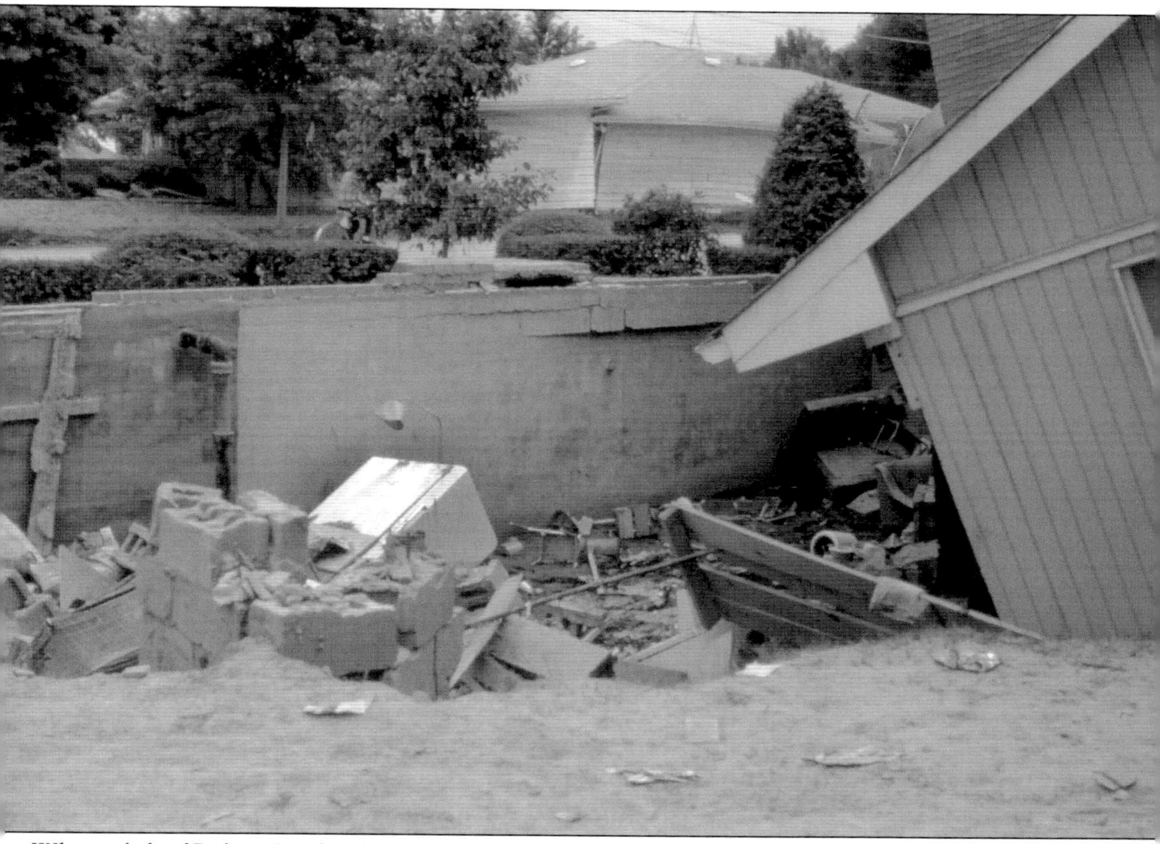

What is left of Robert Jacobs's home in Riverside Park, Wilkes-Barre, is visible here. A friend of Jacobs said that seeing this home upset him the most. The house was completely knocked off its foundation and had to be torn down. Absolutely nothing was salvageable from the home, although a thief did steal the flood-soaked air-conditioner from the window. As with many homes in the area, especially this part of Wilkes-Barre, which was particularly hard hit, the only option was to tear the structures down and rebuild. Many residents decided to relocate to areas outside of the flood zone. One woman moved to California, leaving everything behind. After the waters receded, she orchestrated the sale of her property from across the country. She was willing to trade the risk of earthquakes, mudslides, and fires instead of enduring another flood. (Courtesy of Sheldon Glahn.)

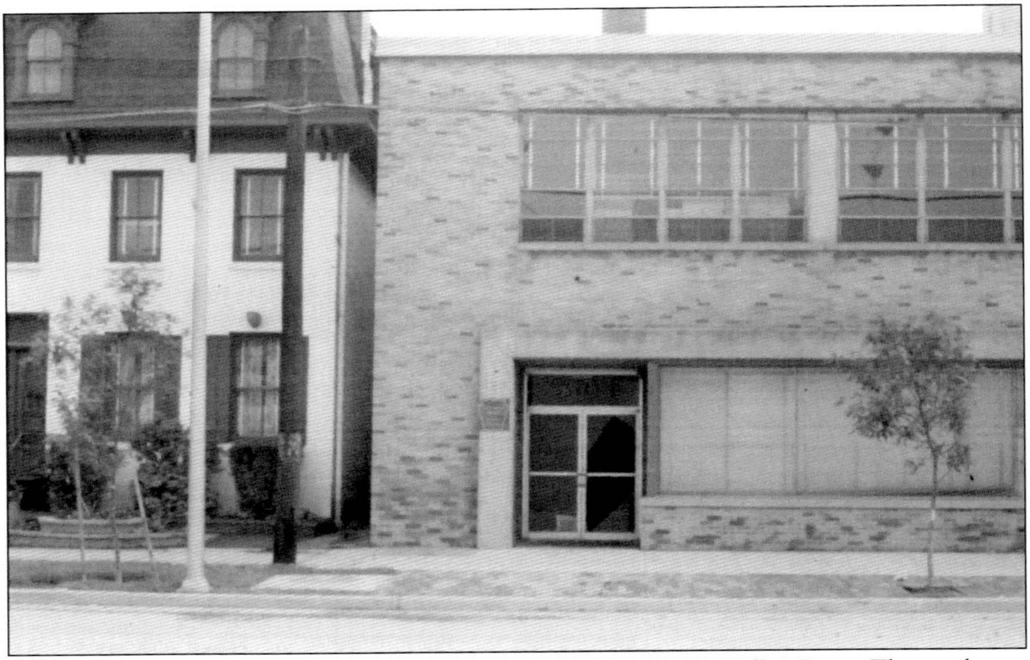

These photographs show the Office of Vocational Rehabilitation in Wilkes-Barre. The employees had only been in this location for six months when Hurricane Agnes caused the Susquehanna River to rise and damage the office. The previous office was on the third floor of another building, which many noted when viewing the damage. Although the state threatened to move the office due to the fact that the landlord refused to clean it, the office employees offered to repair the building. Employees had to throw out thousands of case files, as well as replace carpets and walls and clean. However, they were able to move back into the location within several months. (Both, courtesy of Sheldon Glahn.)

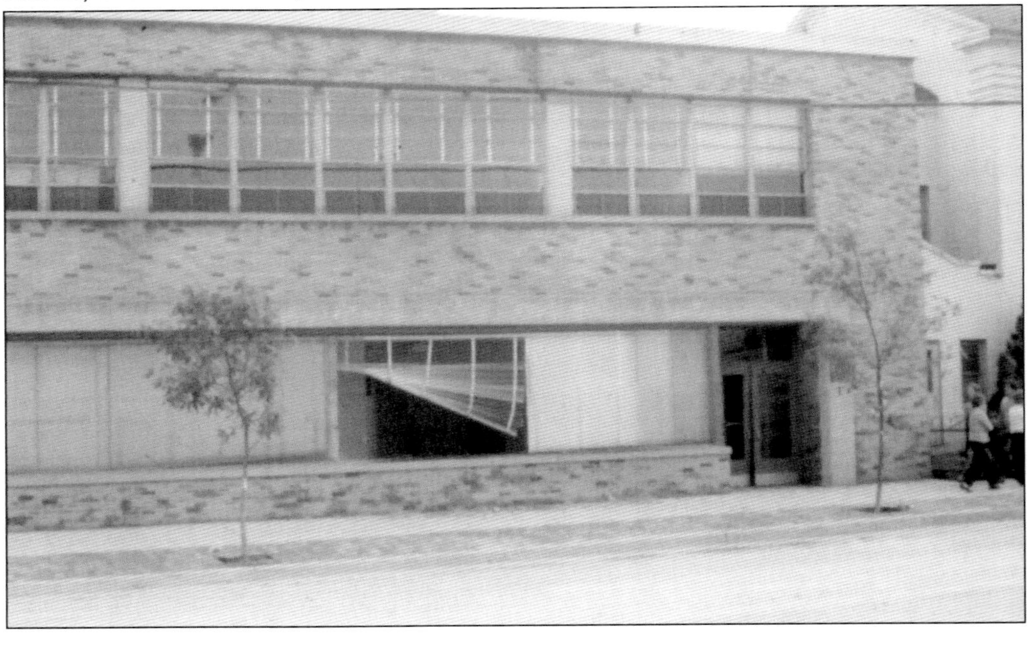

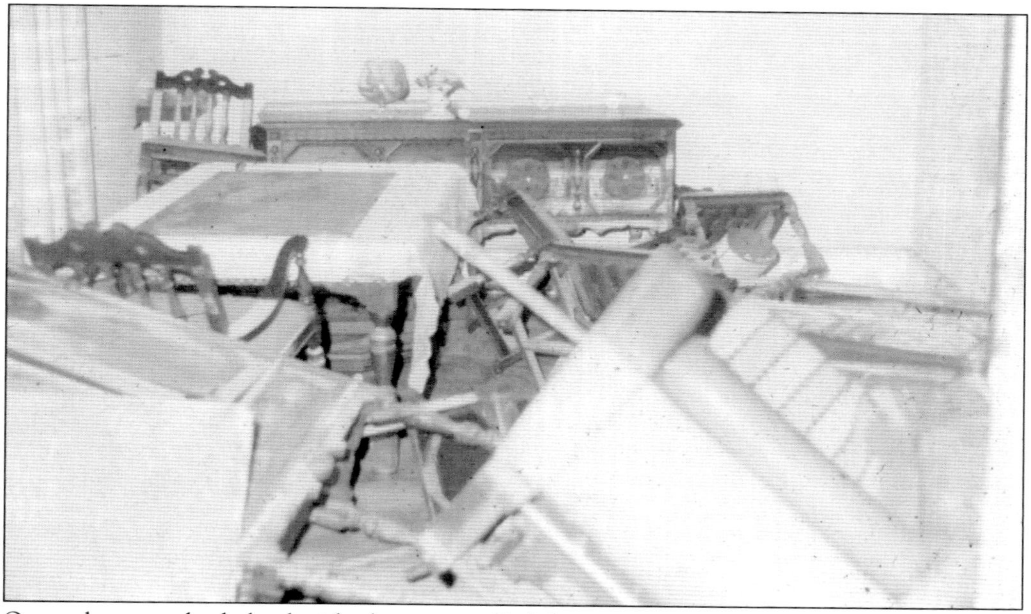

One volunteer who helped with cleanup recalled the resignation residents felt as they realized how many of their possessions were lost. "It's like you were helping them throw their life away," Joseph Hizny stated. Hizny, a Pittston resident who suffered no damage to his home, and his friends earned $2.50 an hour helping with cleanup. (Courtesy of Sheldon Glahn.)

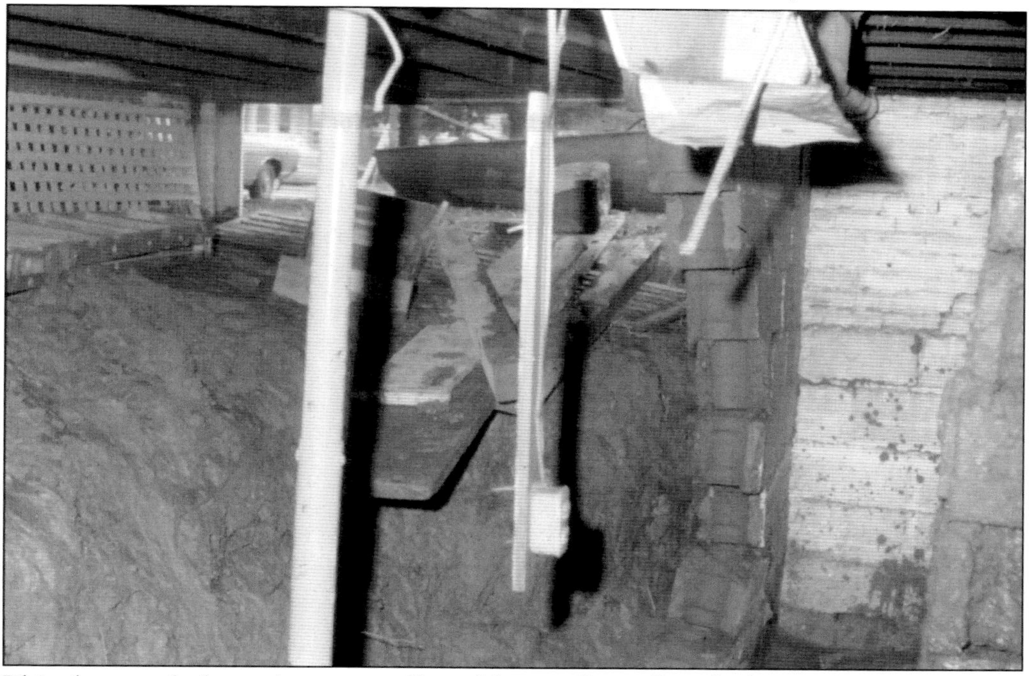

This photograph shows the entire collapsed front cellar wall at the home of Probert Walters. Note the bent cinder block wall and bowed supports. A contractor was able to rebuild the home. First, it was supported temporarily while the wall was rebuilt. Within a few weeks, the structure was safe enough to occupy. (Courtesy of Sheldon Glahn.)

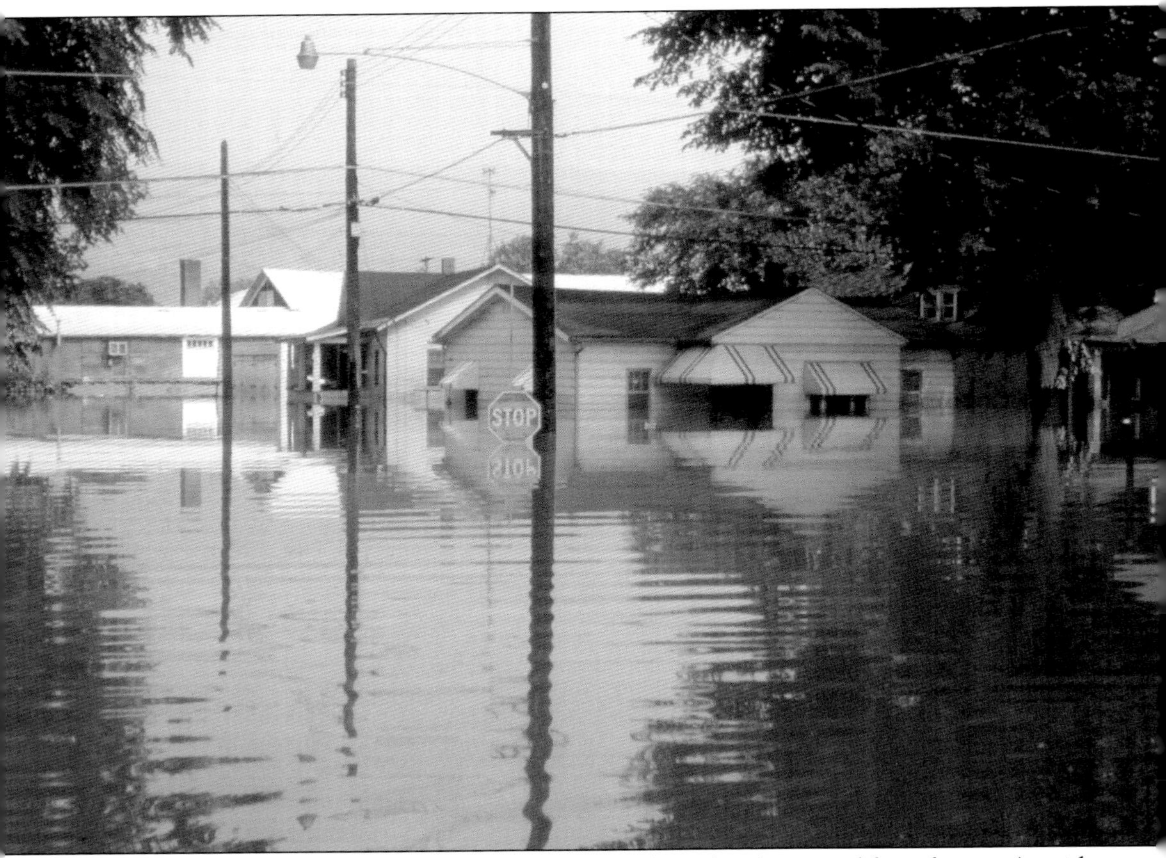

This photograph shows Murray Street in Forty Fort buried under several feet of water. A resident who returned to the area by boat estimated there had to be 12 feet of water, due to it being a low spot. With nowhere to drain or pump to, the water took a long time to recede. Joseph Hizny remembered vividly the carp and other river fish that would become stranded in the puddles and die. The scent was what bothered him the most. It was June, it was hot, and the stench of muddy river water and dead animals permeated the air. Despite this, the most common complaint was still the mud. Residents hauled out bucket after bucket of mud and dumped it into the streets, then hosed their houses down from inside out. To make matters worse, when it dried, the dust was as bad as the mud. "Oh God, the dust," a Forty Fort man exclaimed. (Courtesy of Sheldon Glahn.)

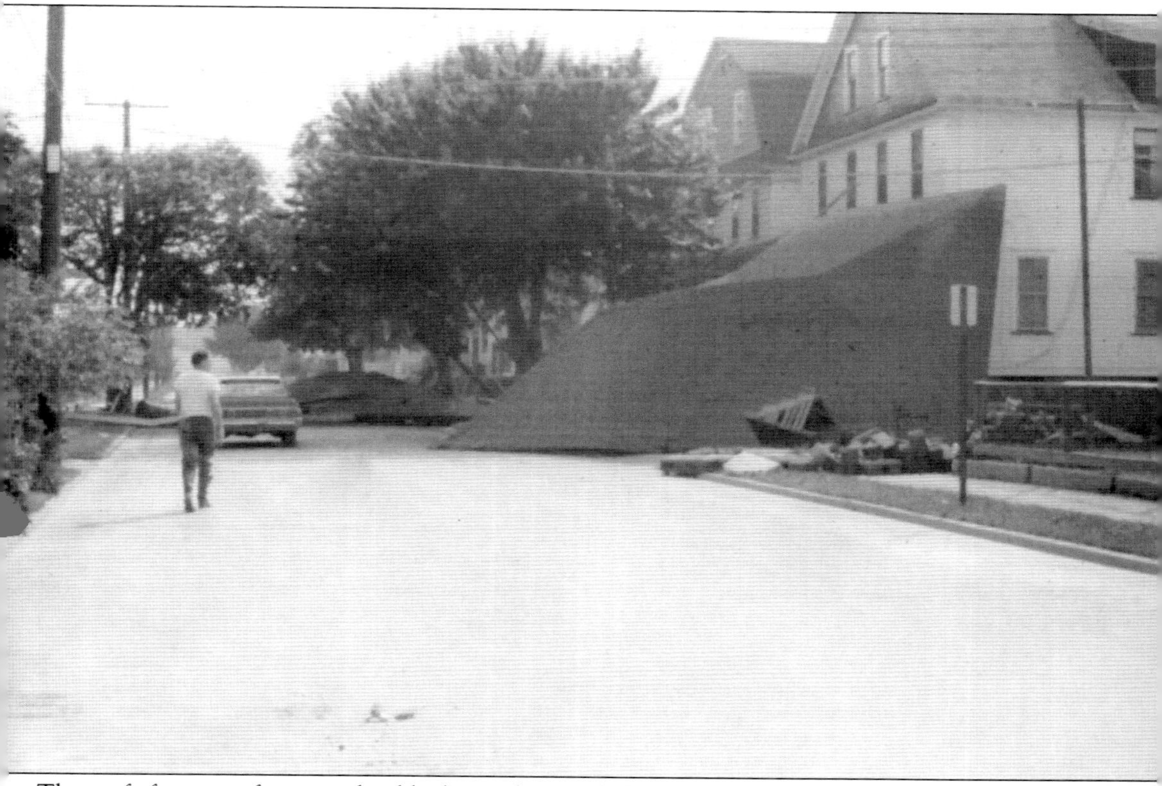

The roof of a garage from another block somehow ended up on South Gates Avenue in Kingston, Pennsylvania. With so much damage and most residents in the flood zone cleaning up their own homes, workers were sought. For $2.50 an hour, young men would be taken by truck to go help. Elderly residents were the usual first stop for those seeking to aid flood victims. One worker recalled that his crew went for lunch, could not get a ride back, and were fired, only to be rehired the next day because workers were so desperately needed each day. While stepping in mud inches thick, the crews worked closely with anyone in need. Government aid was responsible for freeing up funds to help the Wyoming Valley dig itself out. Dan Flood, in particular, even bent the law to make sure his constituents got the help they needed. Privately, even President Nixon was told he could forget about winning Pennsylvania in the general election if he did not visit the area. (Courtesy of Sheldon Glahn.)

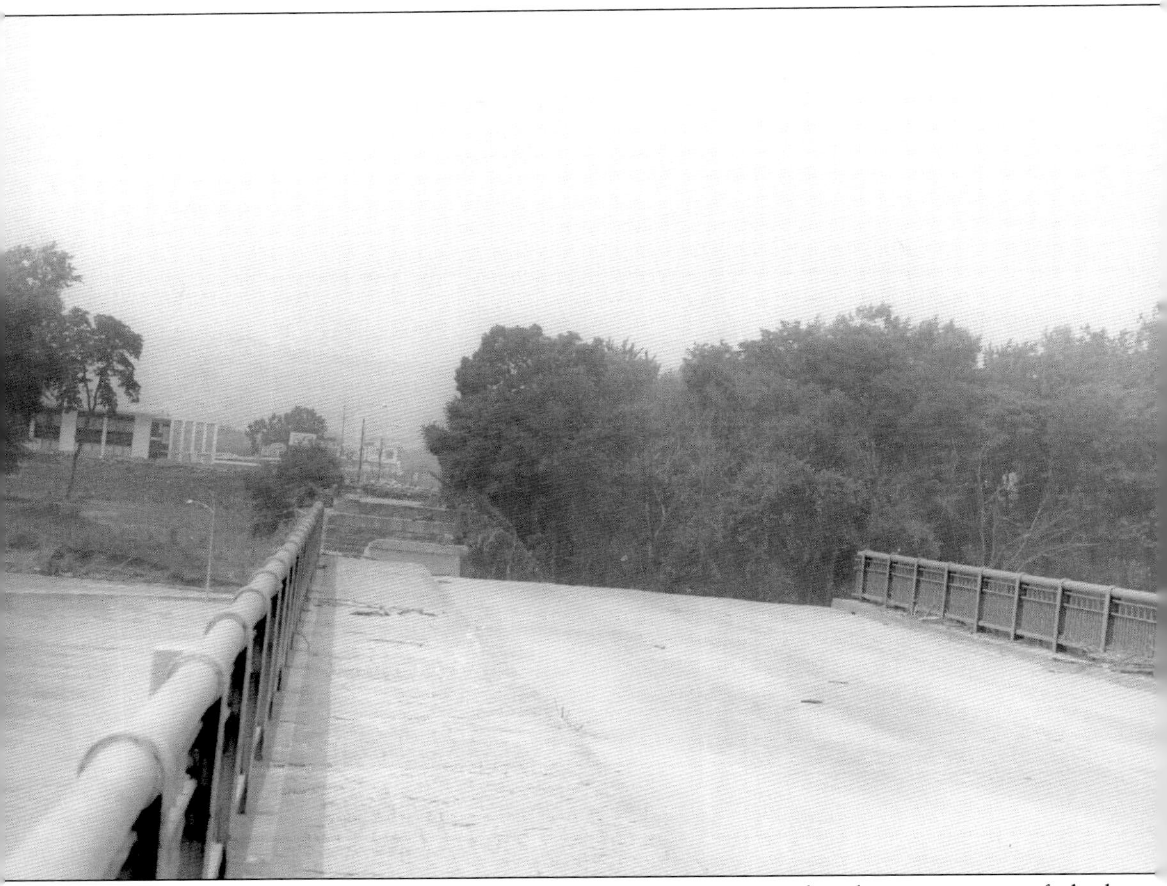

This picture shows a drop-off in the middle of the Pierce Street Bridge, the entire center of which was washed away. James Stinson, a Kingston resident, upon leaving from the Wilkes-Barre side described his vehicle barely making it due to the high water slowing him down. Upon his arrival on the Kingston side, an irate official lambasted and berated him, demanding, "What the hell are you doing?" After responding that he was coming from work, Stinson asked, "Do you want me to turn around and go back?" Crediting his King's College security uniform for helping him look official, Stinson continued to his home. The family was nervous about the rain but did not evacuate until the next morning when the sirens went off. Incredibly, the day of the flood was gorgeous and the sun was shining. But the sirens were an indication to many that things were about to get very bad. (Courtesy of Plymouth Historical Society.)

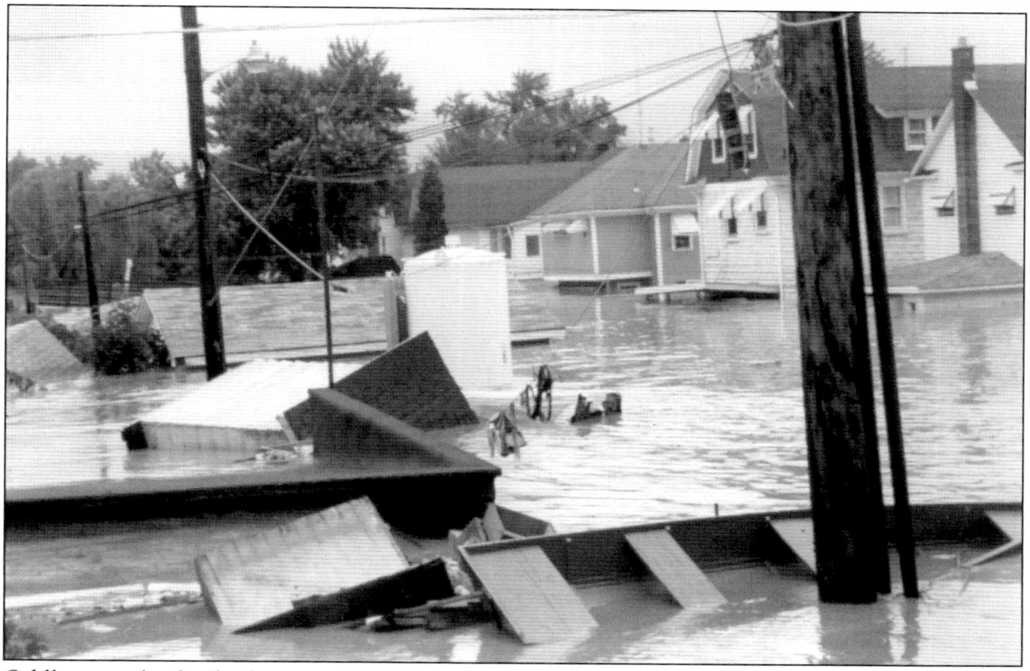

Oddly enough, the farther away some areas were from the Susquehanna River, the higher the water. Of the 6,600 homes in Kingston, only 37 were spared. Water followed the lay of the land, finding its own level. Some houses had water only in the basement, while others were washed away. There was no pattern to the destruction, except that it was immense. (Courtesy of Sister Mary Carmel McGarigle University Archives, Misericordia University.)

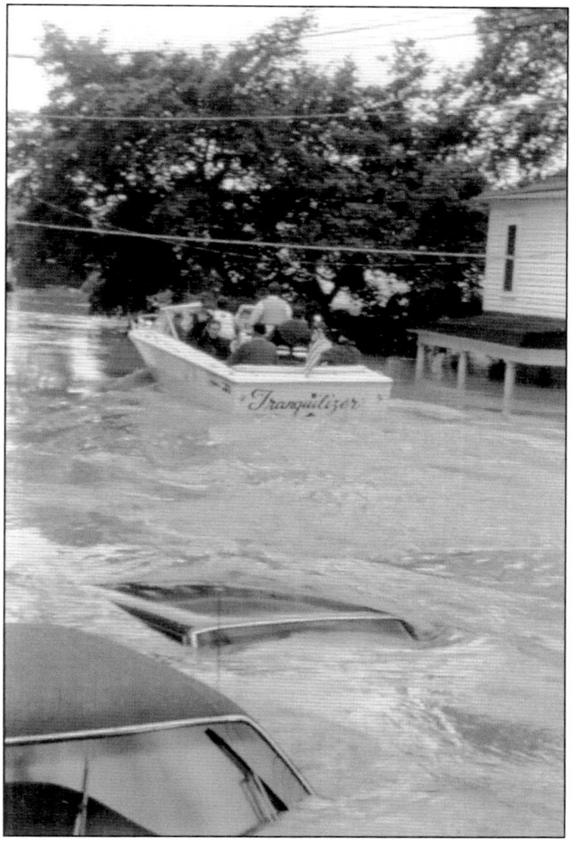

A boat called *Tranquilizer* motors past cars covered with floodwater. Many residents needed a tranquilizer upon seeing the impact of the flood. One worker recalled sleeping in a boat. He had been down all day surveying damage and was so exhausted he put the seats down and took a nap. (Courtesy of Sister Mary Carmel McGarigle University Archives, Misericordia University.)

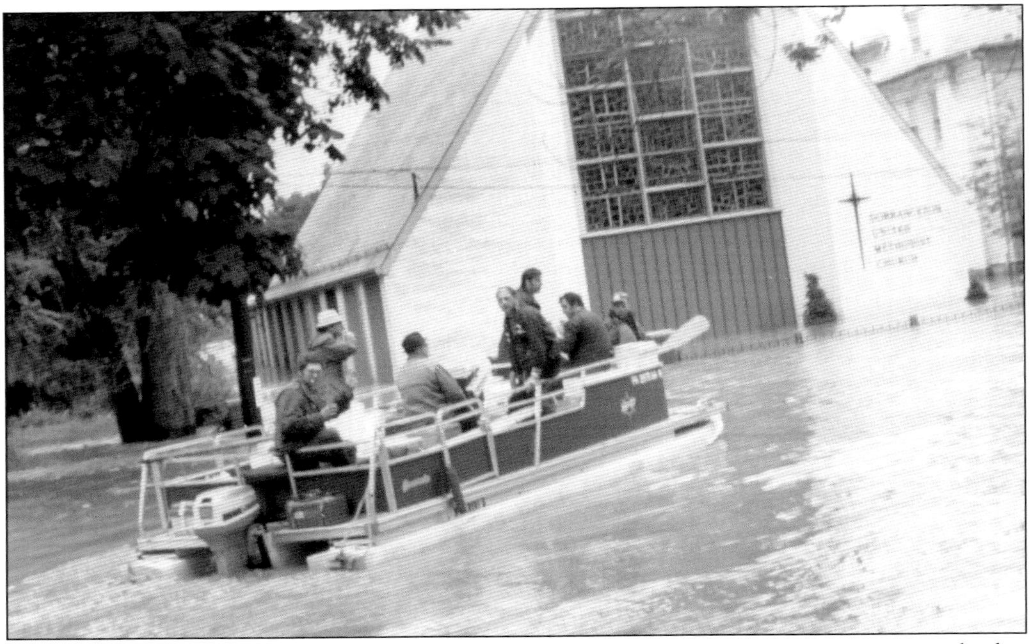

A group of several volunteers in a pontoon-style boat float past the Dorranceton Methodist Church on Wyoming Avenue in Kingston. Across the street, not seen in this picture, would be the Nesbitt Memorial Hospital, which was evacuated. The bill for damage in Kingston and Edwardsville was nearly $200 million. (Courtesy of Sister Mary Carmel McGarigle University Archives, Misericordia University.)

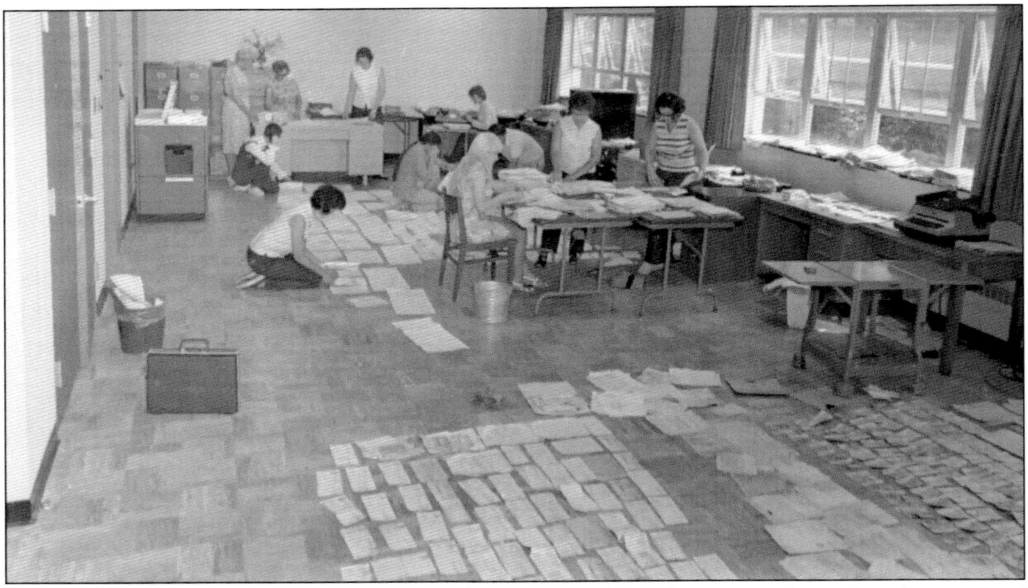

Workers at College Misericordia do their best to sort through paperwork in the aftermath of Agnes. While residents lost mail and personal correspondence, businesses lost important financial records. For many, regular mail service after the flood was a huge morale boost, in that it helped them feel that some aspects of their lives were getting back to normal. (Courtesy of Sister Mary Carmel McGarigle University Archives, Misericordia University.)

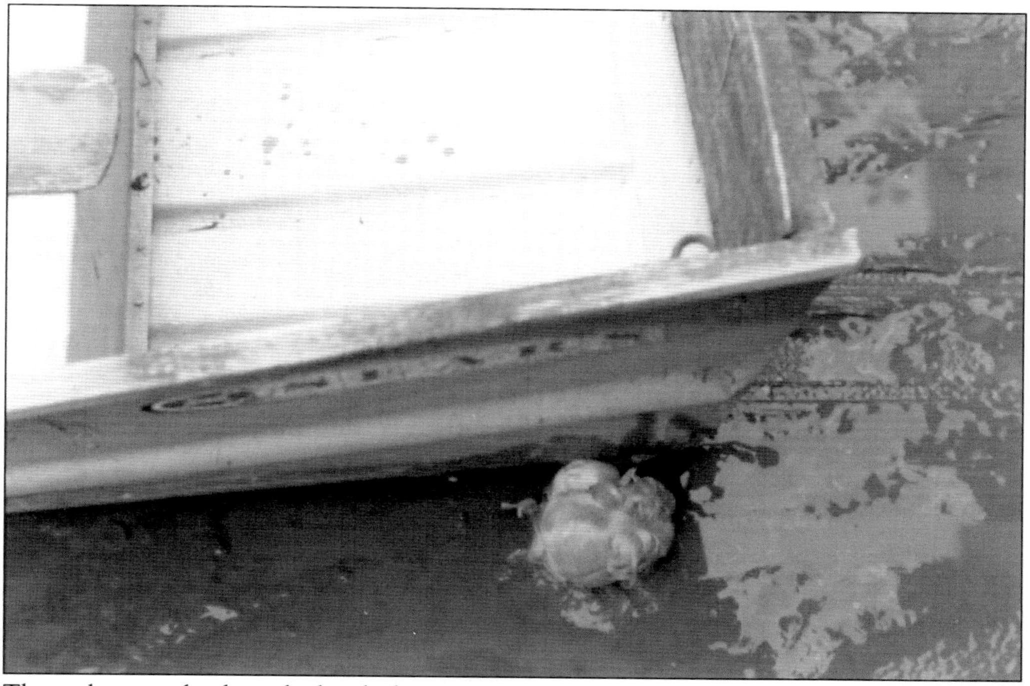

These photographs show the head of a doll and Donald Duck, remnants of the flood. Thankfully, the flood occurred in summer, when children were not in school. For many youngsters, the flood was an exciting time, with midnight evacuations and water filling the streets. One young man's only regret was it had to happen in June, and he did not get to miss school. Children enjoyed playing with band instruments in shelters, meeting celebrities from cleanup crews, and watching the water. Not everyone had fun, however. Some elementary school students were old enough to remember the smell. Others never forgot the bodies from the Forty Fort Cemetery floating down Wyoming Avenue. (Both, courtesy of Sister Mary Carmel McGarigle University Archives, Misericordia University.)

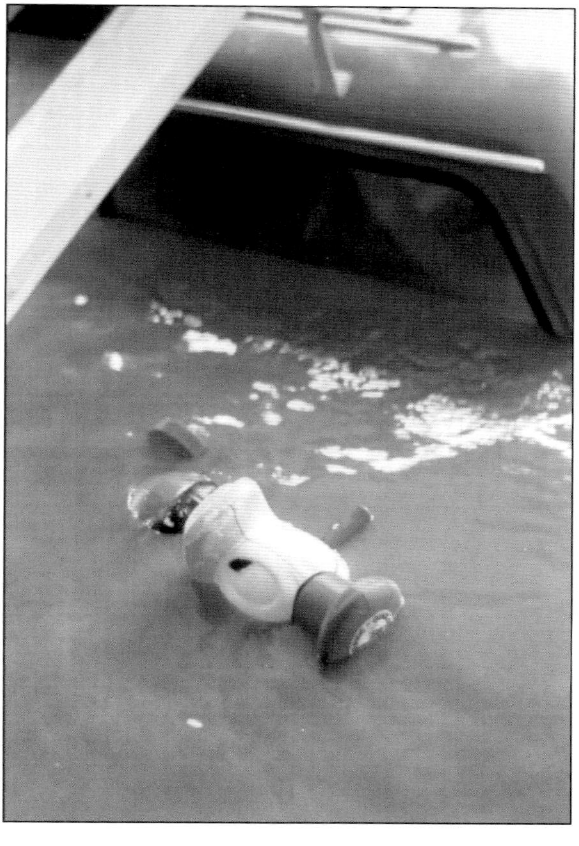

KING'S COLLEGE 3

Wilkes-Barre, Pennsylvania 18702

DEPARTMENT OF CHEMISTRY

		Definite	Probable
1.	X-Ray Diffraction and accessories	$15,000	
2.	Spectrographic Analyzer and acc.	$10,000	
3.	Dark Room and accessories	$ 1,000	
4.	E.P.R. (excluding the magnet)	$29,000	
5.	a. N.M.R. (excluding the magnet)	$22,000	
	b. N.M.R. (with the magnet)		$27,000
6.	a. Magnetic Susceptibility (excluding the magnet)	$ 3,500	
	b. Magnetic Susceptibility (including the magnet)		$ 5,000
7.	Polaroid MP 3 Land Camera	$ 1,500	
8.	D.T.A. and accessories	$ 3,500	
9.	Heath Kit for Instrumental Analysis	$ 2,500	
10.	Balance, Mettler P120	$ 850	

Total Damage
a. Definite $88,850
b. Probable $95,350

This total does not include the air conditioners or dehumidifier that were located in the instrument room. This also excludes the renovation of the room.

Please note that the damage caused in the chemical stockroom to the chemicals and glassware are not included.

Both Kings College and Wilkes University in downtown Wilkes-Barre were hit hard by the flooding. This receipt shows nearly $100,000 worth of damage from a King's College chemistry laboratory. The itemized list shows various X-ray, spectrographic analyzers, and dark room accessories that would need to be replaced. The list is broken into "definite" and "probable." The bottom of the list adds insult to injury, noting that broken glass is not included in the bill, nor is the cost of air conditioners, dehumidifiers, or renovating the room after the flood. Several feet of water submerged both college campuses. (Courtesy of Sister Mary Carmel McGarigle University Archives, Misericordia University.)

Four

For Good Luck
A Flood on Your Wedding Day

For most couples, the joy of starting a new life together is mixed with some anxiety and stress over who to invite, what to serve, and how to pay for it all. For Charles Malpass and his future wife, Mary (Molly) Hourigan, Hurricane Agnes delivered an unwelcome wedding present on what was to be their special day. In between aiding with sandbagging efforts and collecting personal items, it was decided the wedding would still be held, despite a missing veil, gown, bridesmaid, usher, and best man. On June 24, 1972, the future Mr. and Mrs. Malpass gathered with a small group of friends and family at the Gate of Heaven Church in the Back Mountain to make their vows. With a thrown-together menu, mismatched clothing borrowed from friends and family, and some store-bought Pepperidge Farm cakes, a wedding was held.

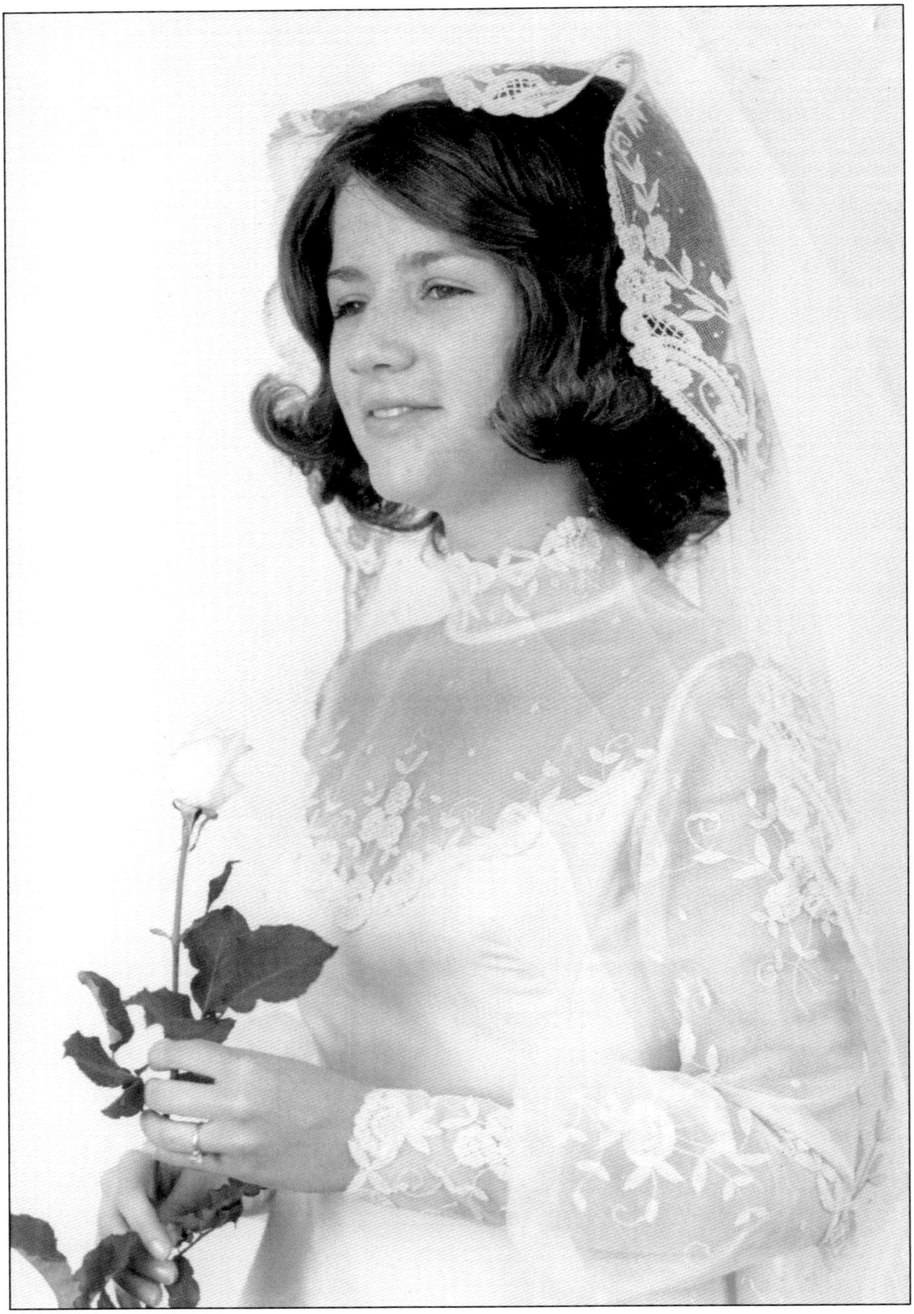

The future Mrs. Charles Malpass is seen in her wedding photograph. In one of the great stories to come out of the tragedy, Mary (Molly) Hourigan could never have imagined while planning her wedding the impact Mother Nature would have on her special day. Her story has been recounted not only in her family, but in local news stories every anniversary of the flood. The wedding was a bright spot in the dark days of the flood for many. She was walked down the aisle by her father, Judge Robert Hourigan, on June 24, 1972, in a borrowed wedding gown on loan from Jane Nicholson. (Courtesy of Charles and Molly Malpass.)

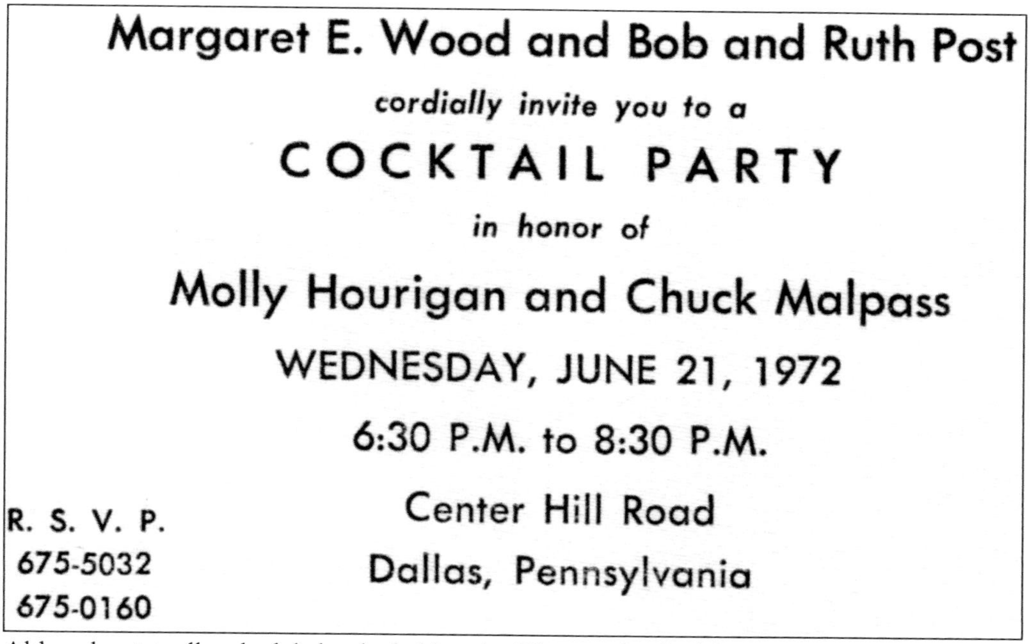

Margaret E. Wood and Bob and Ruth Post

cordially invite you to a

COCKTAIL PARTY

in honor of

Molly Hourigan and Chuck Malpass

WEDNESDAY, JUNE 21, 1972

6:30 P.M. to 8:30 P.M.

Center Hill Road

Dallas, Pennsylvania

R. S. V. P.
675-5032
675-0160

Although originally scheduled to be held at the Westmoreland Club in Wilkes-Barre, Hurricane Agnes forced the bride and groom to move the reception to the home of Robert and Ruth Post, aunt and uncle of the bride. Along with a few bottles of champagne, the menu included Chinese food, pizza, baked ham, and a variety of hors d'oeuvres. The highlight many remember the most, however, was three Pepperidge Farm cakes pressed together and pressed into service as a wedding cake, along with a cake topper from Aunt Ruth's own wedding. Despite the circumstance, Molly Malpass recalled with a smile that Aunt Ruth said it was still the best wedding she ever attended. (Both, courtesy of Charles and Molly Malpass.)

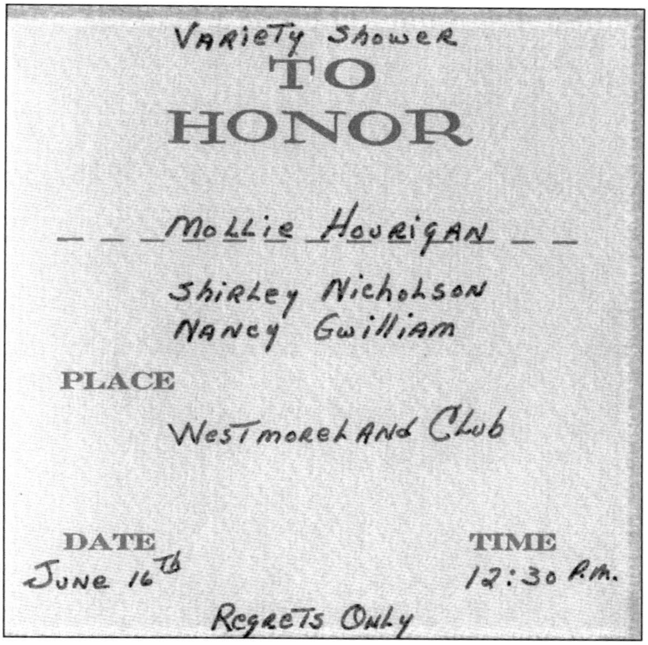

VARIETY SHOWER

TO HONOR

MOLLIE HOURIGAN

SHIRLEY NICHOLSON
NANCY GWILLIAM

PLACE

WESTMORELAND CLUB

DATE
JUNE 16th

TIME
12:30 P.M.

REGRETS ONLY

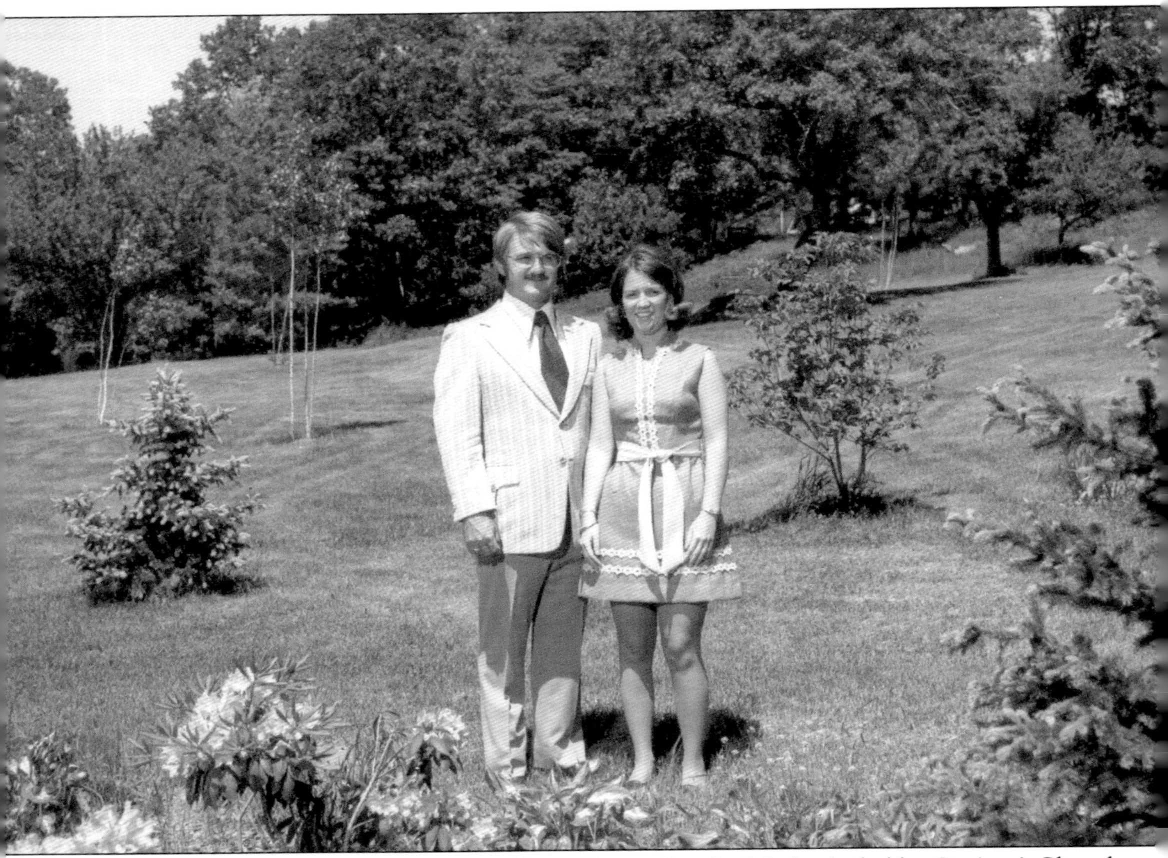

The happy bride and groom are pictured here. Originally scheduled to be held at St. Ann's Chapel, the wedding was moved to the Gate of Heaven Church due to Hurricane Agnes. Molly chose Bonnie Hourigan as maid of honor and Nancy Hourigan and Linda Loughlin as bridesmaids. Floodwater prevented friend Ruth Richards from joining them. On the groom's side, Harry D. Malpass stood in as best man, as his son Harry, the original best man, was stranded in Chicago, unable to get into the flood-ravaged Wyoming Valley. Ushers were Alex Walder and Kurt DeSombre, both wearing borrowed, mismatched suits. Another usher was unable to make it due to the flood. (Courtesy of Charles and Molly Malpass.)

This is the Kingston apartment of Charles and Molly Malpass. The wedding furniture was never to be used by the new bride and groom. Instead, it was thrown to the curb, another pile of refuse amongst the other remnants from Agnes, upon their return from their honeymoon. (Courtesy of Charles and Molly Malpass.)

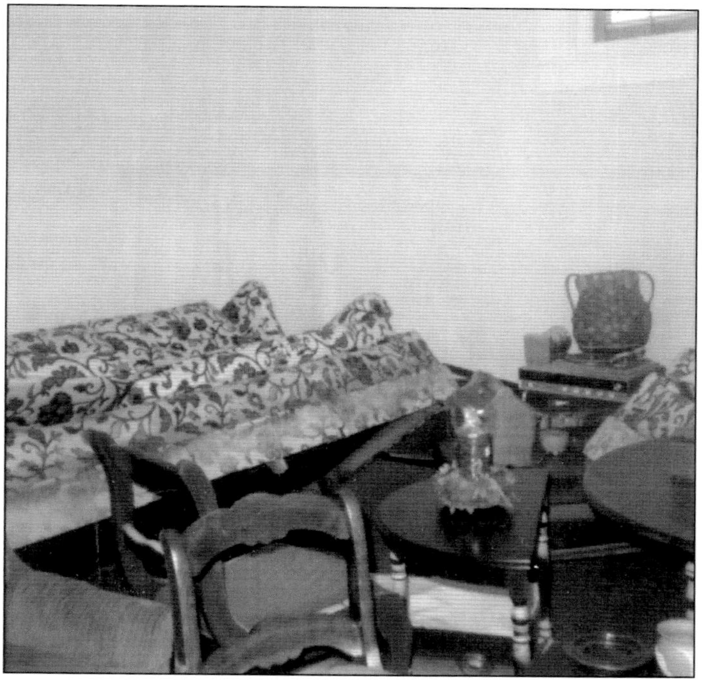

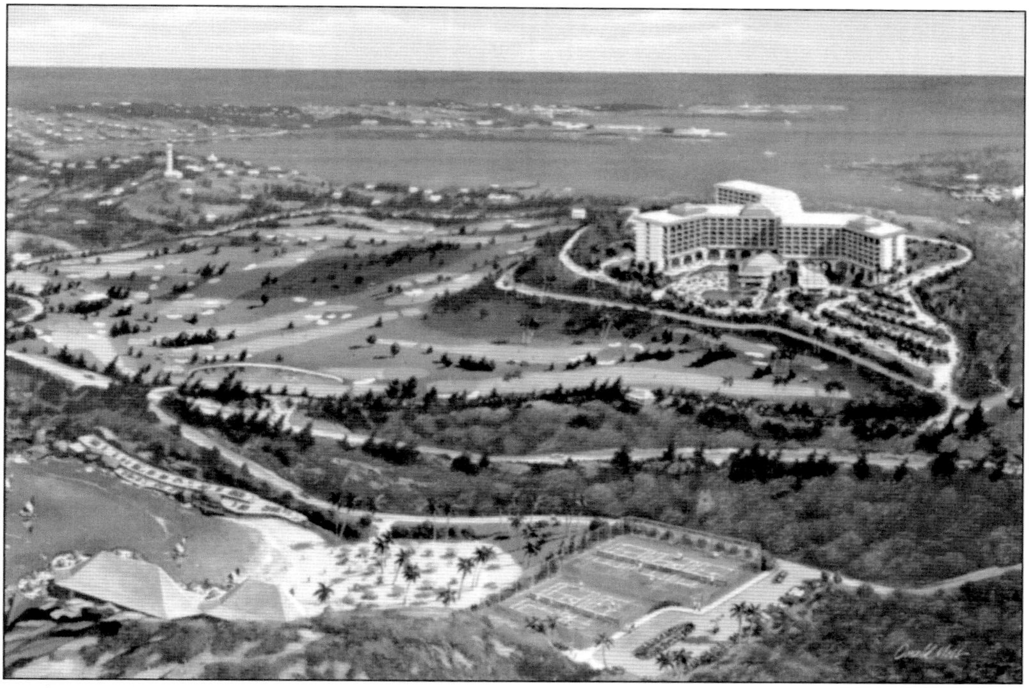

With travel being so difficult, Molly and Chuck Malpass had to drive around the flood-covered valley, through Bloomsburg, and eventually arrive at the airport to go on their honeymoon to the resort pictured on this postcard. After the temporary respite, the newlyweds returned to Kingston, threw out the flood-damaged possessions of their home, and went to live with relatives. (Courtesy of Charles and Molly Malpass.)

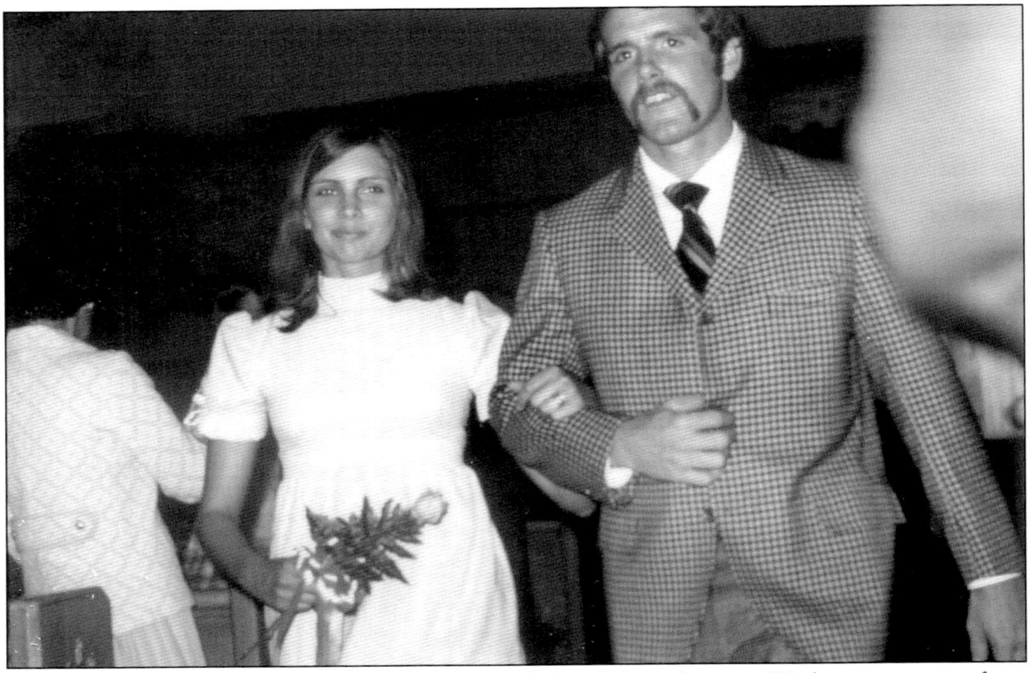

In the above photograph, Alex Walder escorts Linda Loughlin to her seat. With attire ranging from raincoats and boots to mismatched sport coats and borrowed dresses, friends and family joined the bride and groom for a wedding like nothing they could have predicted when their engagement was first made. Below, mother of the bride Augusta Hourigan is escorted by Kurt DeSombre. Echoing the sentiments of many, Chuck and Molly did not know how bad the flood would turn out for the residents of the Wyoming Valley. (Both, courtesy of Charles and Molly Malpass.)

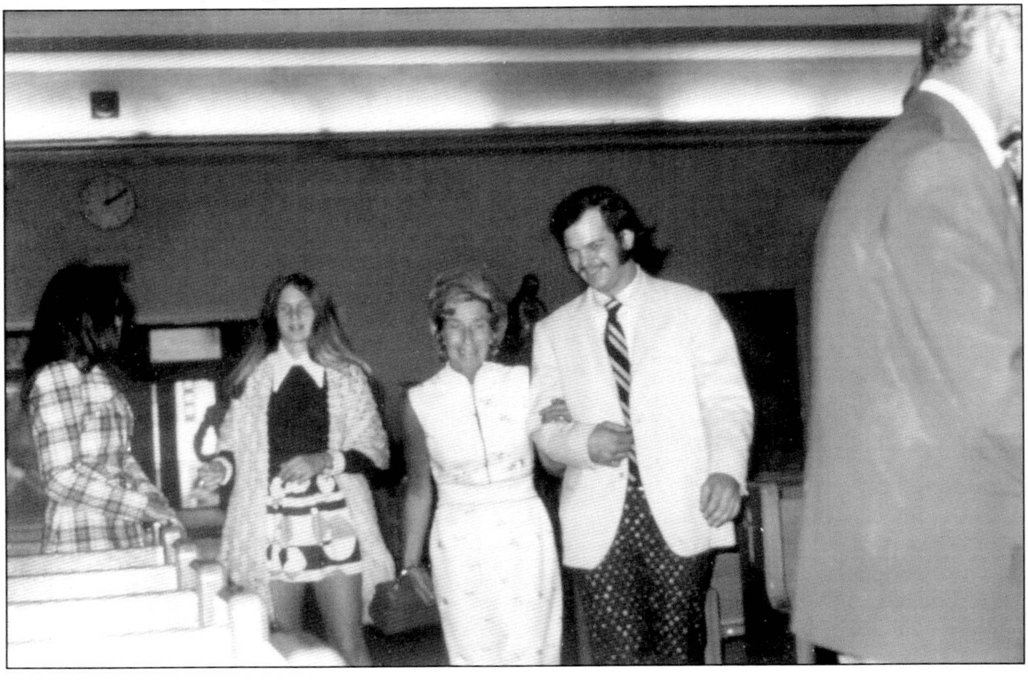

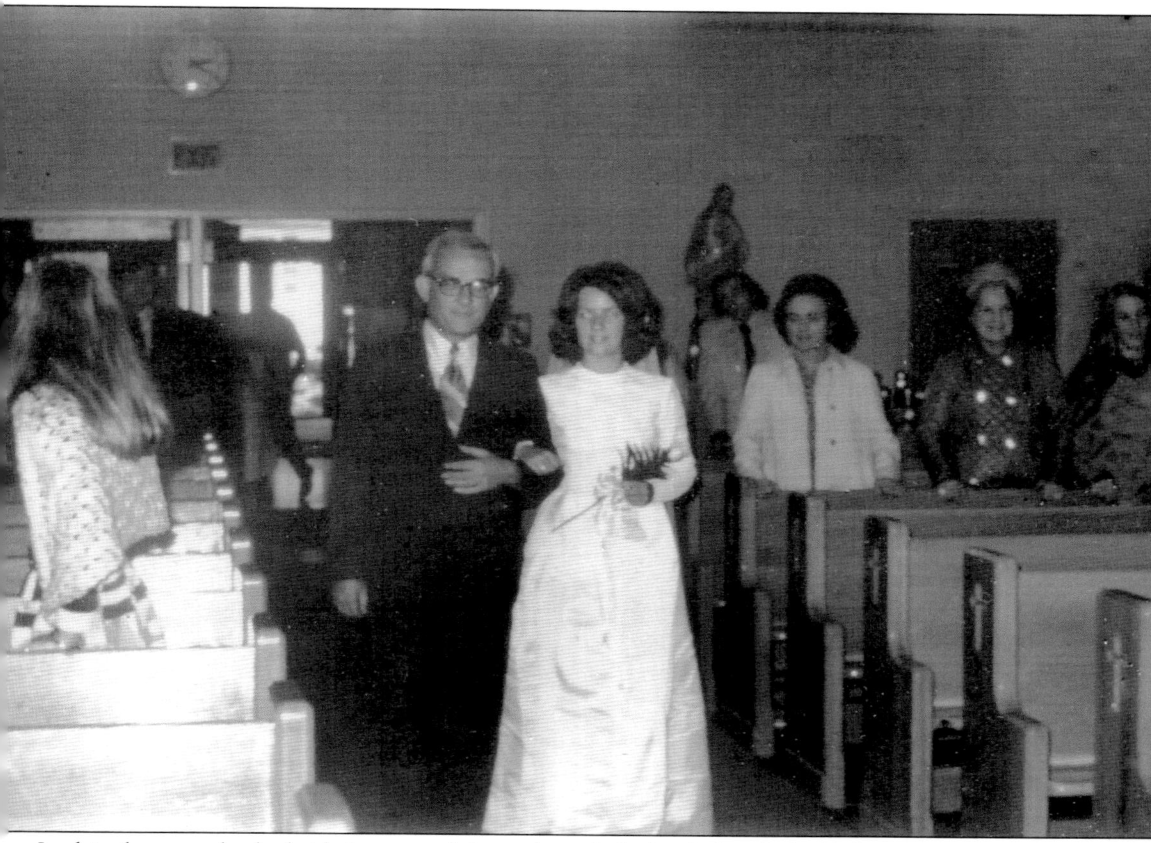

In this photograph, the bride is escorted down the aisle by her father, Judge Robert Hourigan. Her hair had already been set for two days. With the family having been evacuated on Friday, June 23, they had nothing to do but sit around and debate their next move. It was decided late that night that the wedding might as well go on as planned. (Courtesy of Charles and Molly Malpass.)

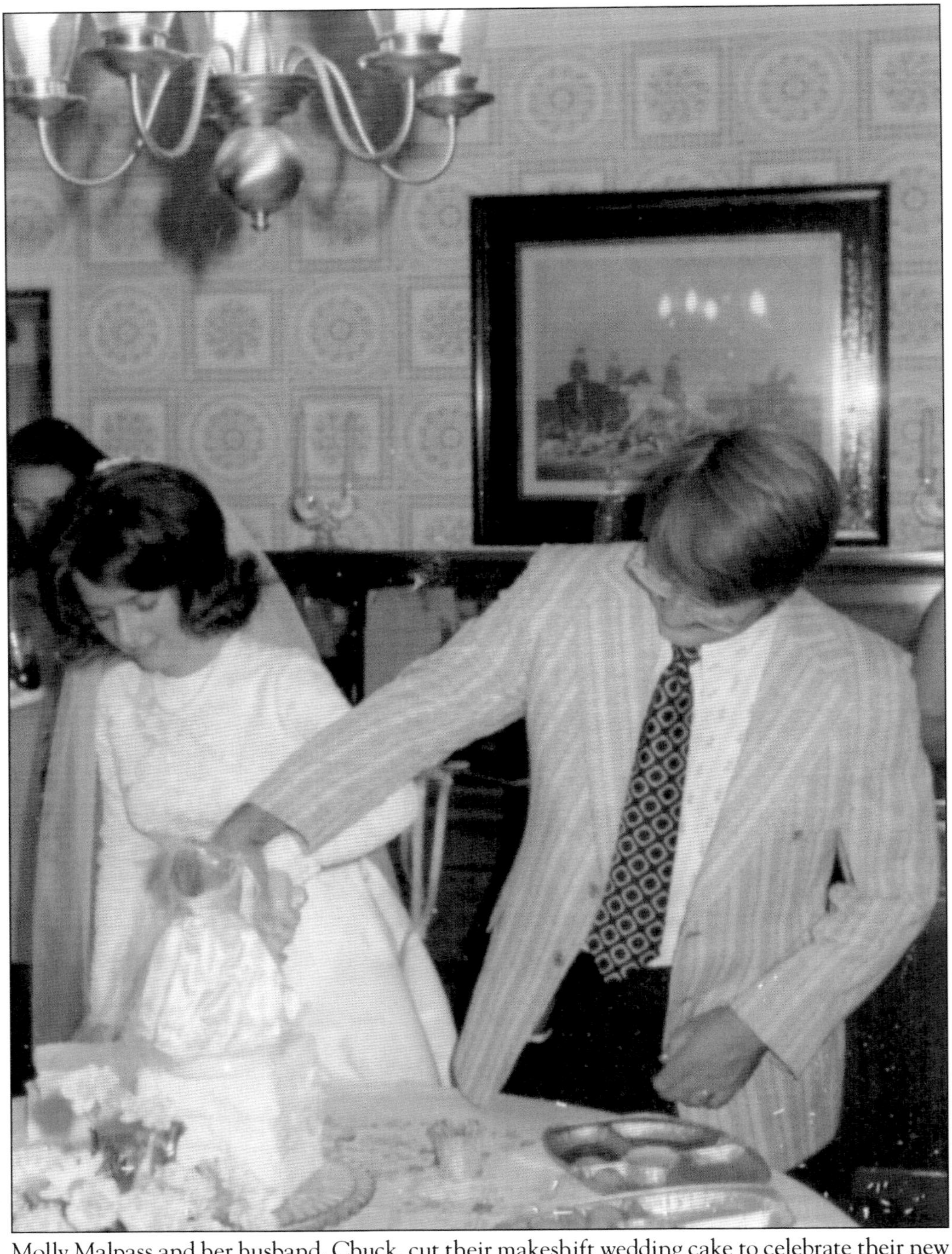

Molly Malpass and her husband, Chuck, cut their makeshift wedding cake to celebrate their new life together as a smaller than planned room of guests looks on. Despite a wedding topper that was borrowed and her husband's tuxedo being replaced by a mismatched suit and tie, the Malpasses tied the knot in front of family and friends. Afterwards, they dined on atypical wedding fare. Though her original veil was lost in the flood, Molly was pleased that her headpiece, a family heirloom, was found and able to be repaired. (Courtesy of Charles and Molly Malpass.)

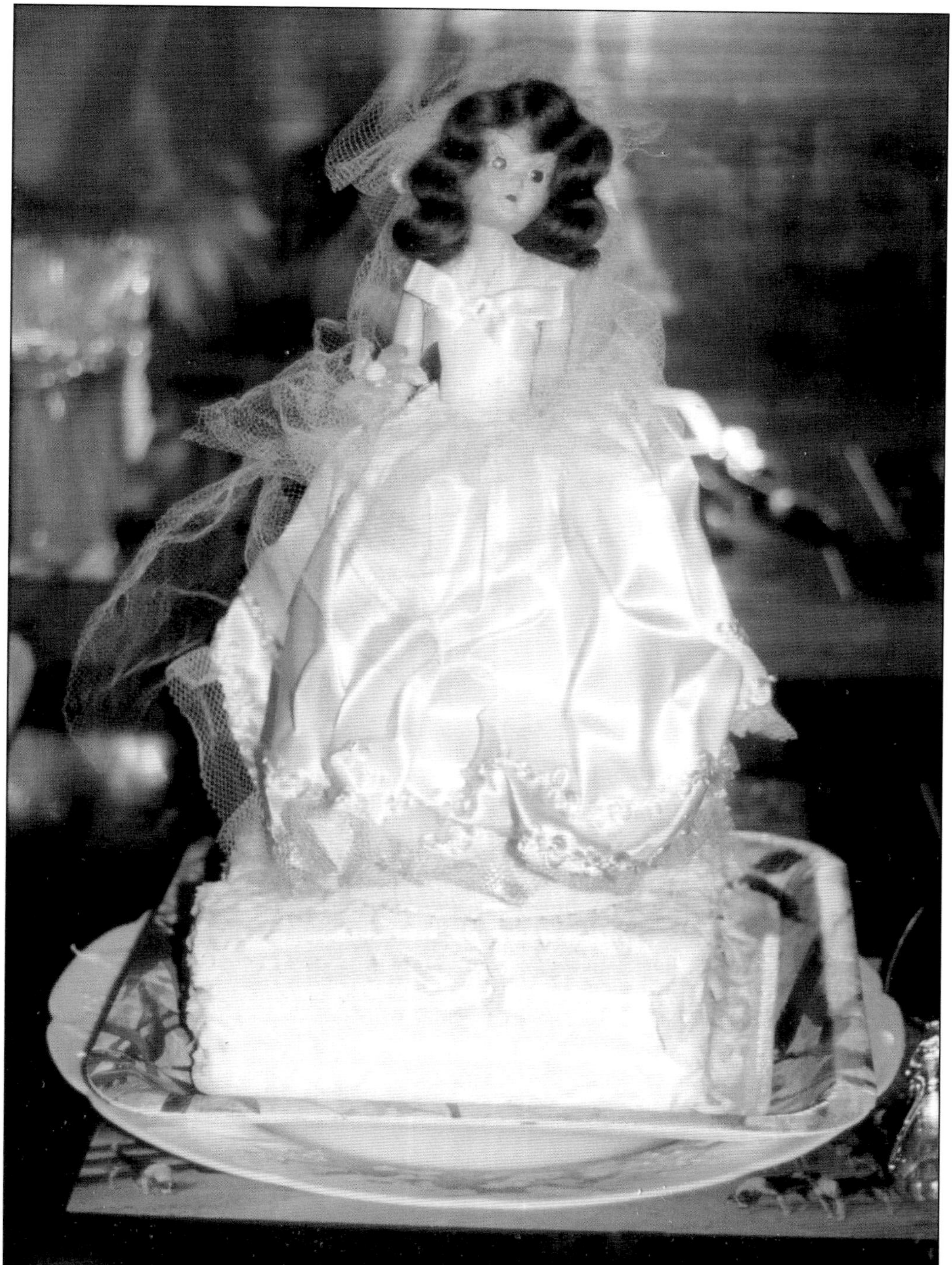

In one of the most memorable events from the wedding, a topper first used by the bride's aunt sits atop store-bought Pepperidge Farm cakes. Unlike most weddings, the night before, the groom was aiding with sandbagging efforts in the valley. At roughly 10:00 that evening, the couple decided to go through with the ceremony. (Courtesy of Charles and Molly Malpass.)

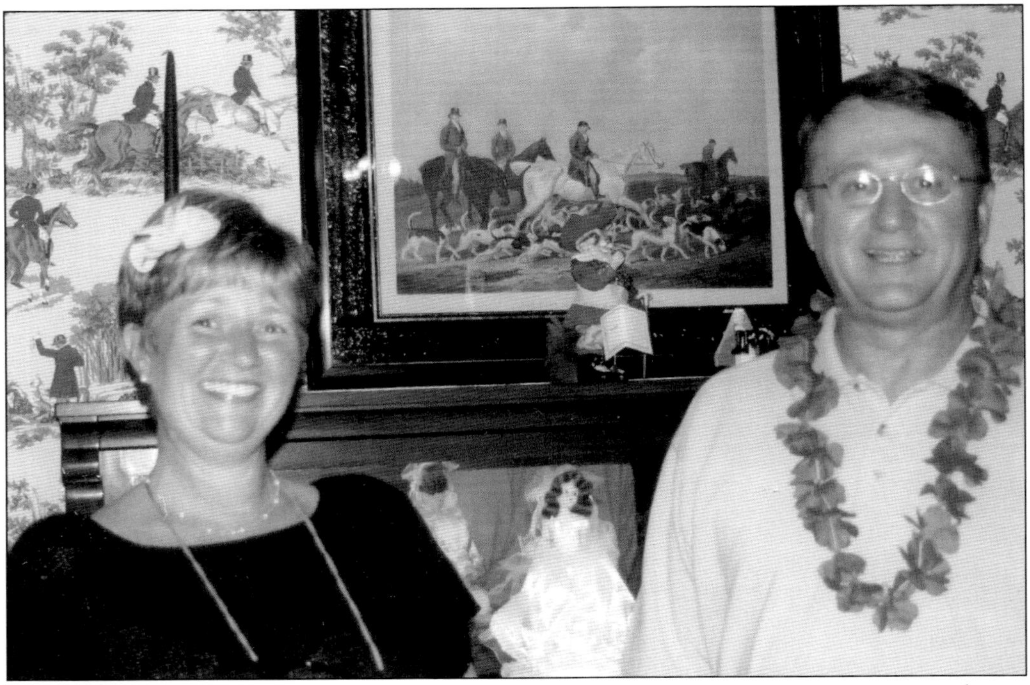

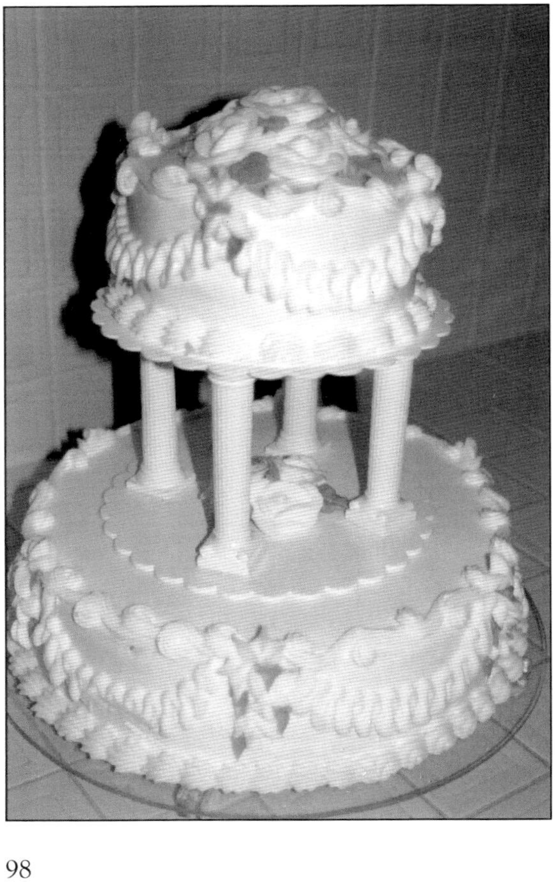

In this photograph, the happy couple celebrates an anniversary during a surprise party given by their daughter three decades after the flood. The infamous borrowed cake topper sits between them. Although their wedding did not go as planned, Chuck and Molly Malpass have grown to appreciate the uniqueness of their story. The rain of the day certainly seems to have brought them good luck. Family and friends surprised them with this party on a night the Malpasses thought they were simply going out for dinner. Chuck and Molly have said time and time again that they have been blessed ever since that day, circumstances withstanding. It truly was an unforgettable event. (Courtesy of Charles and Molly Malpass.)

At the 30 year anniversary party, a more proper wedding cake replaced the three Pepperidge Farm cakes that were used in 1972. (Courtesy of Charles and Molly Malpass.)

Five

College Misericordia

A Campus Becomes A Hospital

The land on which the campus of College Misericordia (now Misericordia University) resides was purchased by the Sisters of Mercy in 1914 and dedicated as an institution of higher learning in 1924. With a name that means "heart of mercy," the college would live up to this billing during the flood of 1972. The contributions of the institute were twofold: It was the temporary location of the Nesbitt Memorial Hospital, and an evacuation center. Over 50 babies were delivered on the campus. The staff provided food and shelter to displaced flood victims while military helicopters landed with supplies.

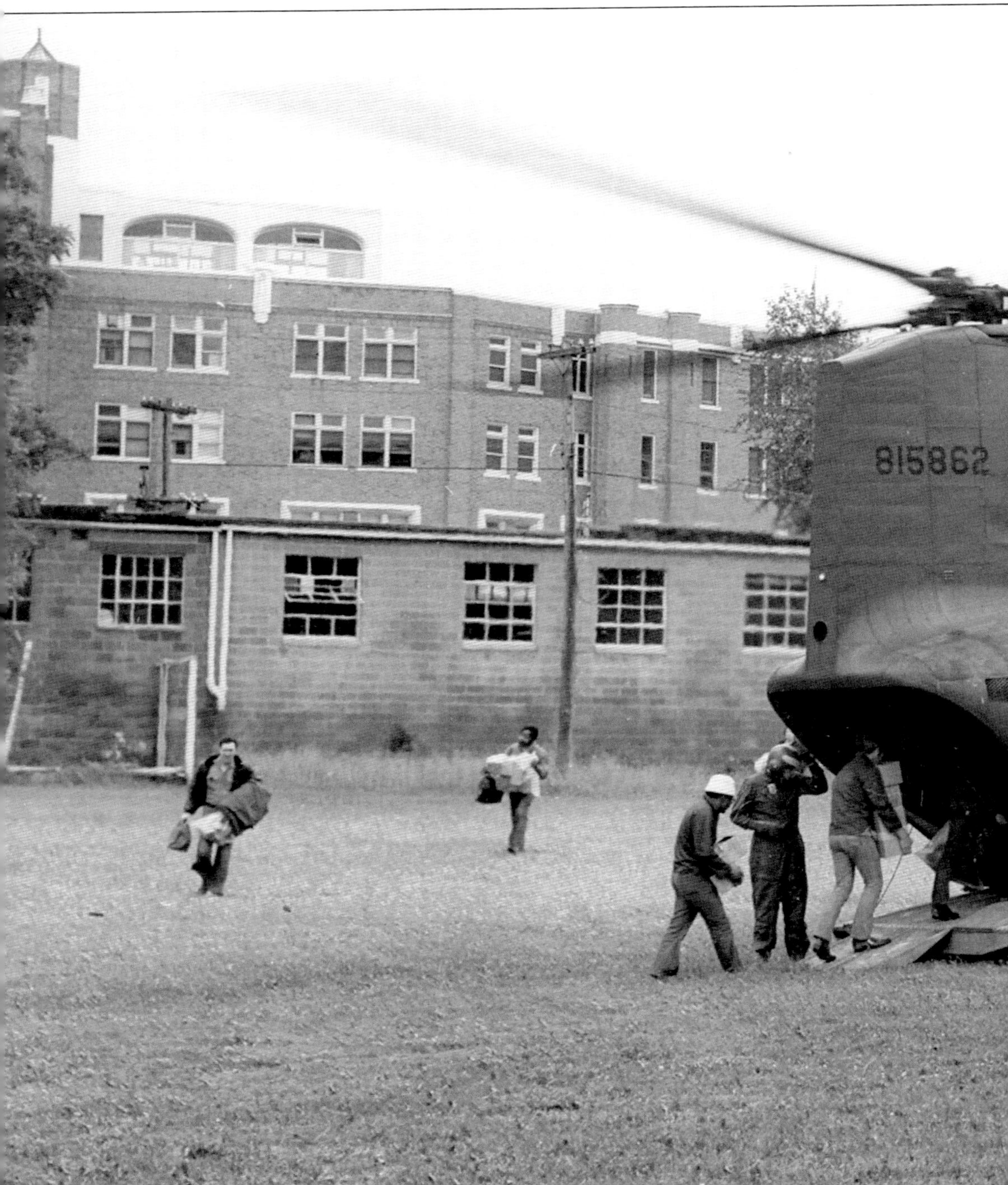

In this photograph, an enormous military helicopter has landed on what is normally a quiet field on the campus of College Misericordia. Over 1,500 people were sheltered at the college during the flood. Sister Miriam Theresa O' Donnell, then president, was instrumental in turning the college into an evacuation center to ease the burden on flood-ravaged victims. Although residents of the Wyoming Valley were experiencing one of the most difficult situations in the history of

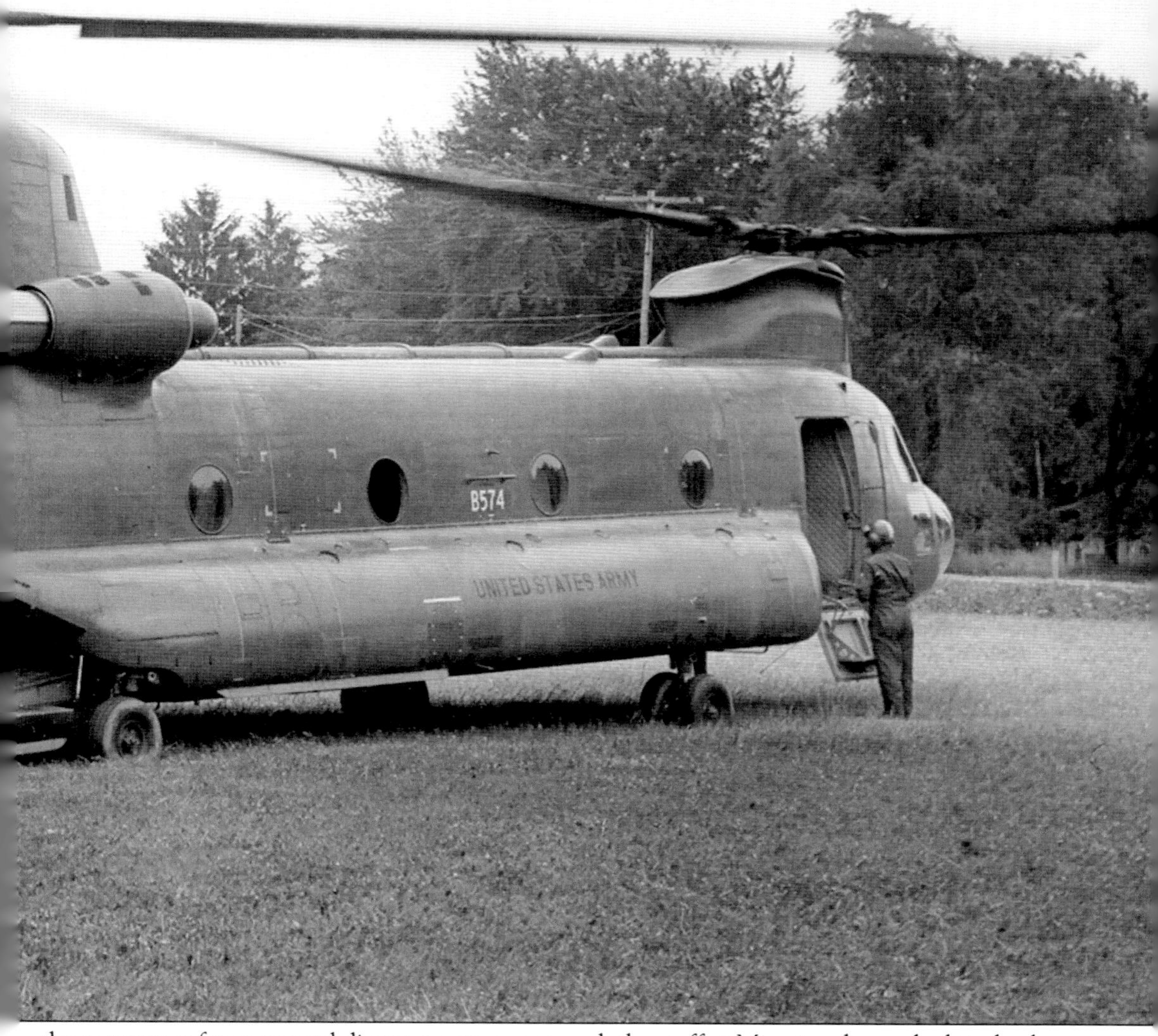

the country as far as natural disasters were concerned, the staff at Misericordia worked tirelessly to provide them with the comforts of home. Helicopters were instrumental in delivering much-needed supplies, as well as transporting expecting mothers to area hospitals. (Courtesy of Sister Mary Carmel McGarigle University Archives, Misericordia University.)

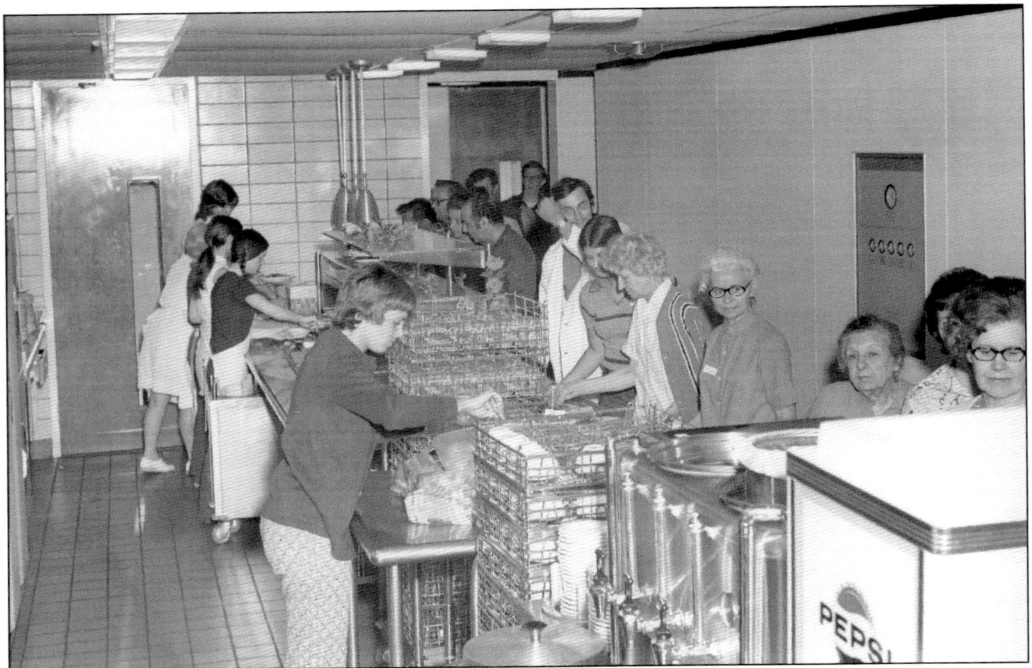

The workers above are doing their best to keep up with the dishes created by refugees who dined at College Misericordia. Three meals a day were served, with some guests stating it rivaled restaurant food: eggs and juice for breakfast, sandwiches for lunch, and even steak and potatoes for dinner. Below, two women wash clothes. Flood victims were eternally grateful, after braving the mud and cleanup all day, to return to the college for a warm meal and relaxing atmosphere. (Courtesy of Sister Mary Carmel McGarigle University Archives, Misericordia University.)

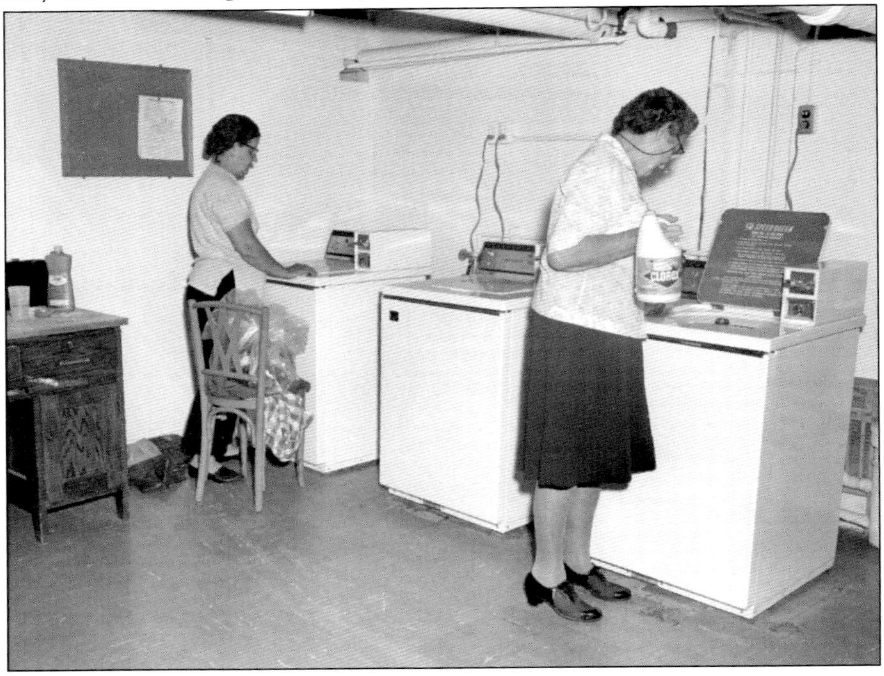

This photograph shows why Nesbit Hospital was forced to evacuate. Located on Route 11 in Kingston between Sharpe and Poplar Streets, floodwater rose halfway up the main entrance. With the exception of a premature infant and a patient awaiting an emergency appendectomy, the entire hospital was moved to the grounds of College Misericordia on Friday, June 23, just as the waters of the Susquehanna River were preparing their onslaught. (Courtesy of Sister Mary Carmel McGarigle University Archives, Misericordia University.)

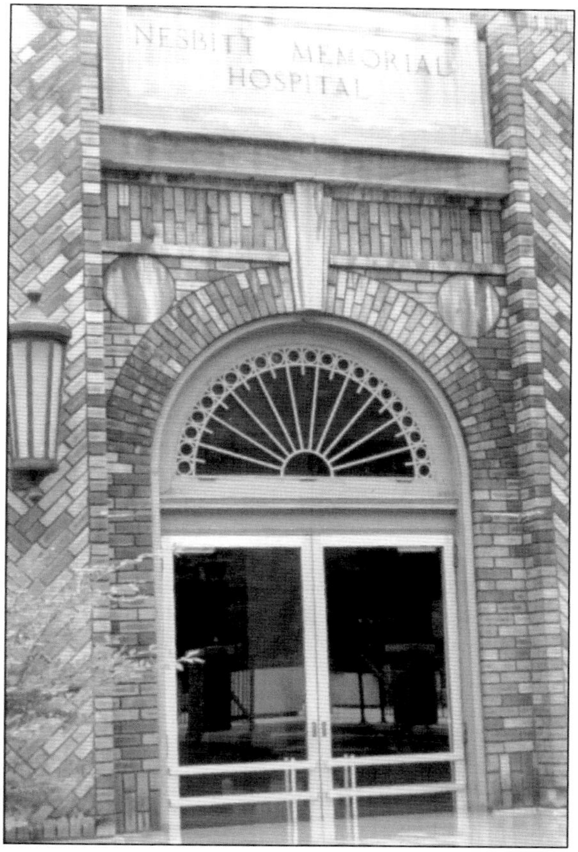

Alumnae Hall at College Misericordia became the temporary home of Nesbitt Hospital. The medical facility was the second evacuation order to come from Hurricane Agnes. Dozens of ambulances transported patients to the makeshift infirmary. (Courtesy of Sister Mary Carmel McGarigle University Archives, Misericordia University.)

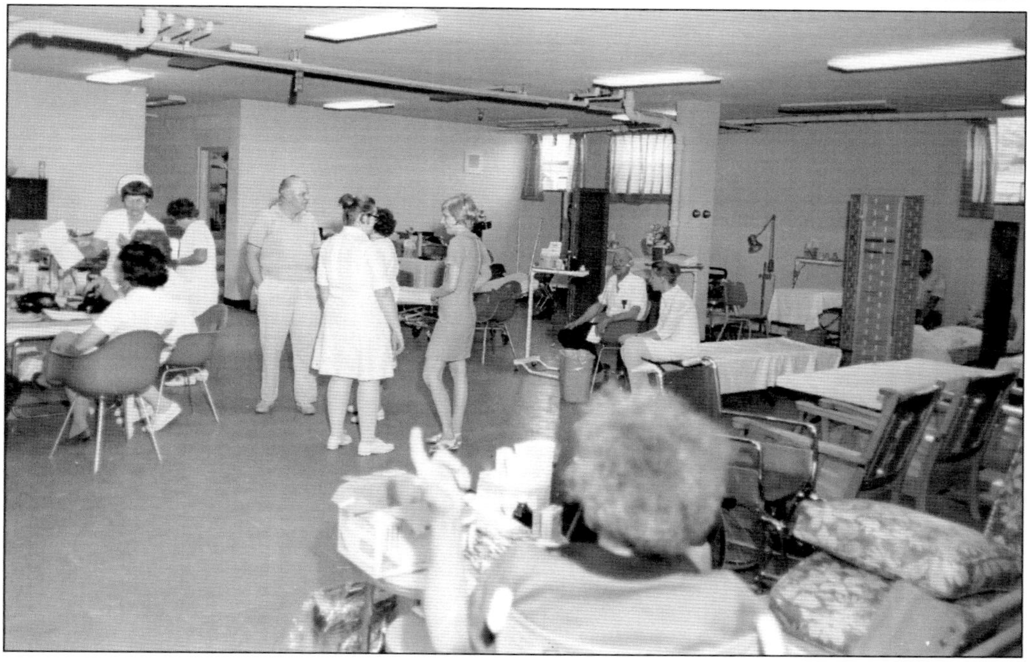

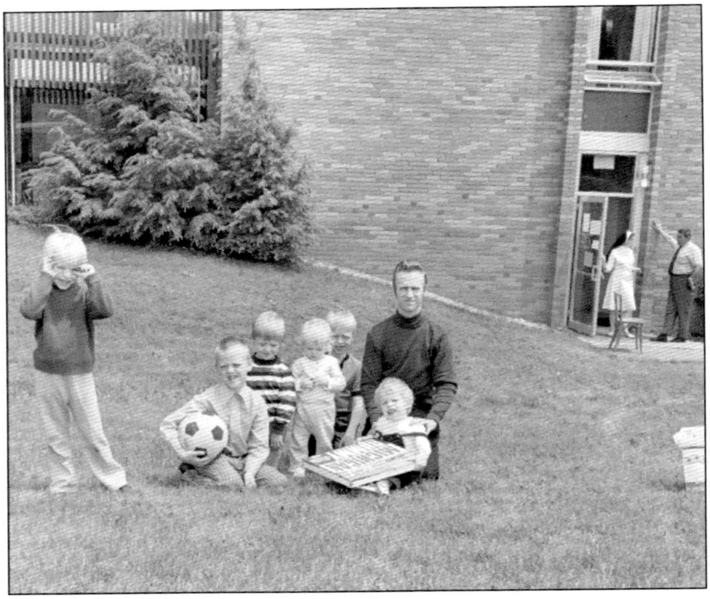

Although most in the Back Mountain were spared the destruction of the flood of 1972, they would be instrumental in the aftermath. In this photograph, a family poses on the grounds of the college. Although their property was damaged, College Misericordia made sure that thousands of people had a roof over their heads and food in their stomachs as they rebuilt their lives. (Courtesy of Sister Mary Carmel McGarigle University Archives, Misericordia University.)

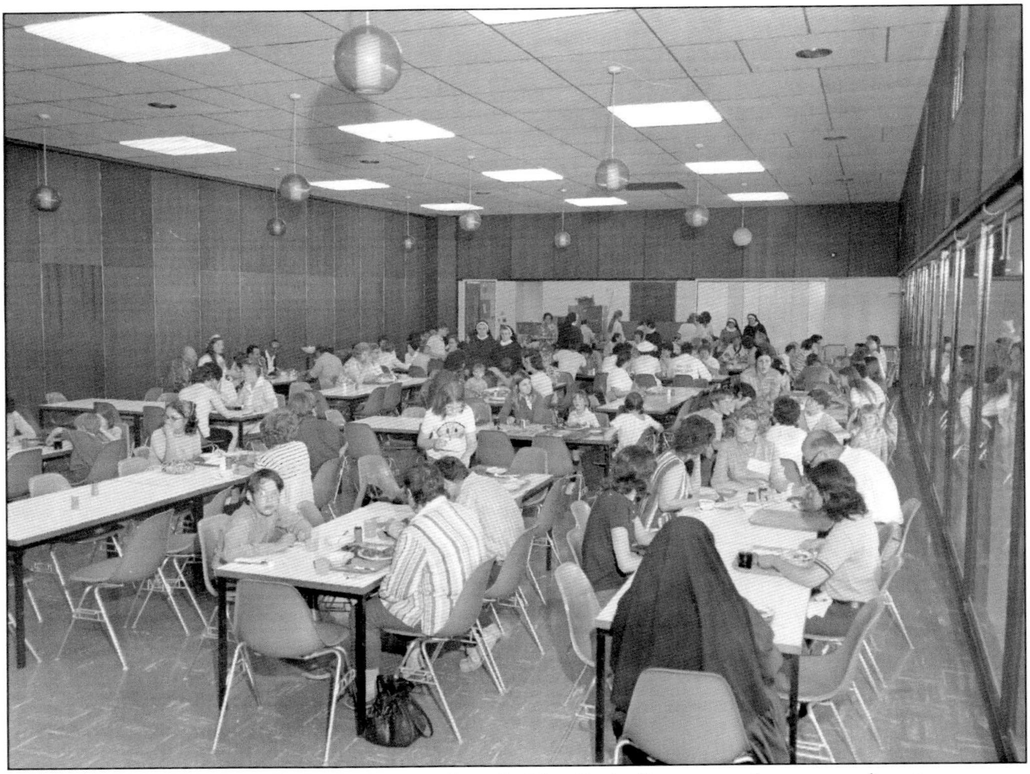

It is perhaps no surprise that a university founded by Catholic nuns, whose very duty is to serve, provided such hospitality to so many people in the aftermath of Hurricane Agnes. Beginning Friday, June 23, 1972, College Misericordia started accepting refugees. Thanks to their self-contained sewage facility, showers and toilets were adequate for the flood victims. (Courtesy of Sister Mary Carmel McGarigle University Archives, Misericordia University.)

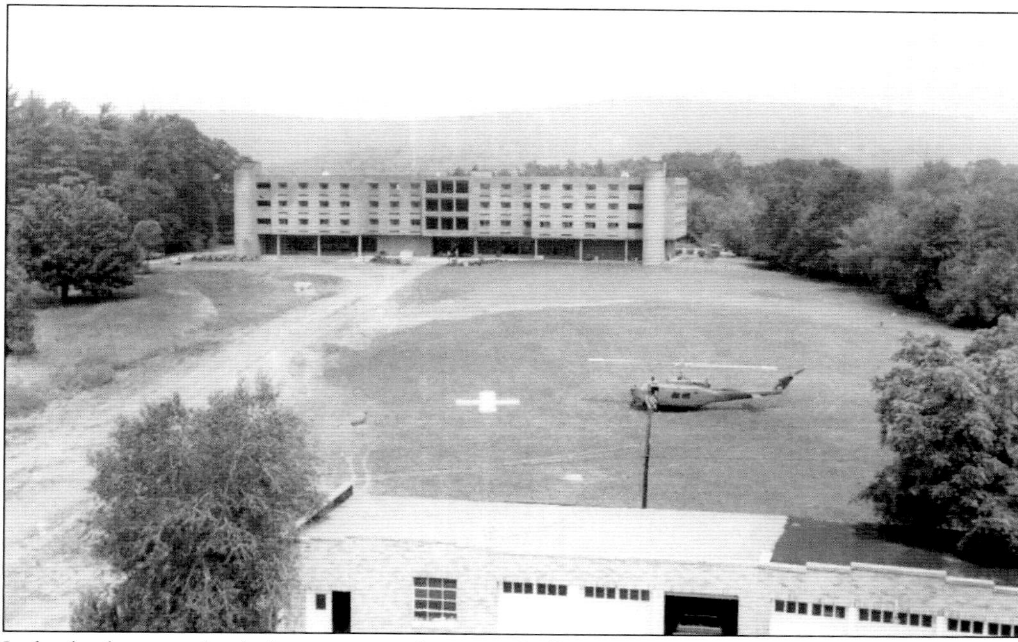

In both photographs, helicopters are shown at College Misericordia. Helicopters were vital in bringing supplies to flood victims, as well as transporting patients from the makeshift hospital to General Hospital in Wilkes-Barre. One such trip involved an expectant mother who was being moved to deliver her baby. While her mother-in-law, a nurse, rode with her in the chopper, the father-to-be had to drive separately because the security officer would not get off the aircraft to make room for him. In the helicopter, the passengers were stunned to see only rooftops, as some neighborhoods were completely under water. Meanwhile, the expecting father and his father drove from Dallas to Bloomsburg, circumventing the entire valley, to finally end up meeting his wife in Wilkes-Barre to witness the birth of his daughter after an emotional reunion with his spouse. (Courtesy of Sister Mary Carmel McGarigle University Archives, Misericordia University.)

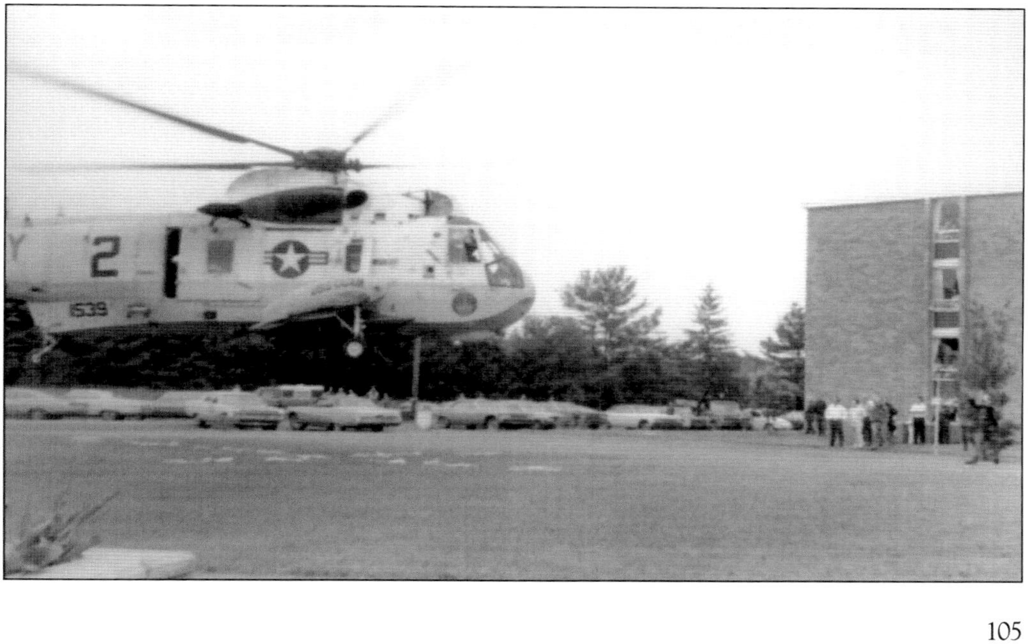

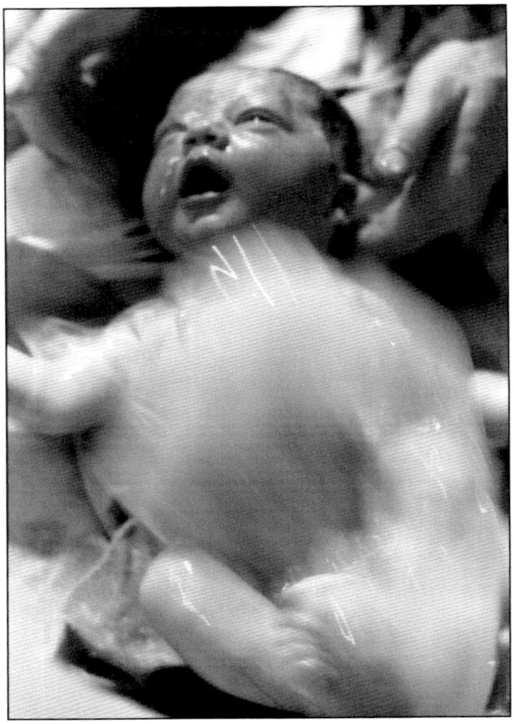

This photograph shows one of the 52 babies born in the makeshift hospital that was College Misericordia. Expecting parents were nervous enough, and to have the birth of their children take place during a flood could be particularly traumatic. Fortunately, most reported that the Nesbitt Hospital staff was outstanding. Although the births were anything but typical, they provided a unique birthday story to be told for generations to come. Many mothers described a relatively relaxed atmosphere, all things considered. When they saw their children for the first time, their happiness temporarily overcame their grief and anxiety of what was happening at home. (Courtesy of Sister Mary Carmel McGarigle University Archives, Misericordia University.)

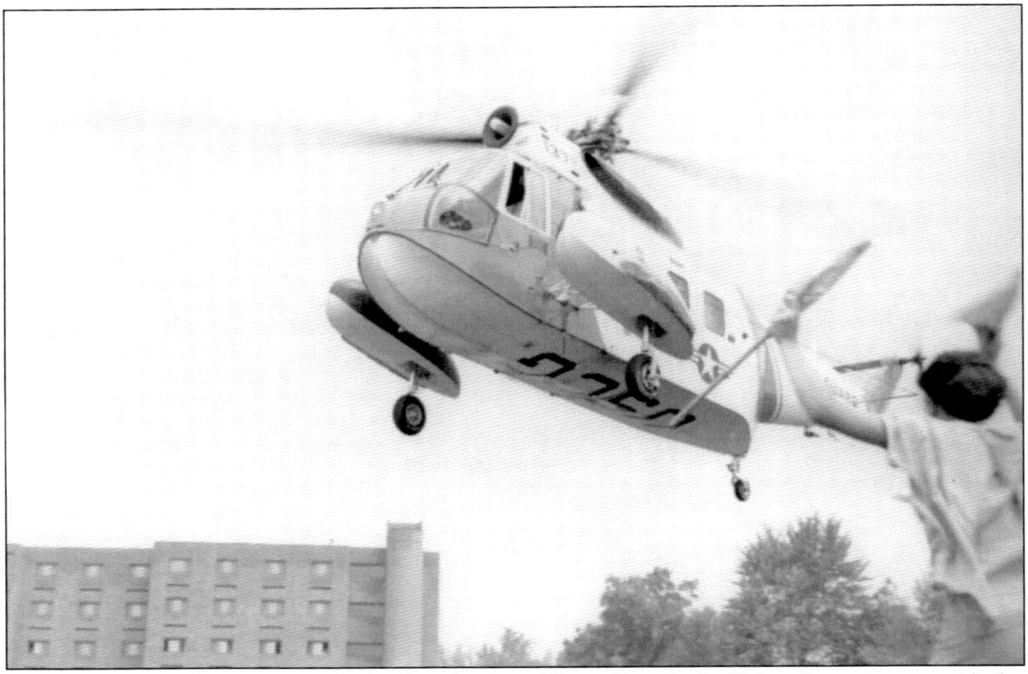

A Coast Guard helicopter is guided in for a landing. The college looked like a busy airport, with the constant take off and landing of helicopters taking residents to hospitals or dropping off supplies. Misericordia graciously told their guests the shelter would be in place "as long as needed." (Courtesy of Sister Mary Carmel McGarigle University Archives, Misericordia University.)

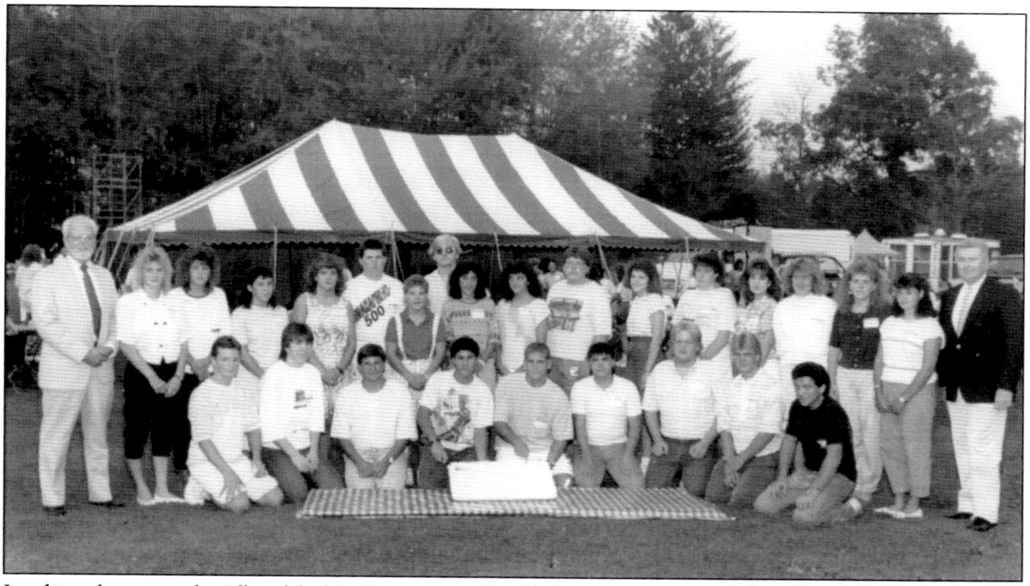

In this photograph, "flood babies" pose on the 16th anniversary of their births. A "Sweet 16" was held for those in attendance and each was offered a scholarship, which many chose to take advantage of. Georgetta Potoski, who was working at Misericordia at the time, suggested the event. (Courtesy of Sister Mary Carmel McGarigle University Archives, Misericordia University.)

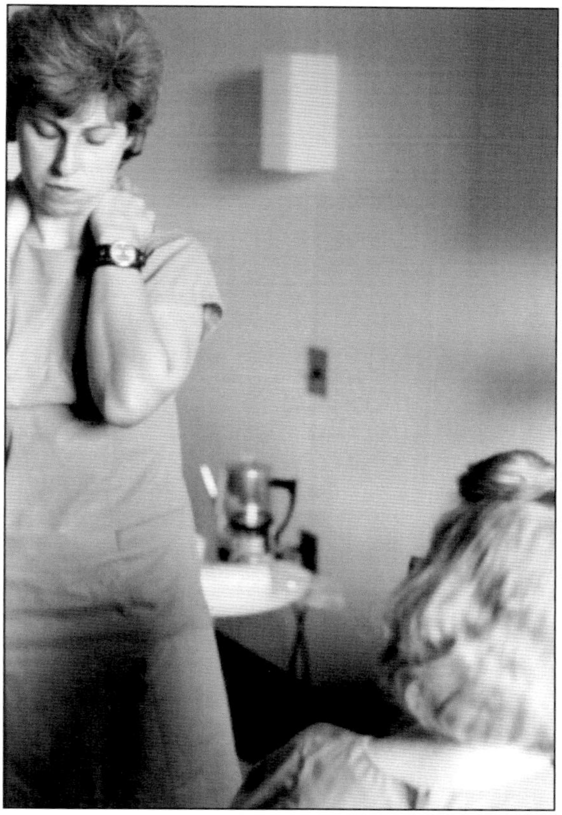

An exhausted nurse rubs her shoulders in her temporary workplace at College Misericordia. Though trying at the time, the birth of so many children during such a catastrophe provided moments of joy. It took only four hours for the staff at Nesbitt Hospital to evacuate into their new home. (Courtesy of Sister Mary Carmel McGarigle University Archives, Misericordia University.)

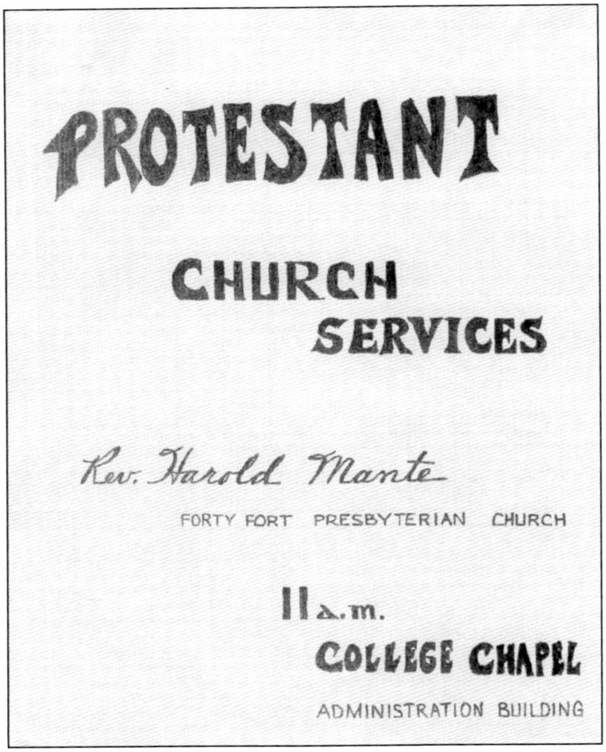

This bulletin advertises church services on campus. Although this worship session was provided by Rev. Harold Mante of the Forty Fort Presbyterian Church, many faiths held services on campus. It was of great comfort to join those of faith during such difficult times. The Presbyterian church was under water in Forty Fort at the time. (Courtesy of Sister Mary Carmel McGarigle University Archives, Misericordia University.)

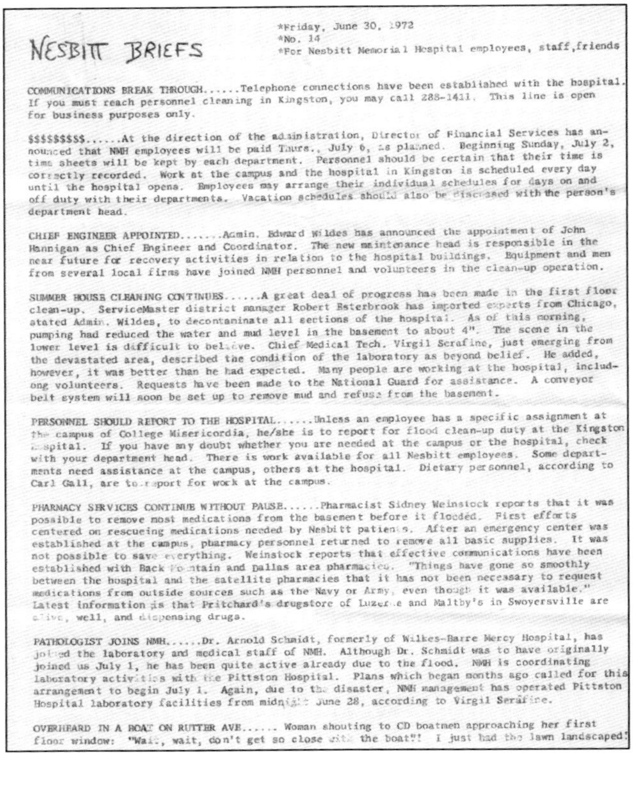

NESBITT BRIEFS

*Friday, June 30, 1972
*No. 14
*For Nesbitt Memorial Hospital employees, staff, friends

COMMUNICATIONS BREAK THROUGH......Telephone connections have been established with the hospital. If you must reach personnel cleaning in Kingston, you may call 288-1411. This line is open for business purposes only.

$$$$$$$$$......At the direction of the administration, Director of Financial Services has announced that NMH employees will be paid Thurs., July 6, as planned. Beginning Sunday, July 2, time sheets will be kept by each department. Personnel should be certain that their time is correctly recorded. Work at the campus and the hospital in Kingston is scheduled every day until the hospital opens. Employees may arrange their individual schedules for days on and off duty with their departments. Vacation schedules should also be discussed with the person's department head.

CHIEF ENGINEER APPOINTED.......Admin. Edward Wildes has announced the appointment of John Hannigan as Chief Engineer and Coordinator. The new maintenance head is responsible in the near future for recovery activities in relation to the hospital buildings. Equipment and men from several local firms have joined NMH personnel and volunteers in the clean-up operation.

SUMMER HOUSE CLEANING CONTINUES......A great deal of progress has been made in the first floor clean-up. ServiceMaster district manager Robert Esterbrook has imported experts from Chicago, stated Admin. Wildes, to decontaminate all sections of the hospital. As of this morning, pumping had reduced the water and mud level in the basement to about 4". The scene in the lower level is difficult to believe. Chief Medical Tech. Virgil Serafine, just emerging from the devastated area, described the condition of the laboratory as beyond belief. He added, however, it was better than he had expected. Many people are working at the hospital, includong volunteers. Requests have been made to the National Guard for assistance. A conveyor belt system will soon be set up to remove mud and refuse from the basement.

PERSONNEL SHOULD REPORT TO THE HOSPITAL......Unless an employee has a specific assignment at the campus of College Misericordia, he/she is to report for flood clean-up duty at the Kingston hospital. If you have any doubt whether you are needed at the campus or the hospital, check with your department head. There is work available for all Nesbitt employees. Some departments need assistance at the campus, others at the hospital. Dietary personnel, according to Carl Gall, are to report for work at the campus.

PHARMACY SERVICES CONTINUE WITHOUT PAUSE......Pharmacist Sidney Weinstock reports that it was possible to remove most medications from the basement before it flooded. First efforts centered on rescueing medications needed by Nesbitt patients. After an emergency center was established at the campus, pharmacy personnel returned to remove all basic supplies. It was not possible to save everything. Weinstock reports that effective communications have been established with Back Mountain and Dallas area pharmacies. "Things have gone so smoothly between the hospital and the satellite pharmacies that it has not been necessary to request medications from outside sources such as the Navy or Army, even though it was available." Latest information is that Pritchard's drugstore of Luzerne and Maltby's in Swoyersville are alive, well, and dispensing drugs.

PATHOLOGIST JOINS NMH......Dr. Arnold Schmidt, formerly of Wilkes-Barre Mercy Hospital, has joined the laboratory and medical staff of NMH. Although Dr. Schmidt was to have originally joined us July 1, he has been quite active already due to the flood. NMH is coordinating laboratory activities with the Pittston Hospital. Plans which began months ago called for this arrangement to begin July 1. Again, due to the disaster, NMH management has operated Pittston Hospital laboratory facilities from midnight June 28, according to Virgil Serafine.

OVERHEARD IN A BOAT ON RUTTER AVE...... Woman shouting to CD boatmen approaching her first floor window: "Wait, wait, don't get so close with the boat"! I just had the lawn landscaped!

Pictured here is a "Nesbitt Brief," which the administration of the hospital provided to employees. Among other things, it addressed rumors, assured workers the hospital would not close, and gave instructions on where and how to report to work and what to do about time off, if needed. It also updated them on the status of the cleaning that needed to take place before the facility could reopen. (Courtesy of Sister Mary Carmel McGarigle University Archives, Misericordia University.)

Six

A Valley with a Heart

Residents Return and Rebuild

Hurricane Agnes delivered a blow to the Wyoming Valley, and in that moment, many residents privately doubted if they would ever recover. Upon seeing what was left, if anything, of their homes and realizing their irreplaceable possessions had been swept away, many residents added their tears to the receding waters of the Susquehanna River. However, there is a spirit that seems ingrained deep in the psyche of the citizens of the Wyoming Valley. As aid from the National Guard and American Red Cross arrived, the residents began to rebuild their homes. Ironically, the long-term benefits of the flood outweighed the temporary inconvenience. Some residents used low-interest loans to make their homes better than before the flood. Cities used funds to improve their infrastructures in ways they could have never afforded previously. Although there is no doubt that some residents lost everything and never recovered, the overall economy of the Wyoming Valley after the flood of 1972 was changed for the better.

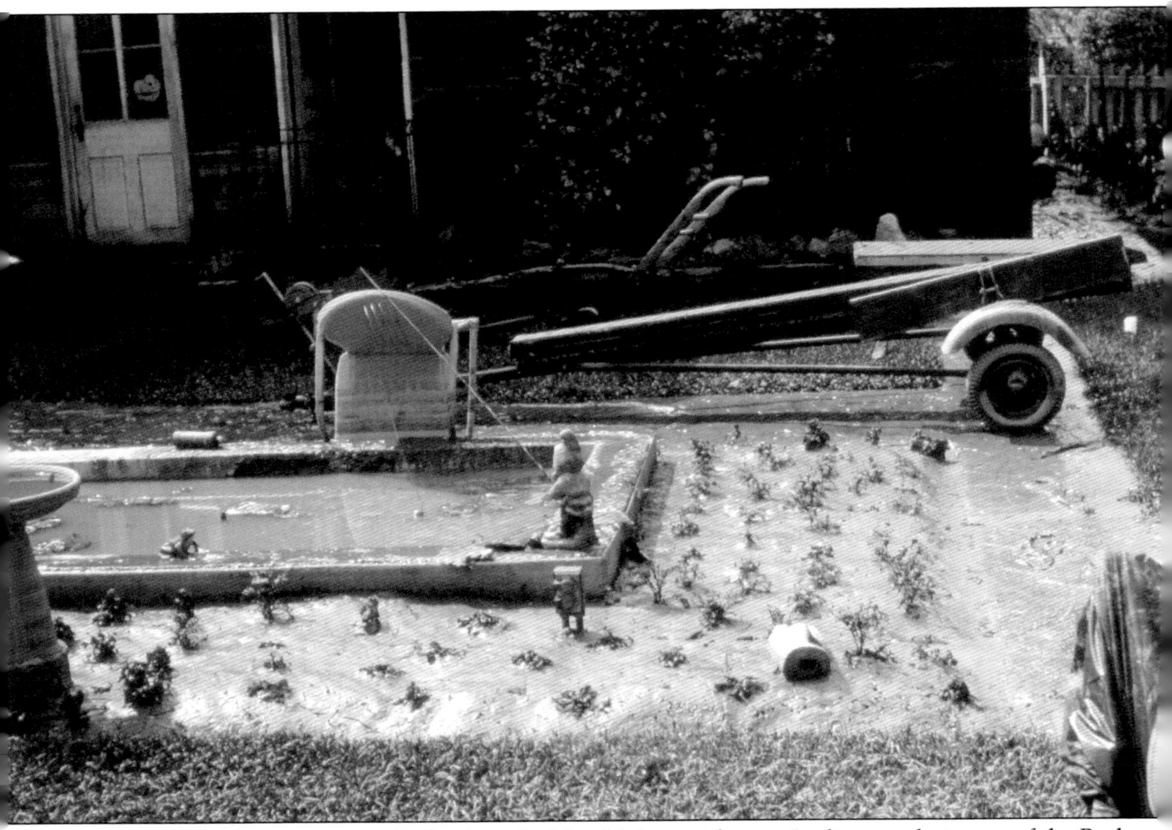

A boat trailer sits empty in the backyard of the Glahn residence. As disaster chairman of the Red Cross, A. Sheldon Glahn coordinated relief for the stricken area. As floodwaters rose, he untied his and his son's boats from their trailers, allowed them to float into the alley behind their garage, and then tied them down so they could be used during the aftermath. A neighbor actually used one of the Glahns' boats to repair his own home while it was still mostly under water. The boat was sent through an open window where, once inside, the man laid on his back, making repairs. (Courtesy of Sheldon Glahn.)

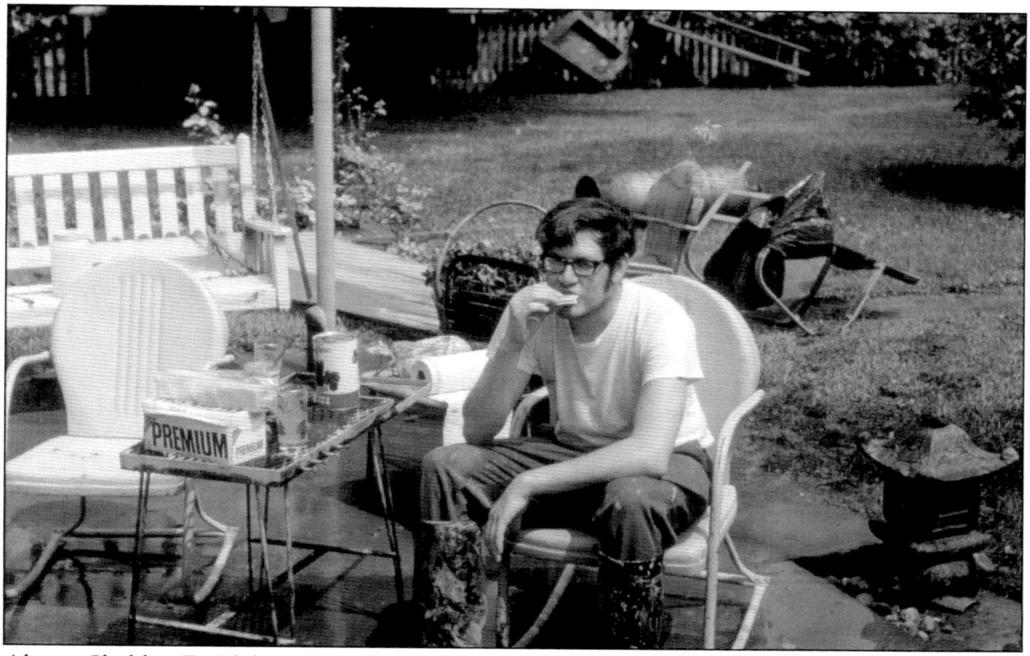

Above, Sheldon E. Glahn takes a break during cleanup to enjoy some saltines and grape drink. During the day, Glahn and his father worked to clean up the junk, sleeping on the dry second floor of their home. They had no power and no potable water. Below, A. Sheldon Glahn enjoys some peanut butter and more grape drink, or "bug juice" as the Glahns referred to it. Supplies were dropped by helicopter to aid those involved in the cleanup. The senior Glahn noted that their spray painted message on the road asking for a radio was still visible years after the flood. The radio, however, was never delivered. (Both, courtesy of Sheldon Glahn.)

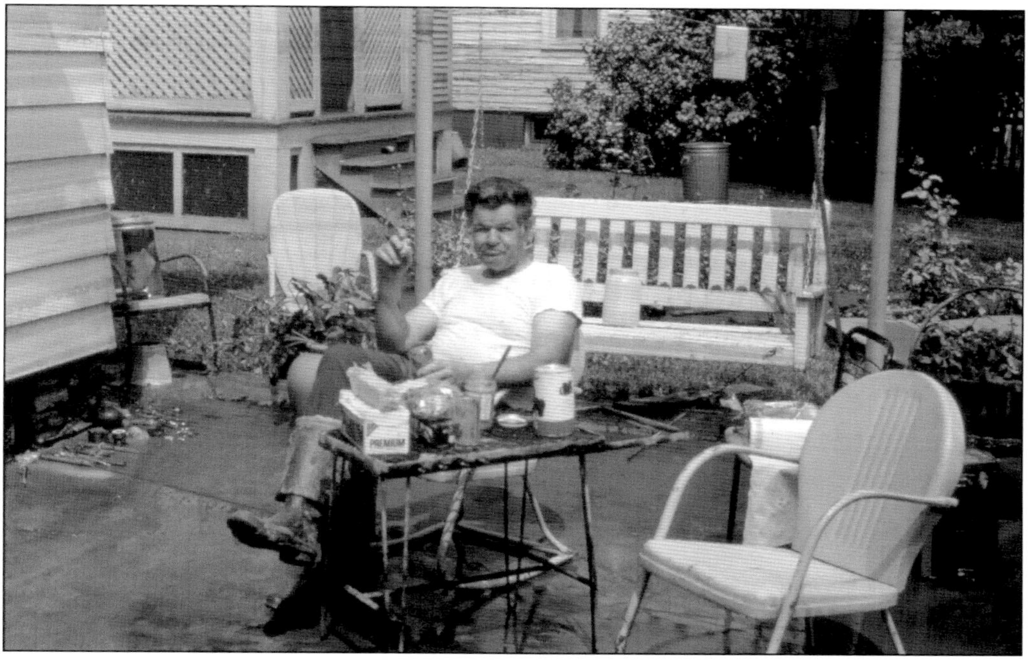

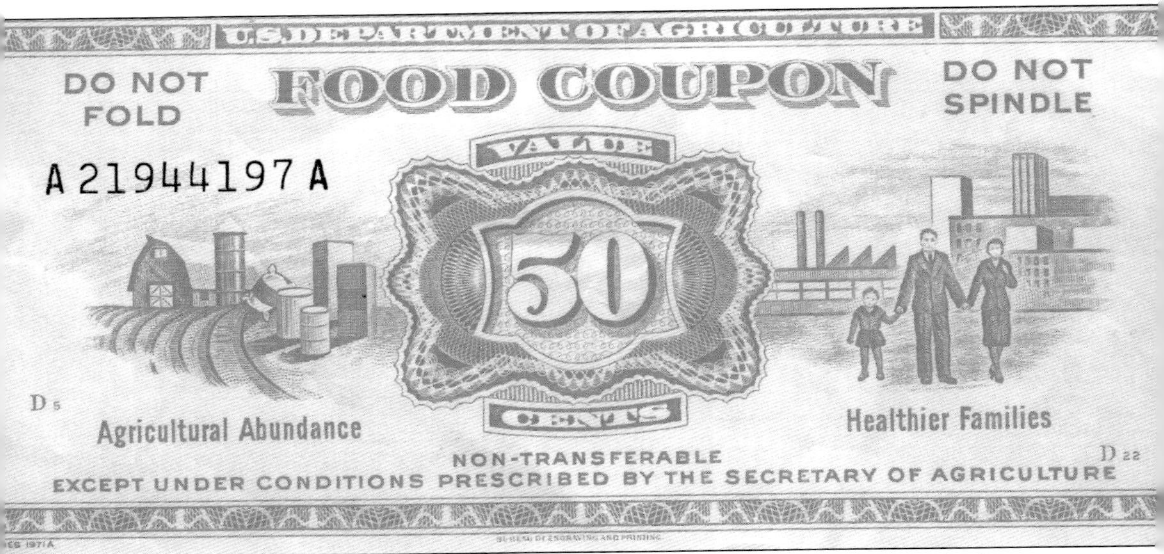

Many of the grocery stores in the valley were destroyed. Each resident was given food stamps, and although some residents expressed humiliation at having to use them, many store owners were sympathetic to their plight. In fact, some store owners allowed the residents to use credit to buy items they needed. Not long after the flood, a shop owner told a customer that every single debt from 1972 had been repaid, proof that the residents of the Wyoming Valley, for the most part, were not looking for handouts. (Courtesy of Charles and Molly Malpass.)

Residents of Forty Fort repair the Hessler home on Bidlack Street. The owner had previously received a leather reclining chair as a gift. In an effort to save the chair, it was hosed down and cleaned to be good as new, or so they thought. After a few days, the smell was just too much, and the piece of furniture had to be thrown away. (Courtesy of Sheldon Glahn.)

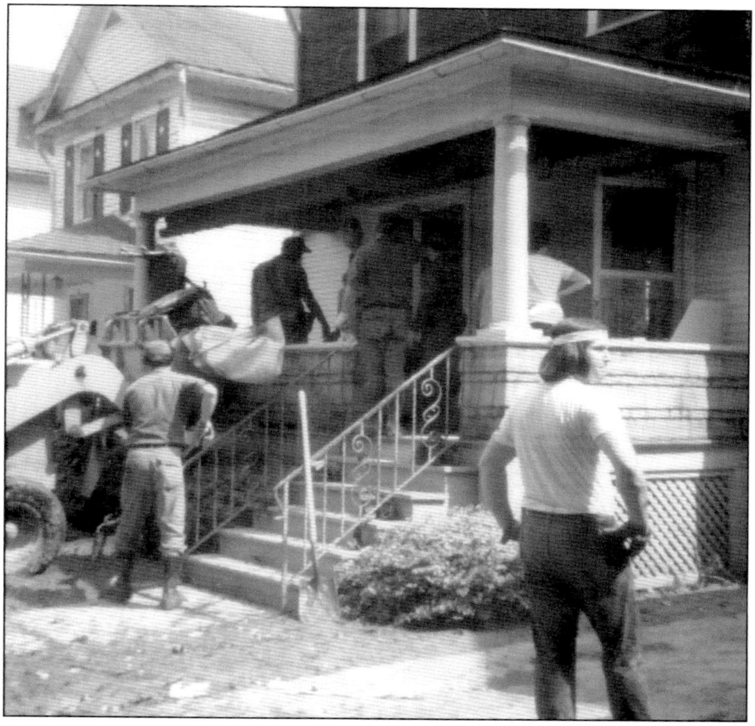

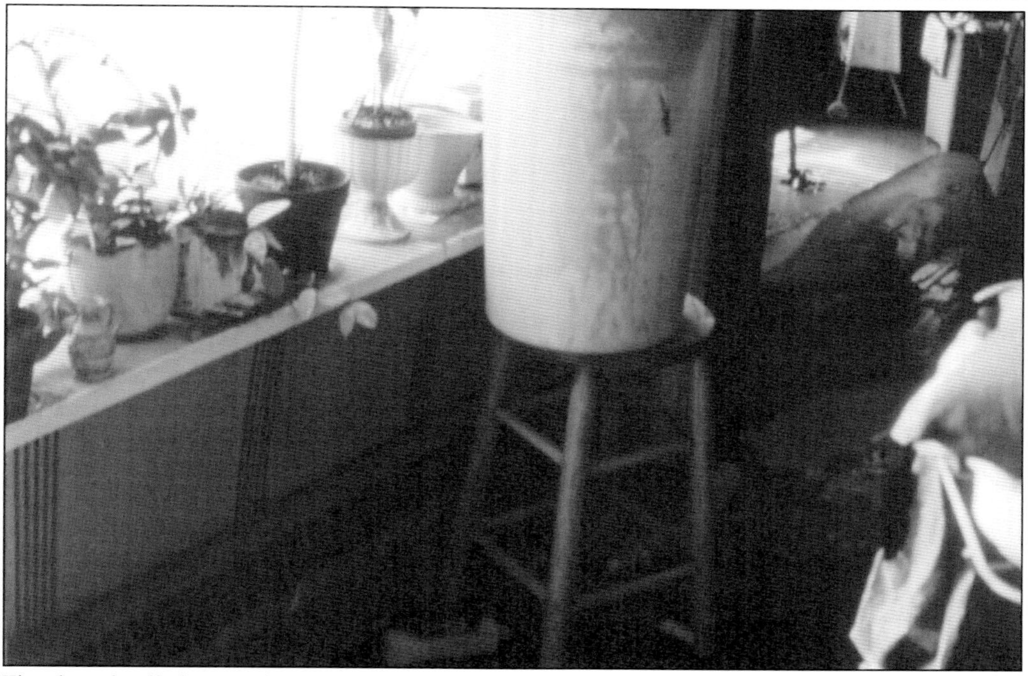

Flood mud still clings to houseplants in this photograph of a back porch. Despite the frustration, citizens learned they had to pace themselves. Many worked all day, only to come home and work more on their own homes in their spare time. Life had to go on despite the mess. (Courtesy of Sheldon Glahn.)

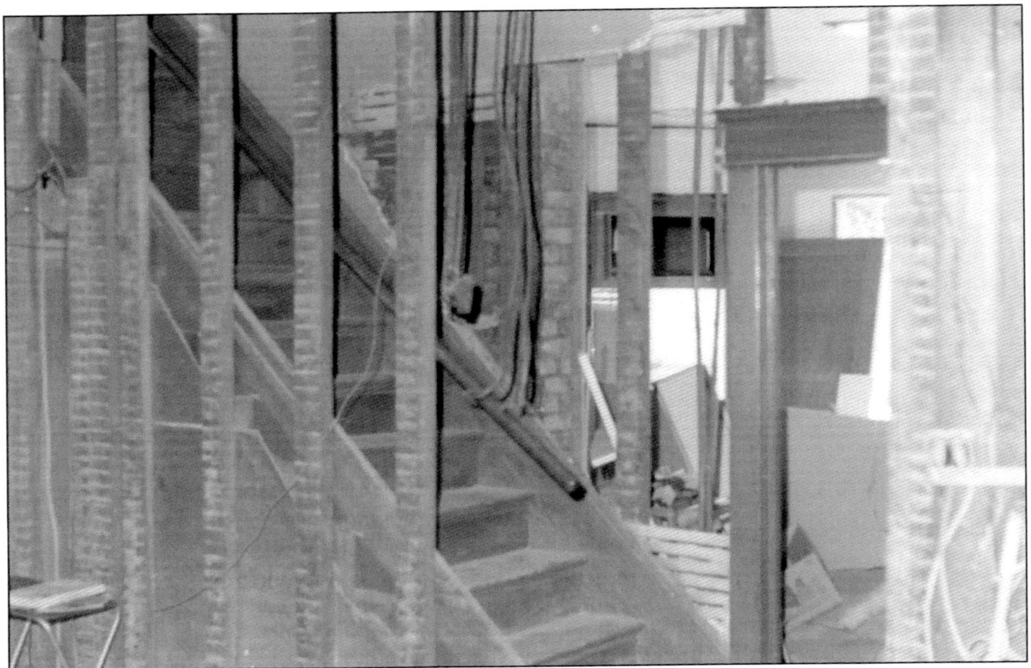

In this photograph, the walls and plaster have been removed. Any part of the structure damaged by Agnes was gutted, and residents began the slow process of rebuilding their homes. For some families, the process took over a year from start to finish. Despite the damage, many did end up making changes to their homes, which they were pleased with in the long term. (Courtesy of Sheldon Glahn.)

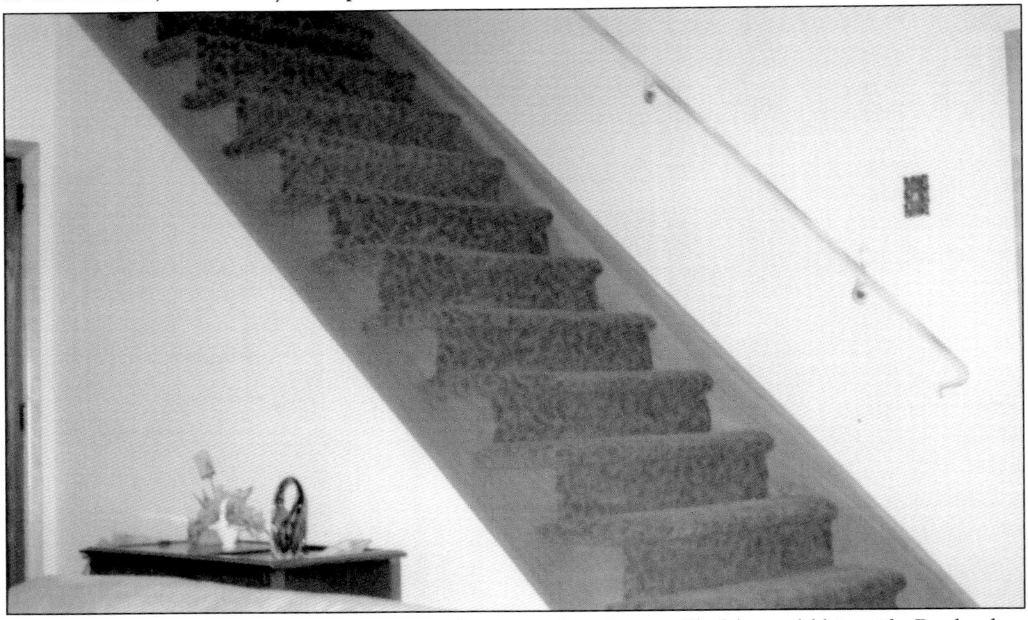

These steps in the Glahn house are as good as new after Agnes. Sheldon told his wife, Ruth, that now was the time to rebuild the home exactly as she wanted, if she did not mind the temporary mess. Government loans with one-percent interest and the first $5,000 free allowed residents some financial freedom in fixing their properties. (Courtesy of Sheldon Glahn.)

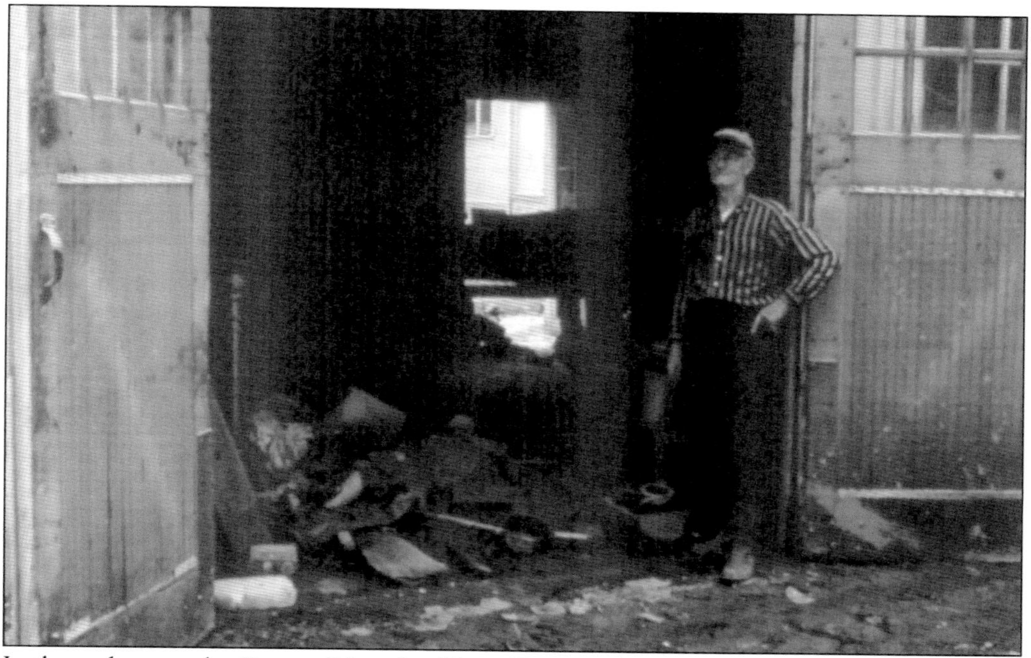

In these photographs, Eugene Edwards of Forty Fort stands near his garage, taking a break from cleaning to pose for a picture. Edwards, an electrician by trade, fixed every blender, toaster, or other appliance that was submerged in floodwaters. Upon their return home, it was suggested that Edwards witness the damage before his wife. He was visibly shaken at having seen up close what the Susquehanna River did to his residence. With his wife having already suffered a heart attack, Edwards put her in the car, and they drove to a relative's home in New Jersey without her ever setting foot inside her home. The Edwards stayed in New Jersey for several weeks, returning only after significant repairs had been completed. Mildred Edwards was still upset when she saw the condition of her semi-repaired home, reaffirming her husband's decision not to show her the immediate aftermath. (Both, courtesy of Sheldon Glahn.)

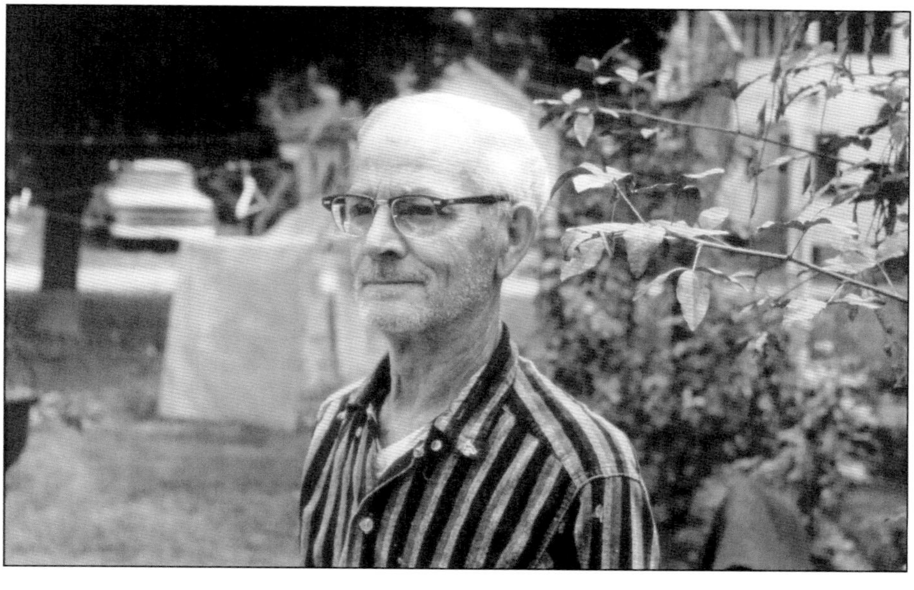

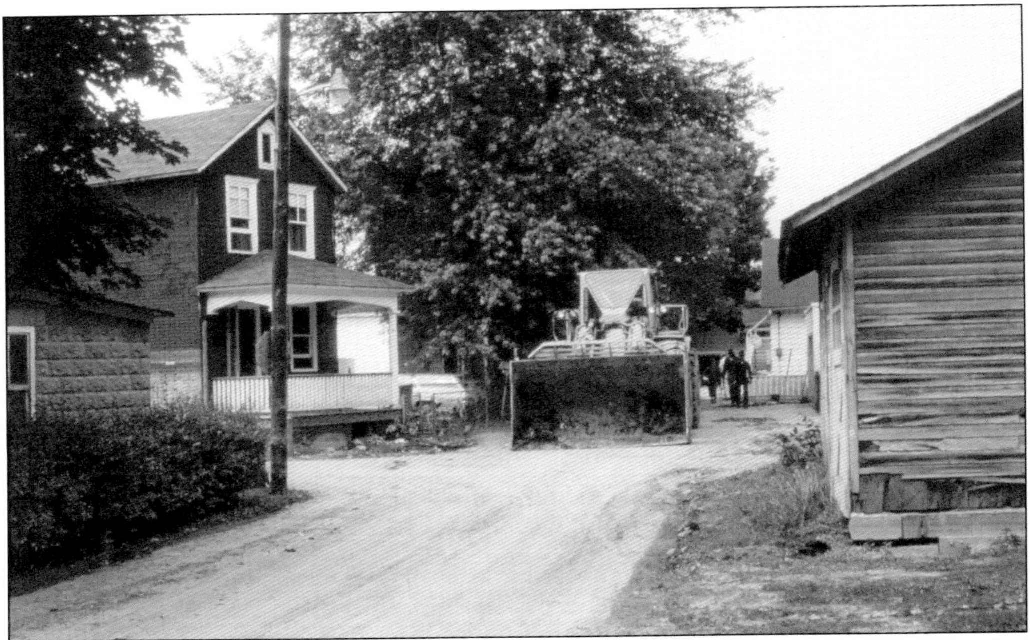

A large bulldozer aids residents in cleaning up the aftermath of Agnes. A homeowner recalled how her son took several hours to move hundreds of cinder blocks away from their destroyed cellar wall, only to witness the bulldozer come by just as he finished and scoop up the mess in a matter of seconds. (Courtesy of Sheldon Glahn.)

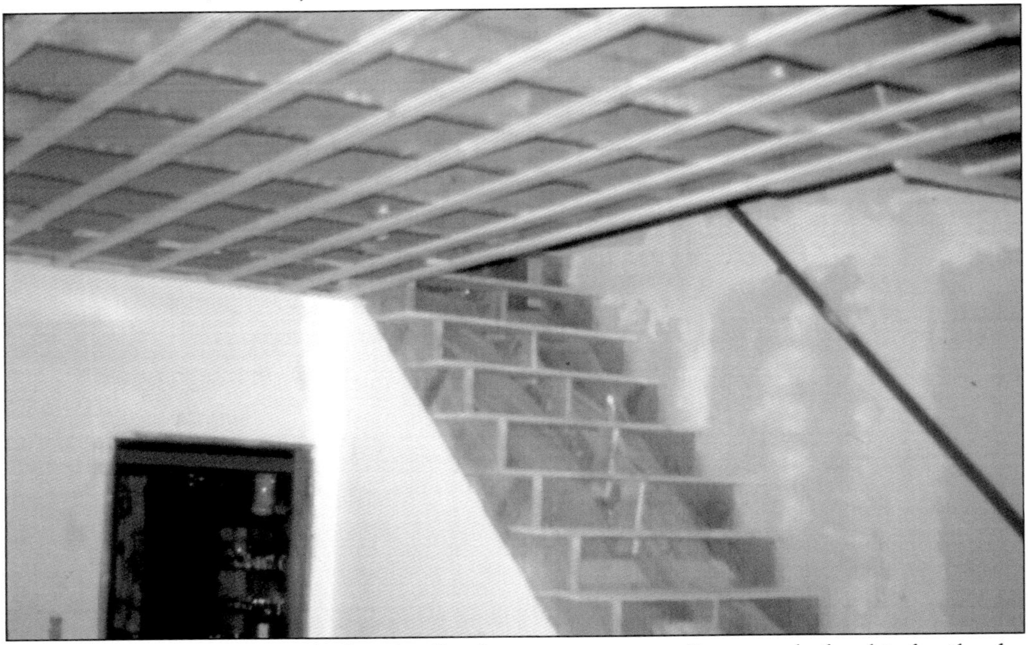

A living room is seen gutted after the floodwaters were gone. Fortunately for this family, the second floor of the home was untouched by the flood. They lived upstairs during the restoration of the first floor. Anything that was touched by mud or water was supposed to be replaced, though that did not always happen. (Courtesy of Sheldon Glahn.)

Ruth Glahn's beauty shop, located in the Glahns' home, is stripped to the studs, having been destroyed by the flood. One positive of the damage was that her husband, Sheldon, a contractor and plumber by trade, told her that the home could be fixed and rebuilt exactly how they wanted it. The entire project took over a year. When asked by the bank how much of a loan he wanted, Sheldon asked for $1 million. Although he did not get it, he felt the one-percent interest rate made the request worth a shot. When asked how much he needed, Sheldon said about $25,000. A neighbor was most excited about the loans, stating that at the age of 80, he was given a 30-year loan with only one-percent interest. (Both, courtesy of Sheldon Glahn.)

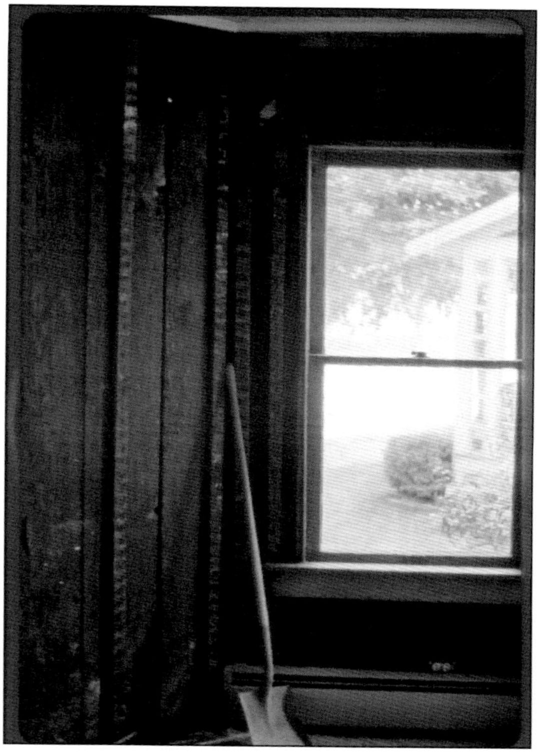

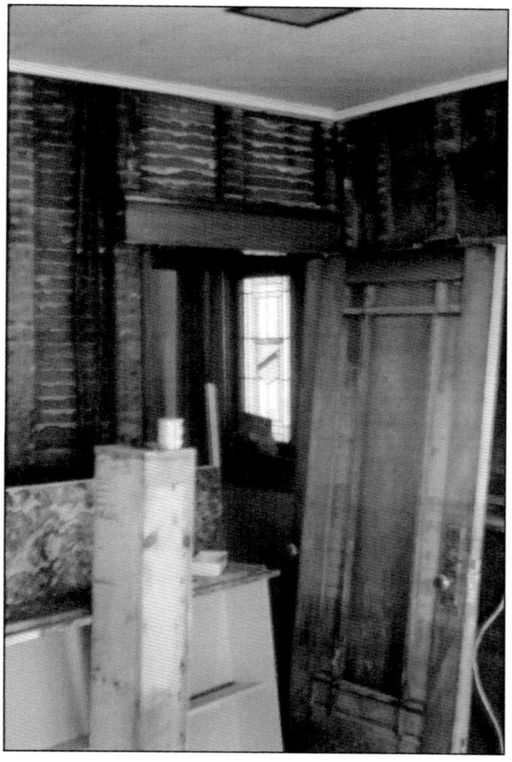

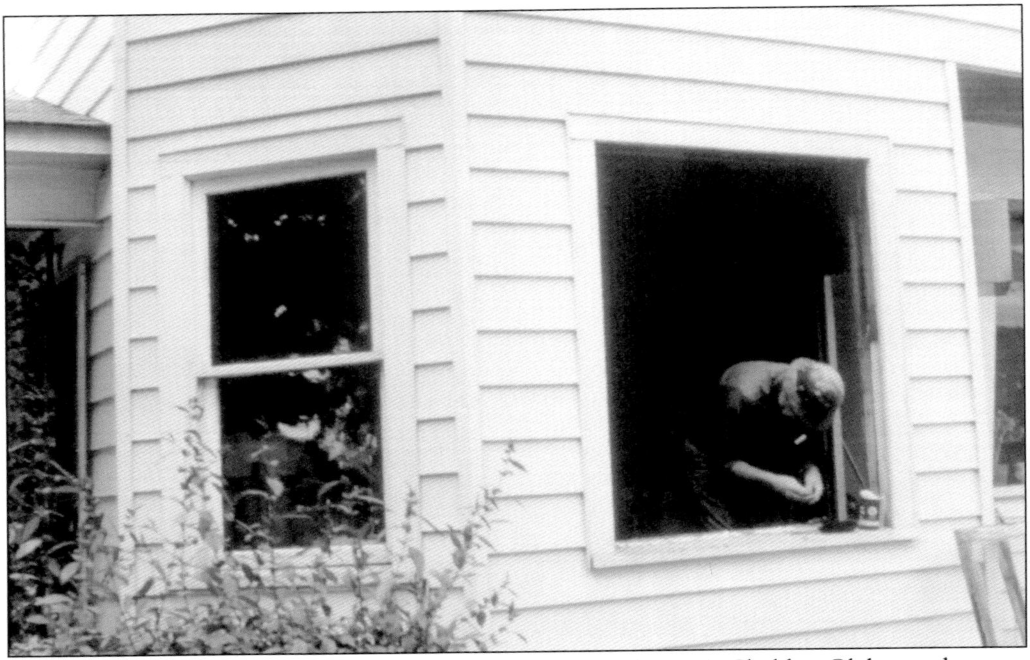

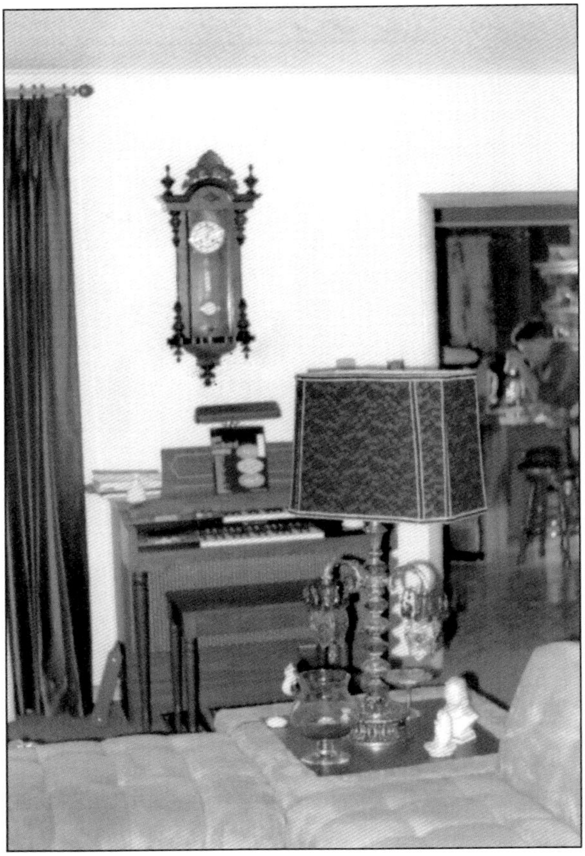

Above, A. Sheldon Glahn works to replace a large window in the front of his house, which he had lived in since birth. As he was working during the day for a company in Scranton, he spent around three hours a night making repairs. He and his son worked most nights stripping plaster, wiring, and trim. They would then install new drywall, windows, doors, ceilings, and whatever else needed to be replaced. Bidlack Street in Forty Fort was one of the last areas to get electricity back. Because of this, the Glahns only used hand tools to work and a hibachi grill to make dinner each night. At left, Glahn enjoys lunch in his newly remodeled kitchen. Despite the mess, new furniture, paint, and hours of hard labor made the damaged house into a home again. Glahn even marked a spot on the wall to show how high the water had been. (Both, courtesy of Sheldon Glahn.)

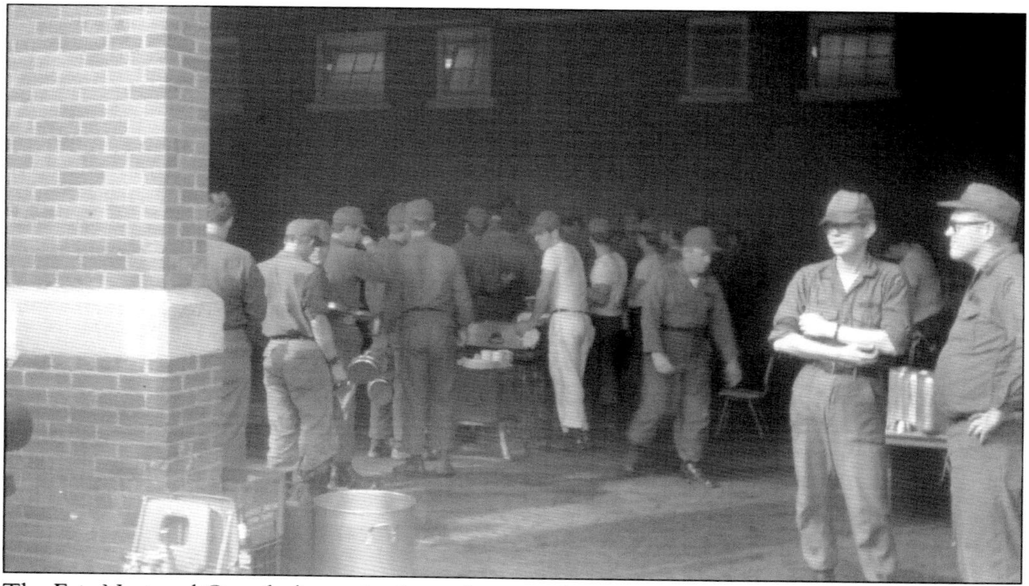

The Erie National Guard, shown in these photographs, was vital in aiding residents in cleaning up from the flood. Their headquarters was the Durkee Street School in Forty Fort. Although martial law was declared, few residents recall any issues. One local store owner, of Eastern European descent, described driving his car up to a post where he was instructed he could go no farther. He brazenly moved a barricade and continued on, saying of the guard, "He have no gun, he no shoot." Despite their efforts in the Wyoming Valley, guardsmen were told they would still have to serve their two weeks' duty later. Many residents protested this to local politicians, and the order was rescinded. The consensus was that the Erie National Guard went above and beyond in helping the residents rebuild their shattered lives. (Both, courtesy of Sheldon Glahn.)

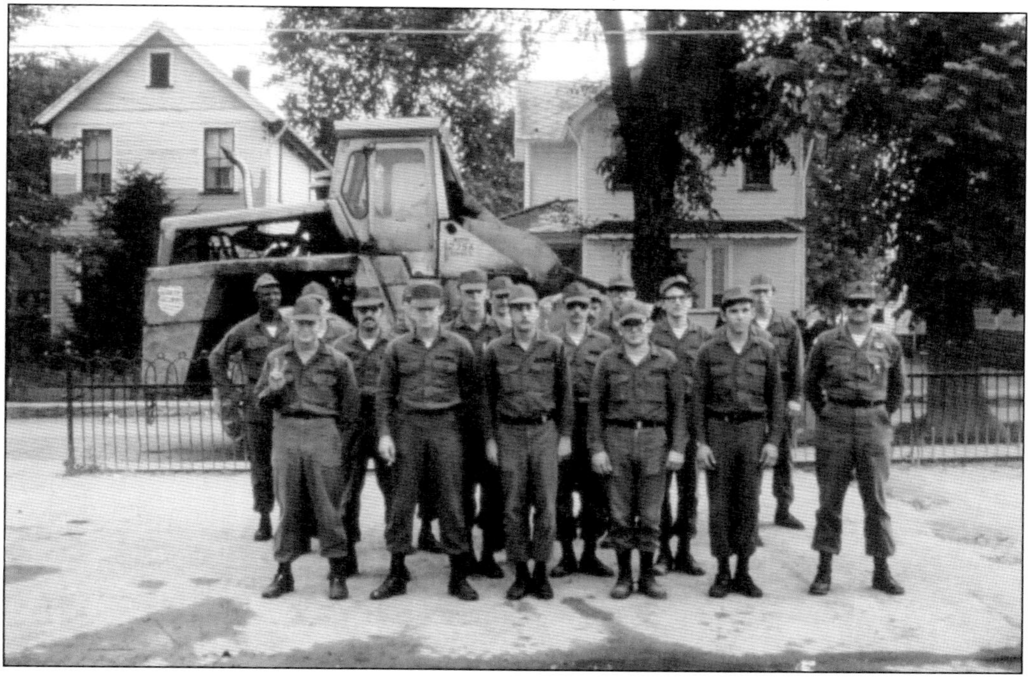

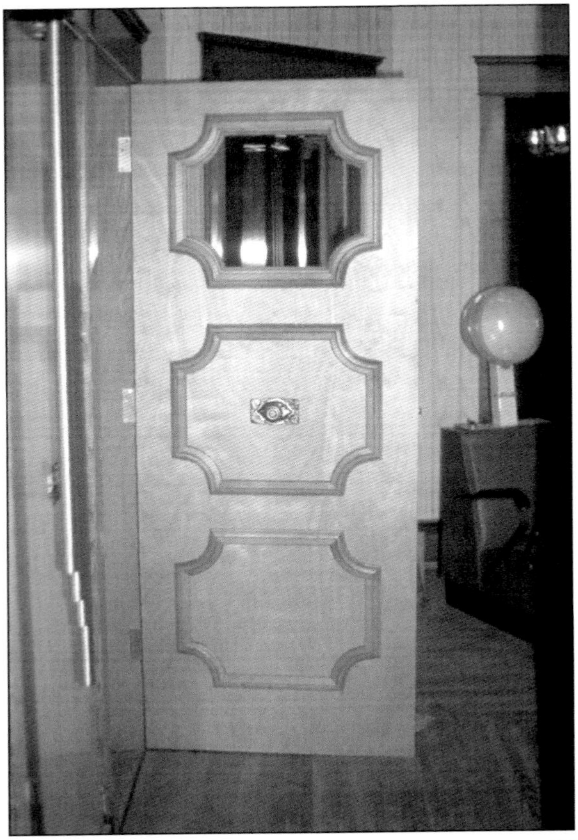

The final touch on this home was a fancy wooden door. Despite being a carpenter, the brother of the owner refused to drill the elongated hole for the lock, fearing he would ruin it. The owner drilled it himself, saying, "If I ruin it, I will go buy another door." (Courtesy of Sheldon Glahn.)

Slowly but steadily, Ruth Glahn's beauty shop, which she ran out of her home, was put back together. Although the walls have yet to be redone, a new sink and chair await future customers. Soon the phone would ring with customers eager to have their hair done. Surely, the flood dominated much of the chatter, as it would for decades to come. An out of town visitor once asked, "What did you guys talk about before the flood?" (Courtesy of Sheldon Glahn.)

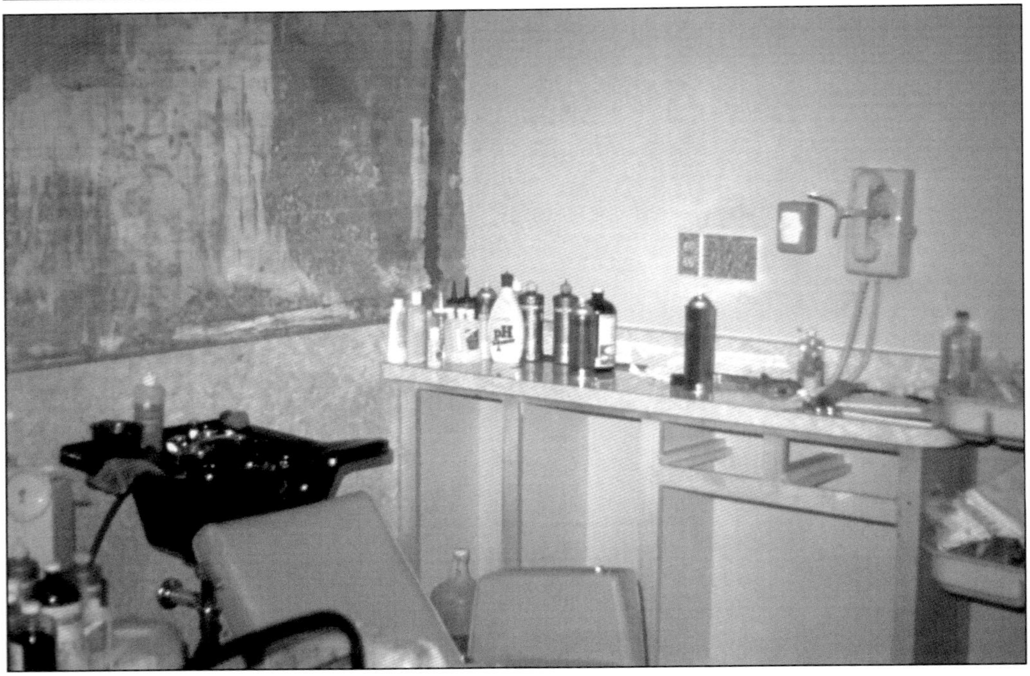

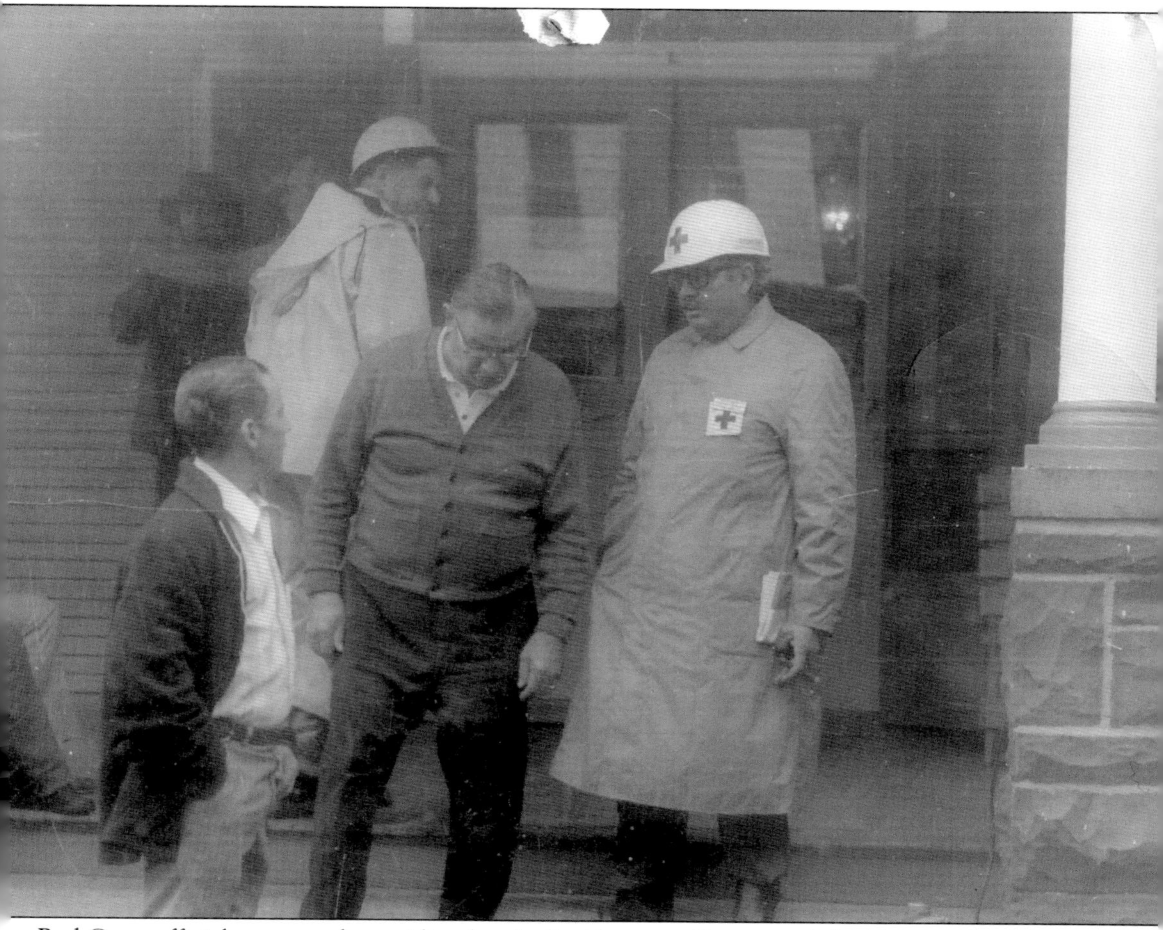

Red Cross officials are seen here aiding locals. Residents could not speak highly enough of the role the charity played in cleanup. Coffee, sandwiches, and other food was provided by mobile trucks. Kitchens were even set up to help feed the masses. Residents received cleaning supplies as well. Much to the anger of some, one woman who did not have a drop of water in her home went down and helped herself to a variety of cleaning supplies and other household items. For the most part, however, citizens were appreciative of the aid and did not take advantage of the situation too much. Those who did and were discovered were prosecuted. (Courtesy of Sheldon Glahn.)

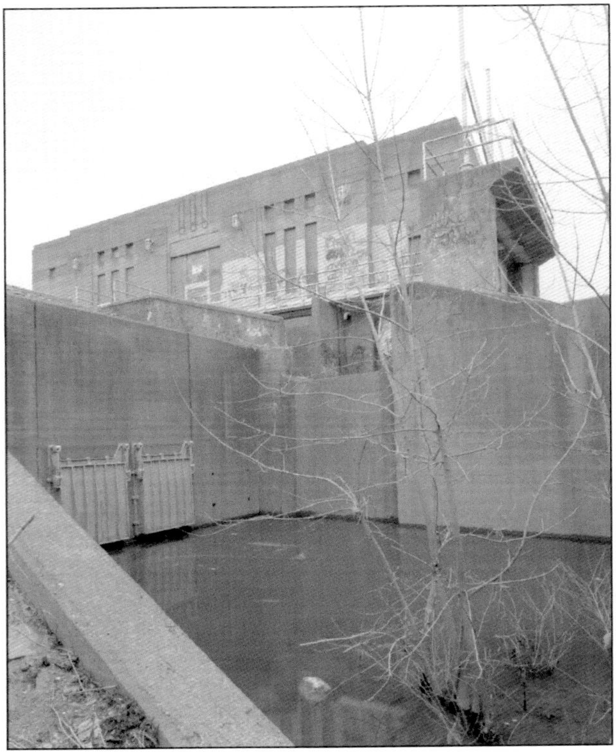

Despite the cost of construction, it is estimated that some $7.6 billion in damages was avoided due to the levy system that stretches from Exeter to Plymouth Township. In 2011, Hurricane Lee caused the Susquehanna River to crest higher than she did in 1972. However, because of the levy system and flood protection devices put in place, such as those in these photographs, the Wyoming Valley was spared the damage inflicted by Agnes. (Both, courtesy of Library of Congress.)

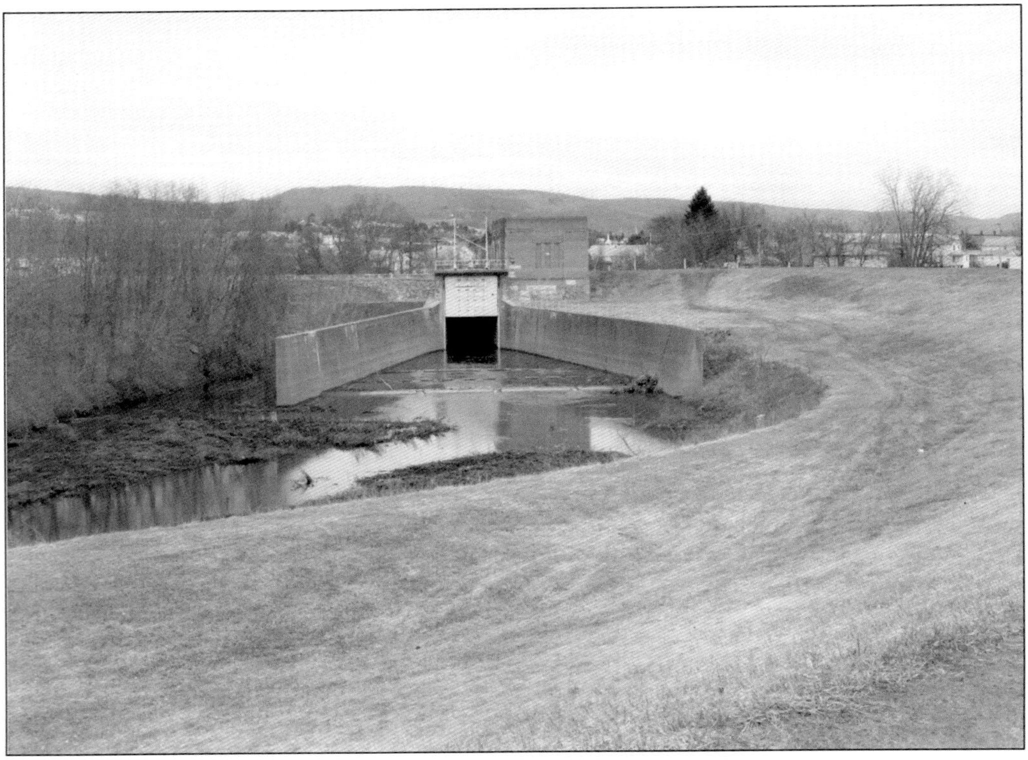

Since 1865, the Susquehanna River has exceeded its natural flood stage 77 times, which is more than once every two years. Because of this, flood protection has always been vital. As a response to the 1936 flood, in which the river crested at 33.07 feet, the levy system was born. Over time, the project has expanded with more pumping stations, recreational areas, and perhaps most importantly, mitigation plans to prevent damage downstream. One negative of protecting the Wyoming Valley is that, as one travels downriver from the 1972 flood zone, flooding inflicts more damage on those communities when the river gets too high. In these photographs, flood control implements are shown in Edwardsville. (Both, courtesy of Library of Congress.)

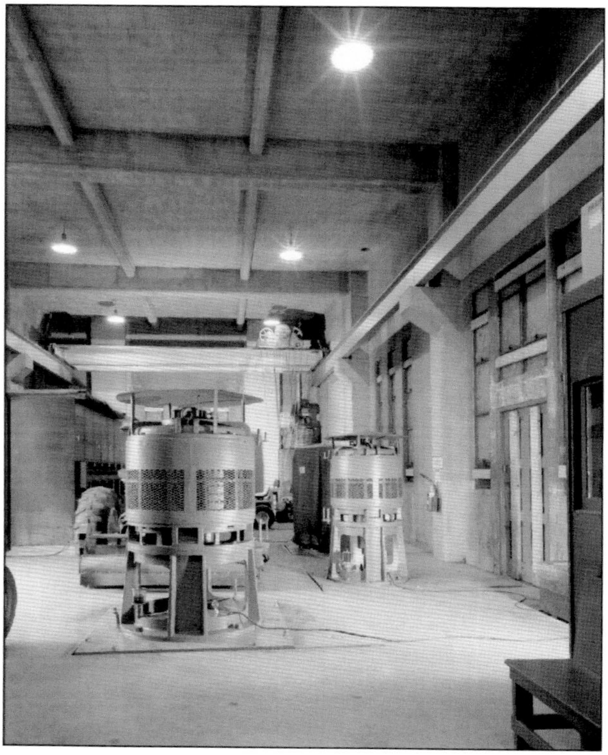

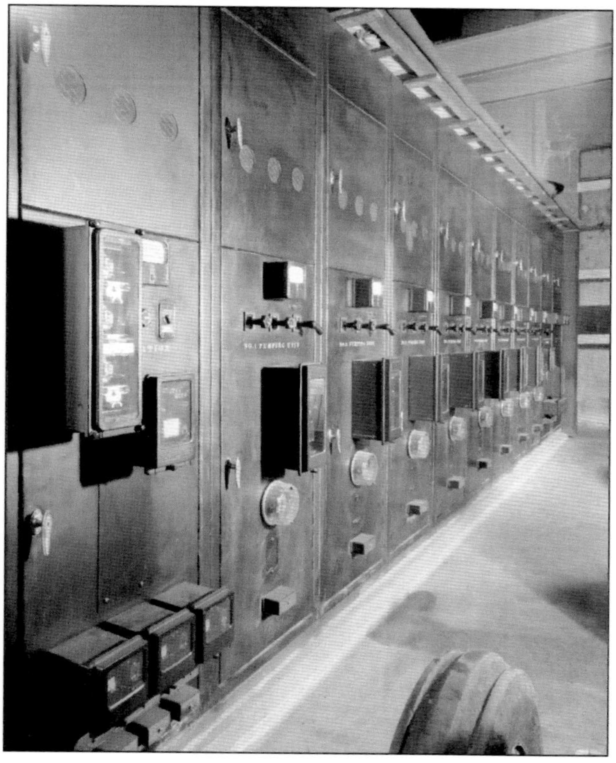

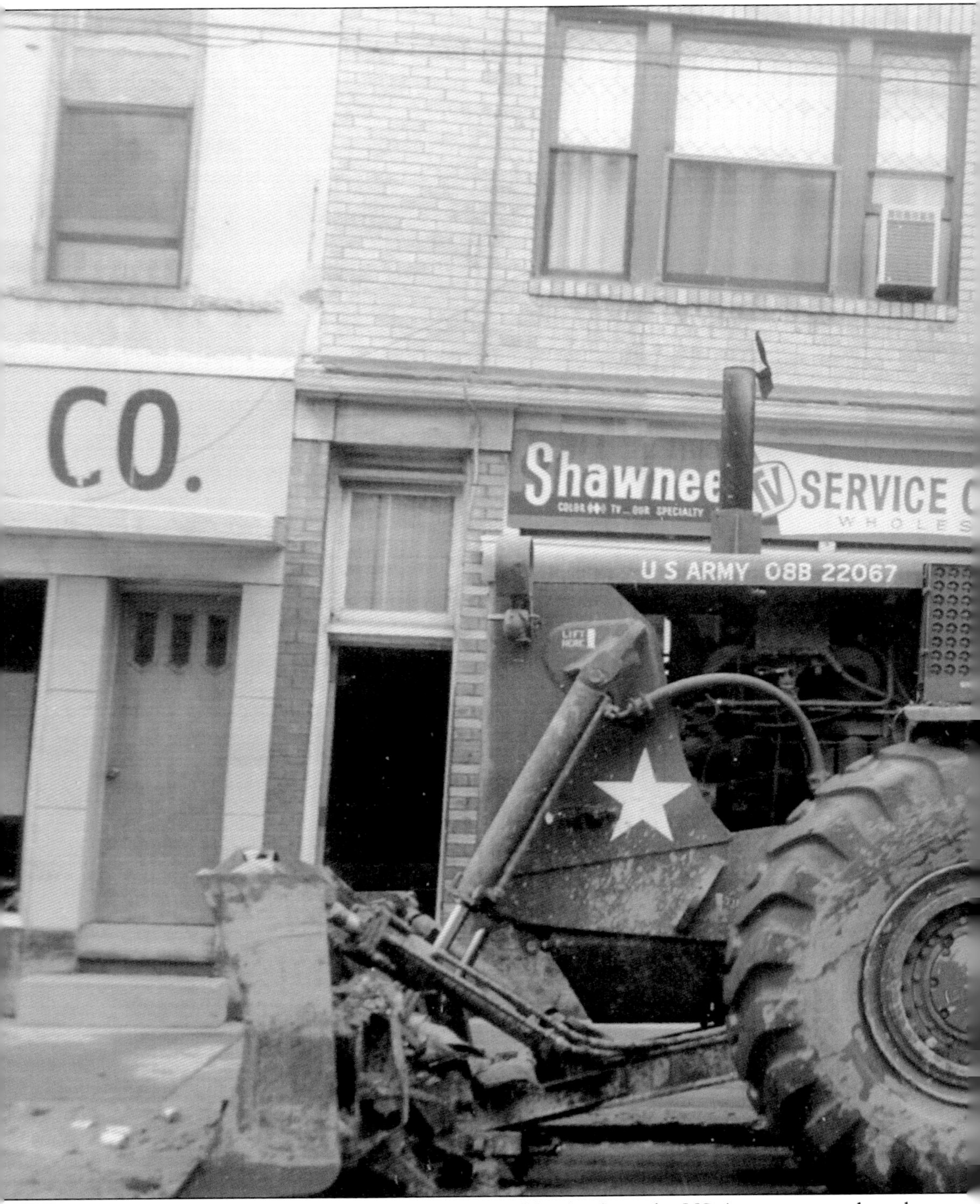

Massive heavy equipment, such as this front-end loader from the US Army, was used to clean up the streets of Plymouth. Although residents of Plymouth were eager to begin cleanup, their efforts were temporarily halted due to the ruptured fuel tanks in Edwardsville, which posed a

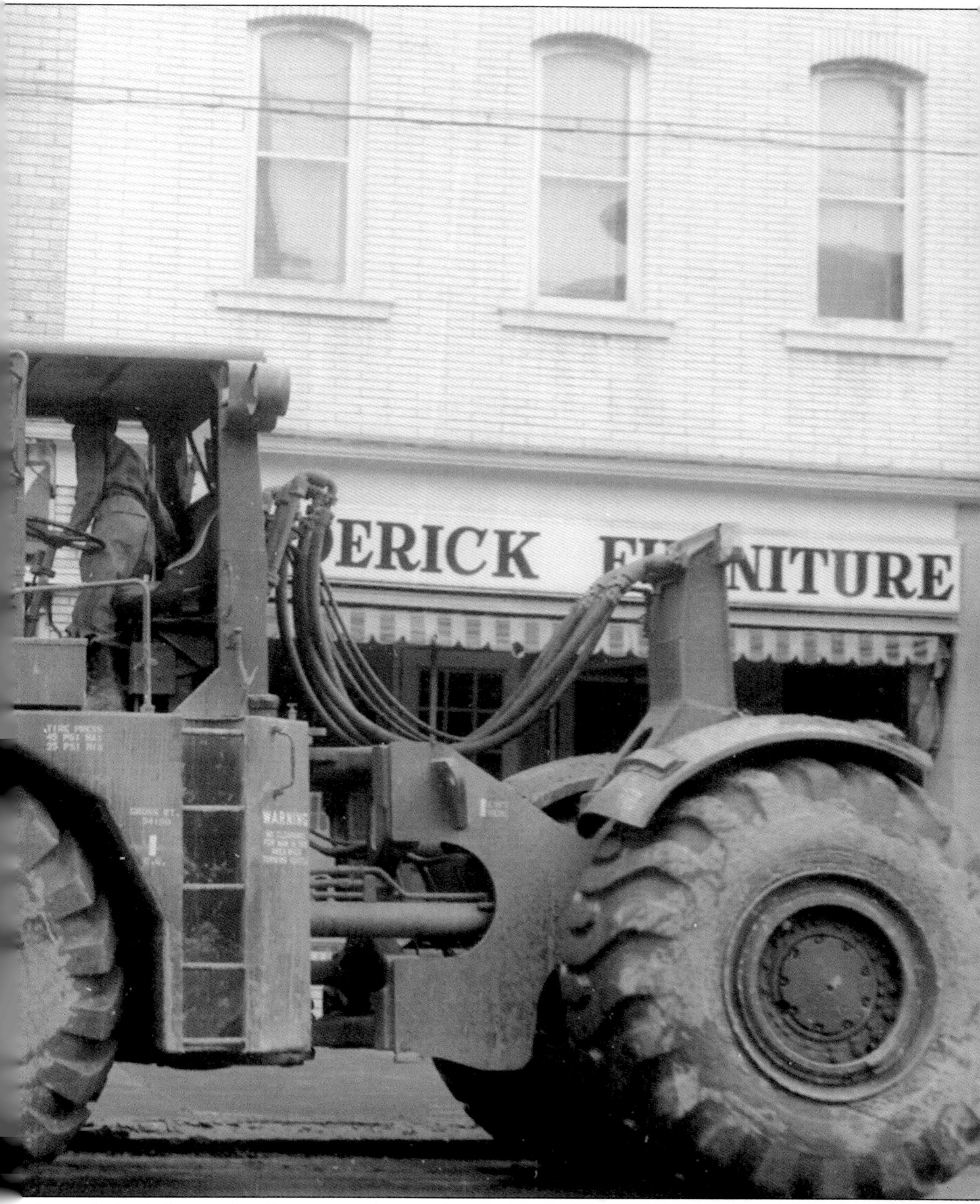

hazard. As fuel mixed with water in the river's current, residents were ordered to pull back, and boats were ordered off the water. The slightest spark could start an inferno that would destroy what was left of Plymouth. (Courtesy of Plymouth Historical Society.)

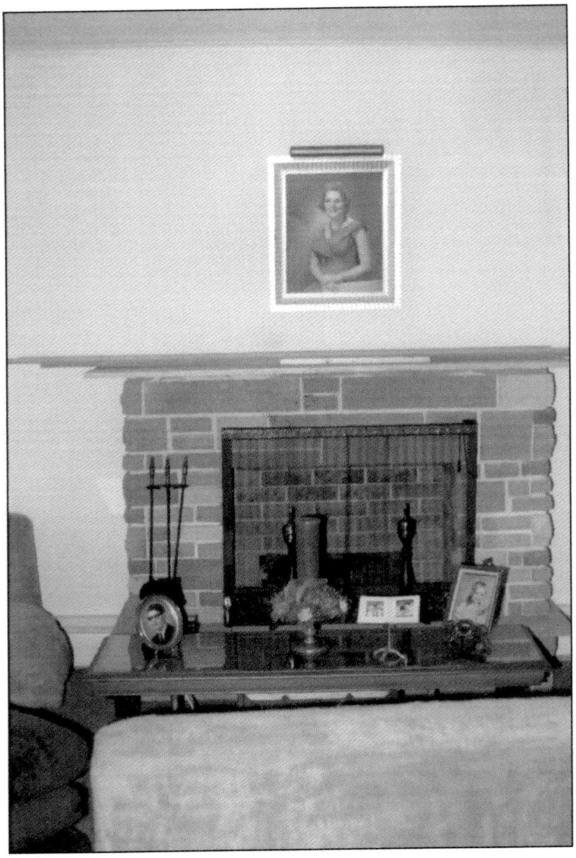

With the floodwaters gone, a picture of Ruth Glahn hangs above a new fireplace in the Glahn home. After a few finishing touches, one would never know this old home once had over eight feet of water in it. Despite a tremendous personal loss, most residents were able to put the flood behind them and being enjoying life again. Although when heavy rain caused the river to rise, they were reminded of what could happen all over again. (Courtesy of Sheldon Glahn.)

Although this is a file photograph of Richard Nixon, the president did make his way to the Wyoming Valley to survey the damage. It is fitting that this photograph shows Nixon at a wedding because, during his tour of the flood-ravaged area, Nixon spent some time with a recently married couple. Since he was not carrying cash, a Secret Service agent provided a gift to the new bride and groom. In addition to Nixon, celebrities such as Bob Hope visited the area, as well as famous athletes from the Philadelphia Eagles, among others. (Courtesy of Library of Congress.)

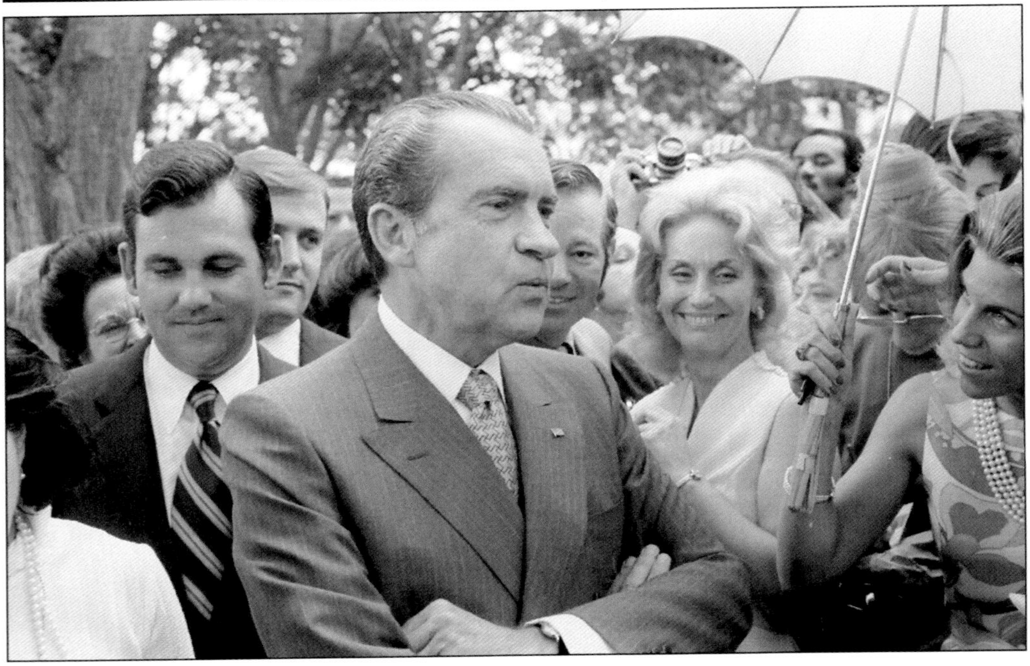

Bibliography

Bolger, J.C., ed. *A Portrait of Agnes*. Dallas, PA: James Kozemchak Sr. and Sons, 1972.

Griffith, W.M., and C.J. Romanelli. *The Wrath of Agnes: A Complete Pictorial and Written History of the June, 1972, Flood in Wyoming Valley*. Wilkes-Barre, PA: Media Affiliates, 1972.

Menichini, M. *After Agnes: A Triumph Over Destruction*. Wilkes-Barre, PA: Times Leader, 1982.

Warnagiris, P.W, and J.J. Rygiel. *The Great Flood of 1972*. Wyoming, PA: Observer-Rygiel Publishing Company, 1973.

Shank, W.H. *Great Floods of Pennsylvania: A Two Century History*. York, PA: American Canal and Transportation Center, 1972.

Smith, W. and Associates. "Flood Control Report Tropical Storm Agnes Wyoming Valley, Pennsylvania." Columbia, MA: Wilbur Smith and Associates, 1973.

Walzer, A., ed. *Agnes Revisited: The Day that Changed our Lives*. Wilkes-Barre, PA: Times Leader, 1992.